D1521853

The Nature of Legal Interpretation

The Nature of Legal Interpretation

What Jurists Can Learn about Legal Interpretation from Linguistics and Philosophy

EDITED BY BRIAN G. SLOCUM

THE UNIVERSITY OF CHICAGO PRESS   CHICAGO AND LONDON

The University of Chicago Press, Chicago 60637
The University of Chicago Press, Ltd., London
© 2017 by The University of Chicago
Chapter 6, "Originalism, Hermeneutics, and the Fixation Thesis," © Lawrence B. Solum
Chapter 8, "Legal Speech and the Elements of Adjudication," © Nicholas Allott and
Benjamin Shaer
All rights reserved. No part of this book may be used or reproduced in any manner
whatsoever without written permission, except in the case of brief quotations in criti-
cal articles and reviews. For more information, contact the University of Chicago Press,
1427 E. 6oth St., Chicago, IL 60637.
Published 2017
Printed in the United States of America

26 25 24 23 22 21 20 19 18 17   1 2 3 4 5

ISBN-13: 978-0-226-44502-1 (cloth)
ISBN-13: 978-0-226-44516-8 (e-book)
DOI: 10.7208/chicago/9780226445168.001.0001

Library of Congress Cataloging-in-Publication Data

Names: Slocum, Brian G., editor.
Title: The nature of legal interpretation : what jurists can learn about legal interpretation
    from linguistics and philosophy / edited by Brian G. Slocum.
Description: Chicago : The University of Chicago Press, 2017. | Includes index.
Identifiers: LCCN 2016041563 | ISBN 9780226445021 (cloth : alk. paper) |
    ISBN 9780226445168 (e-book)
Subjects: LCSH: Law—Language. | Law—Interpretation and construction. |
    Law—Language—Philosophy.
Classification: LCC K487.L36 N38 201 7 | DDC 340/.14—dc23LC record available at
    https://lccn.loc.gov/2016041563

♾ This paper meets the requirements of ANSI/NISO z39.48–1992 (Permanence of Paper).

Contents

Introduction   1
Brian G. Slocum

CHAPTER 1. The Contribution of Linguistics to
            Legal Interpretation   14
            Brian G. Slocum

CHAPTER 2. Philosophy of Language, Linguistics,
            and Possible Lessons about Originalism   46
            Kent Greenawalt

CHAPTER 3. Linguistic Knowledge and Legal Interpretation:
            What Goes Right, What Goes Wrong   66
            Lawrence M. Solan

CHAPTER 4. The Continued Relevance of Philosophical
            Hermeneutics in Legal Thought   88
            Frank S. Ravitch

CHAPTER 5. The Strange Fate of Holmes's Normal
            Speaker of English   105
            Karen Petroski

CHAPTER 6. Originalism, Hermeneutics,
            and the Fixation Thesis   130
            Lawrence B. Solum

CHAPTER 7. Getting Over the Originalist Fixation   156
            Francis J. Mootz III

CHAPTER 8. Legal Speech and the Elements of Adjudication   191
            Nicholas Allott and Benjamin Shaer

CHAPTER 9. Deferentialism, Living Originalism,
            and the Constitution   218
            Scott Soames

CHAPTER 10. Deferentialism and Adjudication   241
            Gideon Rosen

Response to Chapter Ten: Comments on Rosen   272
            Scott Soames

Contributors   283

List of Cases   285

Index   287

Introduction

Brian G. Slocum

L anguage shapes and reflects how we think about the world. It engages and intrigues us. One prominent scholar of language reports
that he has never met a person not interested in language (Pinker 1994).
Yet, our language use seems quite effortless. A typical person comes
into contact with thousands of words in a single day and uses them with
great facility (i.e., seemingly without thinking) (Aitchison 2012). In a
real sense, we are experts on our native languages. For instance, judgments by native speakers of the grammaticality/acceptability of sentences (as well as other linguistic intuitions) have been the major source
of evidence for linguists when constructing grammars (Schütze 1996).

Our language skills also make us unique. One view is that the language faculty governing human communication is markedly different
from that of other living creatures (Hauser, Chomsky, and Fitch 2002).
Viewing the world in linguistic terms is a unique and natural human process. Consider categorization, which more generally is a psychological
process whereby people make judgments about whether an object falls
within a given concept. The ability to categorize is an integral aspect
of human development. Early in their development, humans demonstrate the ability to countenance differences in order to generalize and
form categories based on similarities (Sloutsky 2003). The ability to categorize is beneficial because it allows for the organization of knowledge
through the creation of taxonomies that include smaller classes within
larger ones (e.g., specific creature → Cleveland Bay → horse → animal).
As such, categorization is part of the process of inductive generalization,
where, for example, knowing that a creature has features similar to rec-

ognized members of the category "horse" enables one to characterize the creature as a "horse."

Despite the human language faculty and its natural ability to categorize, as well as the widespread intuition that language users must naturally be experts on the interpretation of their native language, issues of language and meaning, and particularly categorization, have long beguiled judges (and commentators). Consider one of the most famous legal hypotheticals (discussed in hundreds of scholarly papers and books), H. L. A. Hart's (1958, 607) no-vehicles-in-the-park scenario, which asks the following questions:

> A legal rule forbids you to take a vehicle into the public park. Plainly this forbids an automobile, but what about bicycles, roller skates, toy automobiles? What about airplanes? Are these, as we say, to be called "vehicles" for the purpose of the rule or not?

The hypothetical classically frames the challenges caused by the difficulties of categorizing objects and defining words (such as "vehicle") and the consequent fuzziness (often labeled as vagueness) associated with such attempts. The fuzziness associated with most natural language concepts, such as "vehicle," does not undermine most day-to-day verbal interactions, where a high degree of precision is not necessary to successful communication. The requirements of the legal system, however, are different. Interpretive questions (e.g., does a certain object fall within the scope of the "vehicle" concept?) need definite "yes" or "no" answers, and frequently the dispute will involve some object at the margins of the relevant concept (e.g., what about a car without an engine?).

Should a judge feel confident in defining common words in legal texts without the aid of a linguist (or anyone else)? It might seem counterintuitive that speakers would need guidance about the nature and functioning of their native language. This is especially true for judges who are generally well educated and highly trained in the use of language. Judges often state that their own experience and knowledge of language (sometimes referred to by them as "common sense") is sufficient to accurately determine the meaning of words in legal texts. Nevertheless, a judge today would just as likely approach the meaning of the no-vehicles-in-the park provision by consulting a dictionary definition of "vehicle," the key term in the provision. In fact, judicial reliance on dictionaries is extensive and has dramatically increased since 1987 (Brudney and Baum

2013). The manner, though, in which judges have relied on dictionaries has been criticized by linguists and others. Judges are typically motivated to define words in such a way as to avoid uncertainty in application, which assists the judge in reaching the required "yes" or "no" answer in what seems like an objective manner. This may involve selecting a dictionary and treating one of the definitions as though it sets forth necessary and sufficient conditions that when met guarantee membership in the category represented by the word. Defining words through dictionary definitions, and viewing these definitions as providing necessary and sufficient conditions of meaning, may seem to narrow interpretive discretion. The result, though, is contrary to the empirical findings and theoretical work of linguists and psychologists regarding the nature of word meanings (Slocum 2015). The judicial failure to acknowledge this body of linguistic knowledge has come at the expense of accurate definitions.

The famous no-vehicles-in-the-park hypothetical, with its illustration of the uncertainties of word meanings, represents only one aspect of the challenges raised by the use of natural language in legal texts. Indeed, scholars have in various ways critiqued the linguistic methods by which judges determine the meanings of legal texts. Notably, in 1995 Washington University held a conference where linguists and lawyers met to discuss how linguists might approach problems of legal interpretation and whether their expertise could improve legal interpretation. Hart's no-vehicles-in-the-park hypothetical was discussed, as well as a then-recent Supreme Court case involving the scope of modification of adverbs.[1] Some of the linguists, such as Cunningham and Fillmore (1995), demonstrated how they would approach the interpretation of a specific provision. Other scholars, though, were skeptical of the relevance of linguists' expertise to legal texts. Some, such as Popkin (1995), suspected that linguists were attempting to turn legal interpretation into a science by exaggerating the determinacy of language and the relevance of linguistics. Similarly, Poirier (1995) argued, essentially, that there is no reason to defer to the expertise of linguists on matters of language (i.e., the native language users are themselves experts argument). Another argument questioned the legitimacy of theories of linguistic meaning (which constitute much of the study of semantics). Campos (1995, 973, 981), for instance, argued that "texts do not have conventional meanings" and that there is something "troubling" about the "whole idea of attempting to develop comprehensive theories of legal or linguistic meaning." Instead, interpretation always involves "an attempt to discover what the agent meant."

Extended treatment can be given the various arguments mentioned above, but not in this introduction. Similarly, neither this introduction nor the rest of this book attempts to provide a summary and critique of the 1995 conference and all of the arguments made, or assess how views of linguists and the legitimacy of their expertise might have changed over the course of the past two decades. In fact, a focus on linguists is too narrow, as disciplines other than linguistics have made significant contributions to the study of language (and of language and law). For example, philosophers, psychologists, neuroscientists, and others have all made such contributions (some of which are discussed in this book). Thus, the terms of the debate must necessarily shift to a focus on what, if anything, jurists (and others) can learn about legal interpretation from linguistics, philosophy, and other disciplines that study similar issues of language.

For disciplines that study language, such as linguistics (and similar fields), a traditional view could be that the nature of knowledge (and expertise) produced is limited in important respects. The reason is that scholarly research in linguistics is descriptive. The typical scholarly agenda seeks to describe the linguistic world as it is. Thus, linguists, qua linguists, generally do not offer normative views of meaning and communication. Rather, the focus is on descriptive accuracy. Linguists are committed to understanding the ways in which language works, both generally and in special circumstances (such as law). As such, there could be no concerted effort by linguists to exaggerate the determinacy of language (contrary to the assertions of some critics). In fact, just the opposite is the case. As this book discusses in various chapters, linguistic insights can illustrate the ways in which language is complex and frequently indeterminate.

An understanding that linguistics is generally descriptive in nature might suggest the relatively limited value of any project involving the application of linguistic insights to legal interpretation, because legal interpretation, by its very character, calls for normative judgments. In many circumstances, the linguistic content of a text cannot represent its legal meaning. For instance, much statutory language (as well as language in other legal texts) is ambiguous, vague, or otherwise underdetermined. In such situations, the court must disambiguate or precisify (i.e., make more precise) based on considerations other than language. The legal meaning of a text will then depend on interpretive principles and judgments that are based on legal rather than linguistic concerns. Thus, interdisciplinary insights can help explain why the no-vehicles-in-the-park hypothetical presents difficult interpretive issues, but nonlanguage considerations would also need to be considered in order to resolve the many interpretive disputes that would arise when applying the statute. In light of this reality, scholars have distinguished between "interpretation," which represents the linguistic understanding of the provision at issue, and "construction," which represents instances where judges choose meanings that transcend interpretations (Tiersma 1995).

Even in situations not involving ambiguity or vagueness (or some other indeterminacy), the linguistic meaning of a text may differ from its legal meaning. One view is that a particular case will always contain some circumstance not covered by the legal provision at issue, and the provision's silence by itself cannot determine the circumstance's relevance to whether the relevant interest should prevail (Flanagan 2010). The text alone is never decisive because the circumstance, not contemplated by the enactment's linguistic meaning, may be controlling. Circumstances outside the linguistic meaning of a text may therefore always have the potential to control the outcome of a case. For instance, most, if not all, judges agree that if applying the linguistic meaning of a text would cause absurd results, some other meaning should control (Manning 2003). Another long-standing, interpretive position, hotly debated since the Supreme Court's famous decision in *Holy Trinity Church v. United States*, 143 U.S. 457 (1892), is that if the purpose of the enactment is at odds with its linguistic meaning, a meaning consistent with the purpose should control.

The recognition that legal interpretation is ineliminably normative in character does not entail that descriptive insights about language are of limited importance to legal interpretation. Indeed, a foundational defense of interdisciplinary insights about legal interpretation should illustrate the value of such knowledge. Thus, in chapter 1, Brian G. Slocum addresses the value of linguists' expertise to legal interpretation by examining the determinants of meaning of legal texts. Even if aspects of legal interpretation are normative, the meaning of a legal text is generally dependent on objective determinants of meaning that relate to how people normally use language (both inside and outside of the legal context), and which may be said in part to constitute the linguistic meaning of the text. The necessity of relying on objective determinants of meaning holds even under a methodology of interpretation that posits that the drafters' intentions constitute the meaning of the text (Slocum 2015). In light of this view of legal interpretation, it follows that experts on language should be able to contribute to any process that seeks to advance a better understanding of the nature and role of language in legal interpretation.

Even scholars who discount in some ways the value of interdisciplinary insights often come to the same conclusion that these insights can improve legal interpretation. In chapter 2, for instance, Kent Greenawalt argues that philosophy of language and linguistics cannot tell us exactly how interpretation by judges, other officials, and citizens should proceed and cannot provide any overarching reasons for rejecting an interpretive approach that otherwise seems attractive. The reason is that interpretation may be affected by factors that interdisciplinary insights cannot resolve, such as textual ambiguity, vagueness and general, open-ended terms, results that are absurd or that conflict with general social values, and situations that were unforeseen by the drafters. Nevertheless, Greenawalt believes that the philosophy of language and linguistics can contribute in various ways to our understanding of legal language. Greenawalt argues that the philosophy of language can do the following: (1) identify the core features of language and communication and provide insight into what takes place when legal provisions are interpreted, (2) suggest possible approaches and provide analogies from nonlegal contexts, (3) describe why certain approaches are tenable or untenable, (4) indicate which approach should be favored or provide reasons that could count for or against certain approaches, and (5) provide insights into why some forms of interpretation seem attractive apart from their merits.

Interdisciplinary descriptions of language, even when specific to law, might not be sufficient to constitute complete theories of legal interpretation, but the broad implications of such knowledge to an appropriately sophisticated and accurate account of legal interpretation should not be minimized. As Lawrence M. Solan explains in chapter 3, by examining the variety of linguistic issues that arise in interpretive disputes, "we can come to some conclusions about how the architecture of our language faculty influences our ability to govern ourselves under a language-centric system of laws." Language is comprised of various subsystems and interactions, and failures in the system can produce interpretive issues in the legal context. As indicated earlier in this introduction, conceptual systems allow humans to express in language their intended concepts. Often, though, the word chosen creates a situation where the real-world object (either tangible or intangible) at issue is at the border-line of the concept, requiring a legal determination of whether the object falls within the scope of the concept (e.g., is a car without an engine still a "vehicle"?).[2] Such situations, involving vagueness, occur far more often than situations involving syntactic or semantic ambiguity, which are more purely linguistic phenomena. As Solan argues, the frequency of disputes involving vagueness (along with other examples discussed in the chapter) illustrates that our language faculty has limitations and that these limitations constrain our ability to govern ourselves under a rule of law in which language is paramount.

As indicated above, interdisciplinary descriptions of language from nonlinguists can also serve to help develop an accurate understanding of legal interpretation. In chapter 4, for instance, Frank Ravitch argues that it is the limited, descriptive quality of philosophical hermeneutics that makes it valuable in understanding legal interpretation. Ravitch explains that understanding philosophical hermeneutics dictates nothing norma-tive. Any normative approach must be based on some other theoretical foundation. Understandings of how people interpret language, however, can help normative approaches. There is no absolute method of interpre-tation, and each interpreter brings his or her own preconceptions into the act of interpreting a text. These preconceptions are influenced by the tradition, including social context, in which the interpreter exists. The interpreter's tradition(s) provides her with a horizon that includes her in-terpretive predispositions. This horizon is the range of what the inter-preter can see when engaging with a text. The concept of *dasein*, or be-ing in the world, captures this dynamic. We exist in the world around us, and that world influences how we view things. Thus, our traditions and context are a part of our being. One of Ravitch's arguments is that unless we know how judges and other players in the legal system experience in-terpretation, any normative approach will only succeed in the long run when there are closely shared horizons between those seeking to effec-tuate policy and those making and interpreting the law.

Another argument in favor of the relevance to legal interpretation of interdisciplinary insights about language is that some legal interpretive principles by their very description seem to invite the application of lin-guistic insights. For instance, the ordinary meaning doctrine, perhaps the most foundational principle of legal interpretation, provides that judges are to assume that legal language is governed by the same general principles of language usage that apply outside of the law. Thus, according to Justice Oliver Wendell Holmes (1899), legal texts are to be interpreted by the standard of the "normal speaker of English." The "normal speaker of English" was intended by Holmes to represent the need for legal interpretation to be oriented toward external, objective determinants of meaning and away from reliance on authorial intent. Yet, as Karen Petroski examines in chapter 5, although the "normal speaker of English" has been referenced by judges, there has been no elaboration of the figure's attributes or significance. Perhaps, as the chapter suggests, judges are uncomfortable admitting that legal interpretation might rest on a fictional standard, even if doing so would represent reality. Maybe, as Petroski argues, elaborating the characteristics of the "normal speaker" might force judges to confront other important issues, such as the differences between legal and nonlegal English.

While some legal interpretive principles by their very description seem to invite the application of linguistic insights, in other legal scenarios the fundamental nature of the interpretive enterprise itself is disputed in a way that makes relevant linguistic expertise. For instance, the determinacy of language is an issue that bears on the legitimacy of certain methodologies of interpretation. Consider constitutional interpretation. Lawrence B. Solum in chapter 6 describes the originalist fixation thesis that claims that the communicative content of the constitutional text is fixed at the time each provision is framed and ratified and that contemporary constitutional practice should be constrained by this fixed original meaning (unless the text is amended). In turn, the constraint principle claims that legal interpreters ought to be constrained by the original meaning when deciding constitutional cases. Of course, scholars disagree about the particulars of the fixation thesis, such as whether what is being fixed is the original public meaning of the text, the original intentions of the framers, or the original methods of constitutional interpretation. Regardless of the particular claim, the underlying assumption is that meaning can be fixed (even if vague or ambiguous) with some reasonable degree of epistemic certainty.

The position that the meaning of a text can be determined at some point in time has obvious implications. As Francis J. Mootz argues in chapter 7, if the original meaning of a text is declared, it will serve as the default meaning, and the normative value of "constraint," advocating in favor of the default meaning, will be posited as a powerful and nearly undeniable premise of the rule of law. Mootz rejects the fixation thesis on ontological grounds, drawing from Hans-Georg Gadamer's contemporary hermeneutical philosophy. Mootz argues that singular and immutable meanings do not exist in our world of "interpretive vertigo." Rather, meaning always is the result of interpretive activity and is never a historical fact that exists independent of an interpreter.

Even if one accepts Mootz's arguments, it does not follow that interdisciplinary insights about language usage are irrelevant to legal interpretation (and note that Mootz's arguments are themselves interdisciplinary insights about legal interpretation). Instead, based on the arguments, various questions of interest to scholars should be examined. For example, if meaning is the result of interpretive activity, what is the psychological nature of this activity? Can the psychological properties be better identified and described? What is the relevance of our language faculty (see Solan's discussion in chapter 3) to this activity? Furthermore, what is the relevance of objective determinants of meaning, such as word meanings and rules of grammar? These objective determinants of meaning are independent of any individual interpreter, although interpreters of course consider them in sometimes idiosyncratic ways.

Thus far it has been posited that linguistics (and similar disciplines) can offer valuable contributions to legal interpretation because language is an indispensable aspect of legal rules and, as scientific (or at least empirically valid) descriptions of how people use language, linguistic insights can help judges and other legal actors understand the nature of legal language. While greater attention should be paid to such interdisciplinary insights, perhaps the role of disciplines like linguistics can be more revolutionary than has been described thus far. For example, by understanding legal speech as a variety of verbal interaction, as Nick Allott and Benjamin Shaer do in chapter 8, it is possible to reexamine the traditional distinction (described above) between interpretation and construction. If, as the chapter argues, legal interpretation, like verbal interaction (and other meaning-seeking activities), is largely inferential in nature, adjudication (which involves interpretation) is a phenomenon that is far less alien to normal nonlegal language interpretation than legal scholarship sometimes makes it out to be. Furthermore, although judges make creative decisions about the content of the law that go beyond what the legislature intended to convey, decisions involving such things as giving meaning to language that is vague do not necessarily exceed the scope of "interpretation." Rather, such judicial decisions can still be readily understood as part of the inferential interpretive activity, and not outside of it. If so, the scope of interpretation, and the relevance of linguistics, may be broader than many have imagined.

Consider, too, whether the sort of expertise that provides a basis for descriptive claims about language and interpretation naturally allows for more normative claims about the nature of legal interpretation. In chapter 9, Scott Soames, a philosopher, defends a version of originalism that he terms "deferentialism." Deferentialism articulates correctness criteria for the interpretation of legal texts by legally authorized judicial actors. The theory rests on three claims. The first claim is descriptive and is consistent with the narrower conception of interdisciplinary contributions exemplified in earlier chapters of this book. It provides that

> (i) The legal content of a statute or a provision of a written constitution cannot be identified with either the semantic content of the text or the legal or political rationale for its passage; it can be identified with what was said, asserted, or stipulated by lawmakers or ratifiers in passing or approving it.

In describing the claim, Soames argues that meaning exceeds the semantic meanings of the words used and distinguishes what J. L. Austin called perlocutionary intentions (encompassing consequences one expects to follow one's speech act) from what he called illocutionary intentions (encompassing shared expectations one relies on to determine the content of one's speech act). This "pragmatic turn" is an intervention in a longstanding debate among originalists about which features of a legal enactment fix its legal content. While some scholars emphasize original textual meaning and others point to the intentions or expectations of the drafters and ratifiers, Soames explains that the theories miss the key concept of assertoric or stipulated content.

While offering important insights into language, the deferentialist position offers more than a descriptive view of interpretation. The second and third assertions are as follows:

> (ii) In applying the law to the facts of a case, the legal duty of a judge is to reach the verdict determined by the stipulated content, unless (a) that content is vague and, as a result, it doesn't determine a definite verdict, or (b) the content, the surrounding law, and the facts of the case determine inconsistent verdicts, or (c) the contents and facts are inconsistent

      with the rationale of the law, which is the chief publically stated purpose
      that proponents of the law advanced to justify it.

(iii) In cases of type (iia-c), the judicial authority must make new law by ar-
      ticulating a minimum change in existing law that maximizes the fulfill-
      ment of the original rationale for the law.

Deferentialism attempts to balance fidelity to the Constitution with the
authority of the Supreme Court to modify constitutional content when
required by unanticipated circumstances. As the assertions above illustrate, by offering a theory of how judges should proceed when the linguistic meaning of the relevant provision is not determinate (and criticizing some important recent Supreme Court decisions for violating that
theory), deferentialism goes beyond description and offers a normative
view of legal interpretation.

    In chapter 10, in evaluating deferentialism and other theories, Gideon
Rosen further considers interpretive matters that cross the (sometimes
indistinct) line between descriptive and normative. Rosen explains that
a theory of adjudication, which answers the question of what is the legal
content or legal effect of an authoritative pronouncement, is not strictly
a linguistic matter. The legal content of a provision, for example, may
render acts legal or illegal at any given time as a function of its various
linguistic, sociological, and normative features. These factors suggest
that there can be a gap between what a legal provision (literally) says
and what a reasonable, informed interpreter would take the drafters to
have intended to permit or prohibit by means of it.[3] An interpreter thus
faces a choice about what to privilege as the basis of legal content. Furthermore, there are two ways to frame (mis)interpretations that change
the content of the law. One way is to assert that the legal content of the
given provision is different after the interpretation than it was prior to it.
A different, more originalist (and deferentialist) way of conceiving of the
change is to assert that the legal content of a provision is its assertoric
content, which is fixed at the time of utterance, but that the provision at
issue was unwittingly amended by the tradition of misinterpretation and
entrenchment (through stare decisis).

* * *

As outlined above, the arrangement of the chapters in this book represents various points on the spectrum of interdisciplinary contributions to

legal interpretation, with perhaps the later chapters manifesting a more ambitious role for interdisciplinary scholarship in legal interpretation theory. To be sure, descriptive accounts of language and interpretation have the potential to impact legal interpretation in profound ways. Interdisciplinary scholars can significantly contribute to legal interpretation by exploring the ways in which the nature and structure of language interposes on legal discourse, and by describing whether legal interpretation accounts for the nature of language in valid and accurate ways. Yet, readers of this book should also consider whether scholars that bring a perspective from another discipline might legitimately and productively use their expertise to offer accounts of legal interpretation that are more normative in nature. If the answer is "no," there will nevertheless remain a considerable area in which interdisciplinary insights should be relevant to legal interpretation. If the answer is "yes," the possibilities of interdisciplinary insights to legal interpretation are significant indeed, and greater than many have imagined.

Notes

1. The case that was discussed is United States v. X-Citement Video, Inc., 513 U.S. 64 (1994). This case is discussed in chapter 1.

2. For at least one court, the answer is "yes." See United States v McKlemurry, 461 F.2d 651 (5th Cir. 1972) (holding that a car body without an engine was a "motor vehicle" within the meaning of the National Motor Vehicle Theft Act).

3. Flanagan (2010, 257) describes an utterance's literal meaning as the "proposition you would attribute to it if you referred to just the symbols in question and the appropriate community's conventions on linguistic meaning, i.e. to the appropriate set of rules for the meanings of words and sentence construction."

References

Aitchison, Jean. 2012. *Words in the Mind*. West Sussex, UK: Wiley-Blackwell Publishing.

Brudney, James, and Lawrence Baum. 2013. "Oasis or Mirage: The Supreme Court's Thirst for Dictionaries in the Rehnquist and Roberts Eras." *William and Mary Law Review* 55:483–579.

Campos, Paul F. 1995. "This Is Not a Sentence." *Washington University Law Quarterly* 73:971–82.

Cunningham, Clark D., and Charles J. Fillmore. 1995. "Using Common Sense: A Linguistic Perspective on Judicial Interpretations of 'Use a Firearm.'" *Washington University Law Quarterly* 73:1159–214.

Flanagan, Brian. 2010. "Revisiting the Contribution of Literal Meaning to Legal Meaning." *Oxford Journal of Legal Studies* 30 (2): 255–71.

Hart, H .L. A. 1958. "Positivism and the Separation of Law and Morals." *Harvard Law Review* 71:593–629.

Hauser, Marc D., Noam Chomsky, and W. Tecumseh Fitch. 2002. "The Faculty of Language: What Is It, Who Has It, and How Did It Evolve?" *Science* 298 (5598): 1569–79.

Holmes, Oliver Wendell. 1899. "The Theory of Legal Interpretation." *Harvard Law Review* 12:417–20.

Manning, John. 2003. "The Absurdity Doctrine." *Harvard Law Review* 116: 2387–486.

Pinker, Steven. 1994. *The Language Instinct: How The Mind Creates Language.* New York: HarperCollins Publishers.

Poirier, Marc R. 1995. "On Whose Authority: Linguistics' Claim of Expertise to Interpret Statutes." *Washington University Law Quarterly* 73:1025–42.

Popkin, William D. 1995. "Law and Linguistics: Is There Common Ground?" *Washington University Law Quarterly* 73:1043–45.

Schütze, Carson T. 1996. *The Empirical Base of Linguistics: Grammaticality Judgments and Linguistic Methodology.* Chicago: University of Chicago Press.

Slocum, Brian. 2015. *Ordinary Meaning: A Theory of the Most Fundamental Principle of Legal Interpretation.* Chicago: University of Chicago Press.

Sloutsky, Vladimir M. 2003. "The Role of Similarity in the Development of Categorization." *Trends in Cognitive Sciences* 7 (6): 246–51.

Tiersma, Peter M. 1995. "The Ambiguity of Interpretation: Distinguishing Interpretation from Construction." *Washington University Law Review* 73: 1095–101.

CHAPTER ONE

The Contribution of Linguistics to Legal Interpretation

Brian G. Slocum

1. Introduction

Is the expertise of linguists relevant to the interpretation of legal texts? If so, can this expertise contribute to a more sophisticated understanding of legal interpretation than currently exists? This chapter addresses the value of linguists' expertise to legal interpretation by examining the determinants of meaning of legal texts. In one view, the meaning of a legal text should have little to do with objective theories of meaning (i.e., how people normally use language). Instead, each instance of interpretation requires an archaeological-type dig for the meaning that the author(s) intended, or an interpretive process that focuses on neither language nor authorial intent. In another, conflicting, view, the meaning of a legal text is dependent at least somewhat, and sometimes entirely, on objective determinants of meaning that relate to how people normally use language (both inside and outside of the legal context), and which may be said to in part constitute the "linguistic meaning" of the text. Linguists are experts on various aspects of language and communication, including the inferential reasoning processes through which a speaker's meaning is ascertained. The application of this knowledge to the interpretation of legal texts can greatly increase our understanding of legal interpretation (see chapter 8 for an example of the application of such expertise). Nevertheless, the question of what jurists can learn from linguistics is particularly salient if objective determinants of meaning are aspects of legal interpretation, as these objective determinants involve a multitude of language phenomena about which linguists are experts. It might seem incontrovertible that objective determinants of meaning are aspects of the legal meaning of a legal text. Even so, the question of the usefulness of linguistics is particularly important and interesting if objective features of language are, in fact, *significant* determinants of legal meaning.

It is intuitive that the work of those disciplines that study language and how it is used, such as linguistics (as well as philosophy and psychology), should have some influence on how judges interpret legal texts. The extent, though, to which these nonlegal academic disciplines have actually influenced the interpretation of legal texts is debatable, and detailing the possible influences is beyond the scope of this chapter. Rather, this chapter primarily addresses the controversial normative issue of whether the discipline of linguistics (in which philosophy of language and related disciplines will be included for purposes of succinctness) *should* influence the way that judges interpret legal texts.[1] This chapter will assume that linguists are experts on language and that their expertise exceeds that of the typical judge. If one doubts this (obvious) assumption, a single chapter would not likely convince the doubter otherwise.

Despite the expertise of linguists, and the inherently linguistic nature of legal texts, some have questioned whether the expertise of linguists can benefit legal interpreters. Solan (1995, 1069–70), for example, notes that "[t]o the extent that judges need to interpret statutory or other language in performing [their] tasks, they are as able as anyone else to do so without the help of a linguist, and linguistic theory tells us that this is so."[2] Solan, though, has been prolific in using linguistic theory to explain the various ways in which judges fail to understand how language works. In addition, many linguists have filed amicus curiae briefs with the Supreme Court explaining how some aspect of language should be understood. In any case, instead of detailing the various ways in which judges fail to understand (at least explicitly) various aspects of language, or extolling the expertise of linguists and listing the ways in which linguistic expertise has influenced judges, this chapter will address the importance of linguistic meaning to legal interpretation as a way of establishing the relevance of linguists' expertise to legal interpretation.

The argument made in this chapter proceeds as follows. The second section describes how courts, as an empirical matter, focus on linguistic meaning when deciding cases. The third and fourth sections explain that the position that the linguistic meaning of a provision is of "little value" to the interpretation chosen by the court fails to appreciate the ineliminable relevance of linguistic meaning to any plausible theory of textual interpretation. The fifth section argues that determinants of meaning that are based on generalized notions of intent, such as the ordinary meaning doctrine, are necessary due to the inadequacies of confining interpretation to a search for actual authorial intent and the consequent need to focus on the language of the text. The section describes how the ordinary meaning doctrine reflects epistemic uncertainty about authorial intent and is an important aspect of the sequential nature of judicial decision-making. The sixth section argues that criticisms of so-called "plain meaning" decisions may correctly criticize the interpretation chosen by the court but often overlook that the criticized interpretation was based on an erroneous (or at least disputable) view of language. Finally, section seven offers a conclusion and explains that far from exaggerating the determinacy of language, linguists can illustrate its indeterminacy and, if their expertise is taken seriously, force courts to explicitly acknowledge their policy choices.

For purposes of explication, this chapter will distinguish amongst several terms. The "legal meaning" of a text is the authoritative meaning given to it by a judge. The legal meaning may differ from the "linguistic meaning," which refers to the meaning communicated by the language of the text in light of the appropriate context of the communication. A typical determinant of linguistic meaning is "ordinary meaning," which, roughly, refers to the sense that an expression usually has in the context at issue. The "ordinary meaning" may differ, though, from the linguistic meaning.[3] For example, the legislature might stipulate an unusual definition for a term that differs from its ordinary meaning. Similarly, context may indicate that a word should be given a technical or specialized meaning rather than its ordinary meaning.

Like "ordinary meaning," courts often refer to "plain meaning" or the "plain meaning rule." One definition is that the plain meaning rule dictates that statutes are to be interpreted according to the ordinary meaning of the relevant language, unless the terms are otherwise defined in the statute (Tiersma 1999). The plain meaning rule, though, has been used by judges to peremptorily declare textual language to be clear, and its use has consequently been criticized by scholars as representing a simplistic view of language. One criticism is that the plain meaning rule views statutes as commonly being unambiguous and capable of being straightforwardly applied in specific cases based on considerations only of language (ibid.). Contrary to this conception of the plain meaning rule, though, the linguistic meaning of a text, even in context, may be ambiguous or vague. A search for the linguistic meaning of a legal text should not therefore assume a high degree of confidence in people's potential to communicate successfully, at least in a narrow, determinate sense. To the contrary, as this chapter argues, an epistemically modest view of the determinacy of communication should be concomitant with any determination of meaning.

2. The Linguistic Nature of Legal Interpretation

Based on judicial practice, one should conclude that linguistics can contribute to theories of legal interpretation and that judges should be interested in these insights. Courts often frame interpretive disputes in terms of linguistic meaning, even when nonlinguistic concerns are also relevant. Consider the issue of scienter in criminal cases, which was discussed by some of the participants in the 1995 Washington University conference (discussed in the introduction). The case that was of interest to the participants was the Supreme Court's then-recent decision in *United States v. X-Citement Video, Inc.*[4] In *X-Citement Video*, the Supreme Court held that a federal child pornography statute, 18 U.S.C. § 2252, includes a scienter requirement regarding the age of the performer in a visual depiction. Section 2252 provides, in relevant part:

(a) Any person who—
(1) knowingly transports or ships in interstate or foreign commerce by any means including by computer or mails, any visual depiction, if—
(A) the producing of such visual depiction involves the use of a minor engaging in sexually explicit conduct; and
(B) such visual depiction is of such conduct;
[. . . .]
shall be punished as provided in subsection (b) of this section.

The court found that the "most natural grammatical reading" is that the term "knowingly" modifies only the surrounding verbs: transports, ships, receives, distributes, or reproduces. Under this construction, the word "knowingly" would not modify the elements of the minority of the performers, or the sexually explicit nature of the material, because they are set forth in independent clauses separated by interruptive punctuation.[5] The court declined, however, to adopt the "most grammatical reading," for reasons involving legal concerns, including the possibility that it would require invalidation of the statute.

From a linguistic perspective at least, the court's decision in *X-Citement Video* was controversial. Two linguists, Kaplan and Green (1995), have argued that the court adopted an interpretation that contradicted syntactic rules. Interpreting § 2252 from a purely linguistic standpoint is, on the surface, fairly straightforward. A modifier, such as "knowingly," within a verb phrase combines with other expressions within the verb phrase to form a larger expression of that same type. Expressions outside of the verb phrase, though, would not be modified by the adverb. Section 2252 contains an if-clause, which is not part of the verb phrase that contains "knowingly" or the noun phrase, "Any person who knowingly distributes a depiction." Semantically, the if-clause can be said to function as a parenthetical, and the meaning of "knowingly" "cannot apply to the meaning of the if-clause, because of the way modification works in English" (1235). Thus, linguistically at least, the Supreme Court's interpretation of § 2252 was erroneous.

Despite the linguistic focus of some of the court's analysis in *X-Citement Video*, various scholars have questioned whether linguistic knowledge should be influential in the resolution of such a case. Poirier (1995, 1033–34), for instance, questions the relevance and permissibility of the expertise of linguists and argues that

> knowingly in a statute does not operate as standard English does. As a lawyer, I knew that the appearance of knowingly in a context I was unfamiliar with should send me scurrying to cases and treatises. I needed to know how it had been treated in that particular area. Issues of intent and responsibility, implicated semantically in various statutes and situations, are too central and too convoluted for there to be a consistent syntactic usage in heterogenous situations over any period of time. Ordinary language and adverbial syntax are the wrong places to start.

Because language in a statute does not operate as does standard English, Poirier (1034) argues that "[w]hen judges say plain meaning, they may not mean plain meaning in a sense that linguists would recognize as ordinary language."

It is true that "plain meaning" and "ordinary meaning" are separate concepts (as briefly described above). One of the problems, though, with arguments such as Poirier's is that judges consistently indicate that language in statutes operates as does standard English. "Plain meaning" might encompass facts other than linguistic meaning, such as judicial precedents, but certainly one fundamental determinant is linguistic meaning. In fact, the scope of "knowingly" (and other terms relating to scienter) in various contexts is still being decided by courts, and these courts often rely heavily (if not exclusively) on linguistic analysis.

The Supreme Court's recent decision in *Flores-Figueroa v. United States*[6] is one salient example of a court focusing on linguistic analysis. In *Flores-Figueroa*, the Supreme Court decided that a federal criminal statute forbidding "[a]ggravated identity theft" requires the government to show that the defendant knew that the "means of identification" he or she unlawfully transferred, possessed, or used in fact belonged to "another person." The relevant part of the statute applies to one who "knowingly transfers, possesses, or uses, without lawful authority, a means of identification of another person."[7] Contrary to the court's statement in *X-Citement Video*, the court in *Flores-Figueroa* noted that "[a]s a matter of ordinary English grammar, it seems natural to read the statute's word 'knowingly' as applying to all the subsequently listed elements of the crime."[8] The court reasoned as follows:

In ordinary English, where a transitive verb has an object, listeners in most contexts assume that an adverb (such as knowingly) that modifies the transitive verb tells the listener how the subject performed the entire action, including the object as set forth in the sentence. Thus, if a bank official says, "Smith knowingly transferred the funds to his brother's account," we would normally understand the bank official's statement as telling us that Smith knew the account was his brother's. Nor would it matter if the bank official said "Smith knowingly transferred the funds to the account of his brother." In either instance, if the bank official later told us that Smith did not know the account belonged to Smith's brother, we should be surprised.[9]

The court continued its analysis by focusing on linguistic meaning, claiming that

the Government has not provided us with a single example of a sentence that, when used in typical fashion, would lead the hearer to believe that the word "knowingly" modifies only a transitive verb without the full object, i.e., that it leaves the hearer gravely uncertain about the subject's state of mind in respect to the full object of the transitive verb in the sentence.[10]

The court even rejected efforts to refocus its attention on nonlinguistic matters, stating that "[t]he Government correctly points out that in these cases more was at issue than proper use of the English language. But if more is at issue here, what is it?"[11]

The court's analysis in *Flores-Figueroa* was consistent with the views expressed in a brief filed by four professors of linguistics, which argued that "linguistics can offer insights and analytical tools that may be helpful in resolving [. . .] the interpretive dispute this case presents."[12] Unfortunately, though, it is not clear that the court's focus on linguistic meaning in *Flores-Figueroa*, and its somewhat perfunctory analysis of linguistic meaning in *X-Citement Video*, combined to provide a framework for handling issues of scienter (and other adverbial scope issues). The court's interpretation in *X-Citement Video* would not be problematic, at least from a linguistic perspective, it if had acknowledged the correct linguistic meaning of § 2252 and explained the circumstances in which that meaning could be overcome by legal concerns. Instead, the court's linguistic analysis was perfunctory, stating simply that it was "reluctan[t] to simply follow the most grammatical reading of the statute."[13] This lack of exposition necessitated the *Flores-Figueroa* case, which dealt with the same issue in a different context. While the *Flores-Figueroa* case focused heavily on linguistic analysis, this sort of analysis is not, of course, sufficient to overcome established interpretive practices. For instance, some state courts have disagreed with *Flores-Figueroa*, indicating that it is inconsistent with their interpretive practices.[14]

Judicial use of linguistic analysis is obviously not limited to issues involving adverbial scope and extends to many issues more commonly encountered. For instance, issues involving word meanings are pervasive, due in part to the nature of legal disputes. A typical dispute often involves deciding whether an object or act falls within the scope of some legal provision, requiring a court to precisely define one or more of the provision's words. Hart's (1958) famous no-vehicles-in-the-park scenario (discussed in the introduction), for example, is a classic situation where a court would rely on linguistic analysis, at least in part, in determining whether a given object (such as a bicycle) falls within the concept "vehicle." In fact, a modern court would likely approach the meaning of the

statute by relying on a dictionary definition of "vehicle." While such judicial reliance on dictionaries has been criticized, the definitional question is often at the core of the court's decision. Furthermore, many of the
criticisms of judicial reliance on dictionaries do not take issue with the
necessity of defining the key words but, rather, argue that the current judicial approach to definitions often results in inaccuracies.[15]

3. The Contribution of Linguistic Meaning to Legal Meaning

Considering that courts often employ linguistic analysis when determining the meaning of texts, it may seem obvious that linguists can and
should contribute to legal interpretation. This is especially true considering the errors of linguistic understanding that courts sometimes make
when interpreting legal texts. Some scholars and judges nonetheless argue that linguistic meaning (and, consequently, linguists' expertise) is
not particularly useful to legal interpretation, at least as a normative
matter of how legal interpretation should proceed. Establishing that linguistic meaning (and, correlatively, linguists' insights) is essential to legal interpretation might, to some, be accomplished by demonstrating (as
was done in the last section) that courts habitually engage in linguistic
analysis when interpreting texts. Nevertheless, critics would undoubtedly concede this point but assert that such reliance on linguistic analysis is undesirable because it leads to erroneous interpretations. Thus, in
order to address these arguments, it must be shown that linguistic meaning is inherently an important determinant of legal meaning due to the
nature of legal interpretation.

At the outset, it must be acknowledged that the linguistic meaning of a text is not always coterminous with its legal meaning, which is
the authoritative meaning given to it by a judge. Courts purport to enforce plain and unambiguous statutory language according to its terms,
but much statutory language (as well as language in other legal texts)
is not plain and unambiguous. Instead, it may be ambiguous, vague, or
otherwise underdetermined. Even in situations not involving ambiguity
or vagueness, the linguistic meaning of a text may differ from its legal
meaning (as was discussed in the introduction). Even when putting aside
a judge's ideological motivations, which may cause the court to distort or
ignore a text's communicative content in favor of the judge's preferred
interpretation, circumstances outside of the linguistic meaning of a text

may therefore always control the outcome of a case. Indeed, it is well accepted amongst scholars that the legal meaning of a text may depend on interpretive principles and judgments that are based on legal rather than linguistic concerns.

The legal meaning of a text is not always an instance of linguistic meaning generally, as other legal principles may require an interpretation that deviates from legal meaning, but this concession does not establish that linguistic meaning should not be a crucial determinant of legal meaning. Some skeptics, though, argue that linguistic and philosophical insights are of limited importance because factors other than linguistic meaning should be determinative of legal meaning. Ross (1995, 1057), for example, makes a representative claim that "linguists' principal expertise—ascertaining how language is used by ordinary speakers of English—is often of *little value* in interpreting controversial non-criminal federal statutes" (emphasis added). Ross (1057–58) argues that with regulatory statutes directed at a small community of lawyers, regulators, and people subject to the specific regulations,

> extrinsic evidence that is known and accessible to this small sub-community—such as legislative history, established norms of construction, and other evidence about the context in which the legislation arose—is more likely than linguistic analysis to help an outside judge shed light on what Congress meant and how the statute is to be understood. Rather than serving as the principal means of interpretation, a *statute's ordinary meaning should be a weak, tie-breaking default factor in most cases*, to be used only when the judge cannot confidently interpret the statute based on extrinsic indicia of the legislation's meaning as understood by legislators and those actually subject to the legislation (emphasis added).

Ross (1058) claims that the above view is heresy because "ordinary meaning is so heavily emphasized by interpreters of all the leading schools of statutory interpretation."

Various aspects of the above critique are inaccurate. First, and perhaps most importantly, linguists' expertise extends beyond issues relating to ordinary meaning. The ordinary meaning doctrine is primarily semantic in nature and thus accounts for linguistic phenomena by relating, via the rules of the language and abstracting away from specific contexts, linguistic expressions to the world objects to which they refer (Ariel 2010). Linguists are equally interested, though, in pragmatics, which accounts for linguistic phenomena by reference to the language user (producer or interpreter) and involves inferential processes (ibid.). In fact, some linguists view interpretation, including legal interpretation, as being best explained by the inferential processes that typically fall under the pragmatics heading.[16] Thus, tying the contributions of linguists to the ordinary meaning doctrine severely underestimates the scope of their expertise.

Furthermore, an additional flaw concerns the erroneous conception of ordinary meaning. It is not true that "established norms of construction, and other evidence about the context in which the legislation arose" are never aspects of ordinary meaning. To the contrary, established norms of construction and contextual evidence can in fact be determinants of ordinary meaning (thus undercutting Ross's efforts to list alternatives to reliance on ordinary meaning). One could of course conceive of an interpretive regime where legal interpreters chose interpretations based on their own conceptions of what the content of the law should be, without regard to the linguistic meaning of the text.[17] Under any plausible theory of interpretation, though, the argument that linguistic meaning is of "little value" to legal interpretation fails to appreciate the ineliminable relevance of linguistic meaning. In order to qualify as "plausible," in the sense that it might be adopted by judges, a theory of legal interpretation must be consistent with the legal practices of the United States and thus make some claim that adherence to the theory is consistent with the proper role of judges as the "faithful agents" of the legislature.[18]

With respect to statutes, one tactic that "little value" proponents use, while purporting to conform to the faithful agent model of judging, is to argue that certain cases establish that linguistic meaning is either misleading or of negligible value in discerning the true intent of Congress. Contrary to the arguments, however, these cases do not establish that linguistic meaning was unimportant to the court's interpretation. Consider, for example, the Supreme Court's decision in *Train v. Colorado Public Interest Research Group*, relied upon by Ross.[19] The *Train* case involved the Environmental Protection Agency's (EPA) claim that it did not have authority under the Federal Water Pollution Control Act ("the act") to regulate the discharge of nuclear waste materials. The operative term "pollutant" was defined in the act as follows:

The term "pollutant" means dredged spoil, solid waste, incinerator residue, sewage, garbage, sewage sludge, munitions, chemical wastes, biological materials, radioactive materials, heat, wrecked or discarded equipment, rock, sand, cellar dirt and industrial, municipal, and agricultural waste discharged into water.[20]

The provision contained two explicit exceptions to the scope of "pollutant" that did not cover the materials in question. There was thus little dispute that nuclear waste materials (as "radioactive materials") were included within the scope of the "pollutant" definition. The problem was that the Atomic Energy Commission (AEC) and its successors under the Atomic Energy Act of 1954 (AEA) already had regulatory authority concerning nuclear waste materials.

In its opinion, which held that the EPA did not have authority to regulate the nuclear waste materials, the Supreme Court noted that the "Court of Appeals resolved the question exclusively by reference to the language of the statute."[21] The court stated that the Court of Appeals was in error in excluding examination of the legislative history of the act. The court cited a precedent, *United States v. American Trucking Ass'ns*,[22] for the proposition that "[w]hen aid to construction of the meaning of words, as used in the statute, is available, there certainly can be no 'rule of law' which forbids its use, however clear the words may appear on 'superficial examination.'"[23] The court reviewed the legislative history of the act and concluded that it favored the conclusion that the EPA did not have jurisdiction over the nuclear waste materials. It reasoned that

If it was not clear at the outset, we think it abundantly clear after a review of the legislative materials that reliance on the "plain meaning" of the words "radioactive materials" contained in the definition of "pollutant" in the FWPCA contributes little to our understanding of whether Congress intended the Act to encompass the regulation of source, byproduct, and special nuclear materials.[24]

*   *   *

Notwithstanding decisions like *Train*, it is a difficult argument that the linguistic meaning of a text should be of little importance to the interpretation chosen by the judge. Indeed, the "little value" position is a minority one even amongst those who are skeptical about the influentialness of linguistic meaning. Instead, it is typical for legal theorists to concede, at the least, that the linguistic meaning of a statute generally acts as a constraint on its legal meaning. Even critics who question the decisiveness of linguistic meaning concede its importance. For example, one such critic, Flanagan (2010, 258), "offer[s] no objection to the idea that enactments' literal meaning is of great assistance in determining their legal meaning." Similarly, another critic, Greenberg (2011, 221), emphasizes that "on any plausible view, the meaning of a statute's text is highly relevant to the statute's contribution" to the legal meaning of the text. Undoubtedly, linguistic meaning is influential because it is difficult to conceive of a realistic methodology of interpretation in which it would *not* be influential. Hence, even those who advocate in favor of methodologies that find facts other than linguistic meaning decisive typically allow for considerations of textual meaning to be significant. For example, the once-influential legal process approach of Professors Hart and Sacks advocates a purposivist approach to interpretation where courts should assume that legislatures are "made of reasonable persons pursuing reasonable purposes reasonably" (Eskridge and Frickey 1995, 1378). Even Hart and Sacks (1994, 1374), though, maintained that in interpreting the words of the statute so as to carry out the purpose a court should not give the words "a meaning they will not bear."

The best argument that can be made in favor of the "little value" theory of *Train* is that the linguistic meaning of the language in the statute did not provide a basis for restricting the scope of its literal meaning, and thus the court determined the meaning on some other basis (specifically, the perceived intent of Congress). The court indicated that legislative history should be consulted "however clear the words may appear on superficial examination," but the "nonsuperficial" contextual considerations did not reveal that the seemingly clear words of the provision were in fact unclear. One example of such a situation is when contextual evidence reveals that a word or phrase has a technical, legal, or other specialized meaning that differs from its ordinary meaning. Hence, the seemingly clear meaning of the provision, based on its ordinary meaning, would be revealed to be unclear, or have a different meaning, based on contextual considerations. In the *Train* case, though, the legislative history provided persuasive reasons, at least in the court's view, to *reject* the linguistic meaning of the provision in favor of a nonliteral meaning. The words remained clear, but the court nevertheless rejected the clear meaning.

Despite the court's reliance on legislative history to select a nonliteral meaning, the "plain meaning" of the words "radioactive materials" must have contributed more than an insignificant amount to the court's understanding of whether Congress intended the act to encompass the regulation of nuclear materials. Suppose, counterfactually, that the definition of "pollutant" in the act did not include "radioactive materials" or any other term that would encompass nuclear waste. Would such a fact not change the court's analysis? Presumably, the court would have still consulted the legislative history of the act, but with the understanding that the linguistic meaning of "pollutant" did not include nuclear waste. Undoubtedly, conflicting or nonexistent evidence of congressional intent would not cause the court to rule that nuclear waste is a "pollutant." In contrast, if the definition of "pollutant" in the act did include nuclear waste, conflicting or nonexistent evidence of congressional intent would not cause the court to rule that nuclear waste is not a "pollutant." The difference in the linguistic meaning of "pollutant" would, thus, be critical to the outcome of the case.

Suppose, instead, that the provision did not include nuclear waste but that the court was considering whether such inclusion was appropriate in light of congressional intent. Would the court have been as willing to reject the linguistic meaning of the provision in order to insert a term as it was in *Train* to reject the linguistic meaning of the provision in order to exclude a term? Even the famous paragon of purposivist decision-making, *Holy Trinity Church v. United States*,[25] involved the court narrowing the scope of the provision rather than broadening it. The court indicated that "[i]t is a familiar rule that a thing may be within the letter of the statute and yet not within the statute, because not within its spirit, nor within the intention of its makers."[26] Note that the court did not assert the inverse.

Certainly, then, the amount of evidence necessary to *confirm* the linguistic meaning of a provision as its legal meaning is less than that necessary to *reject* the linguistic meaning in favor of a nonliteral meaning.[27] This difference should not be underestimated, as the allocation of the burden of proof in a case has a significant bearing on the outcome.[28] Thus, as indicated above, would the court have been as willing to expand the stipulated definition of "pollutant" to include "nuclear waste," if it thought doing so would be consistent with congressional intent, as it was to contract the meaning to exclude it? Various scholars, including perhaps most notably David Shapiro (2000), have observed that principles of legal interpretation tend to operate to restrict rather than broaden the scope of provisions. This tendency is consistent with the views of some linguists and philosophers regarding how language generally works. For instance Stanley (2007, 18) explains that "extra-linguistic context is never called upon to *expand* the content determined by the context-independent meaning of a term in a context." Indeed, "[i]f context could affect the interpretation of words in such a manner that the content they express relative to a context would be inconsistent with their context-independent meaning, that would threaten the systematic nature of interpretation" (ibid.). Even if one is not ready to accept the strength of Stanley's claim, acknowledging that context tends to narrow rather than expand the "context-independent meaning of a term in a context" is sufficient to make the point that the linguistic meaning of a provision, even if rejected, is important to the accepted interpretation.

In contrast to an interpretation where linguistic meaning is given little weight, it is not uncommon for a court to reject the ordinary meaning of a word in favor of some other linguistic meaning. For instance, in *Johnson v. United States*,[29] the court rejected a conventional meaning of "revoke" in favor of an unconventional one, determined in part by broad considerations of purpose and legal consequences. The court remarked that while it was

> departing from the rule of construction that prefers ordinary meaning . . . this is exactly what ought to happen when the ordinary meaning fails to fit the text and when the realization of clear congressional policy . . . is in tension with the result that customary interpretive rules would deliver.[30]

There is an important distinction between the two types of interpretations. In the first, as exemplified by *Train*, the court chooses a meaning that is not restricted by the linguistic meaning of the text. In the second, as exemplified by *Johnson*, the chosen meaning is controlled by the linguistic meaning of the text. Instead of the ordinary meaning of the given word or phrase, which represents the conventional meaning that would likely pertain outside of the legal context, another meaning is selected that represents a specialized or technical meaning. The second scenario thus cannot be counted amongst those cases that reject the linguistic meaning of the text.

4. Other Arguments about the "Contextual" Approach to Interpretation

Even if nontextual sources of meaning are valued, it is a difficult argument that the linguistic meaning of the relevant language should contribute little to the legal meaning of the provision. In fact, the claim is implausible for various reasons. A court may rely on the background of the statute and its legislative history, but it cannot reject basic principles of syntax and semantics and still make sense of the provision. Furthermore, the rejection of the linguistic meaning in favor of a nonliteral meaning in a given case (as happened in *Train*) is not sufficient to establish the general proposition that the linguistic meaning of a provision does, or should, contribute little to its legal meaning. Similarly, a judge looking outside the text to disambiguate language or make it more precise does not further an argument that "plain meaning" is of little relevance to legal meaning. Rather, such interpretations accept the linguistic meaning but must necessarily use nonlinguistic principles in order to give the text a meaning that is sufficient for the purposes of the law.

Ross (1995, 1061) argues that the court's approach in *Train* was "superior to one based on the way the text alone would be understood by ordinary speakers of English," but the case is not the best vehicle for such a comparison. For one, the key term "pollutant" was given a stipulated definition by Congress. Determining the ordinary meaning of a word, which involves lexical semantics, is an area in which linguists and philosophers, as well as some psychologists, have expertise that is relevant to legal interpretation. By enacting a definition, Congress relieved the judiciary of the responsibility of determining the "ordinary meaning" of the word, although of course definitions require interpretation. Importantly, though, as indicated above, the key issue in the case did not involve a dispute regarding the linguistic meaning of the words in the text but, rather, whether the linguistic meaning should prevail. The case thus focused on a narrow range of issues compared to many other cases, and the court's focus on drawing specific insights from the legislative history was not one of the areas in which linguists can be most helpful.

In addition, the argument that the court's "contextual" approach in *Train* was superior to one that would focus "on the way the text alone would be understood by ordinary speakers of English" is not the proper way to frame the debate. There is a false dichotomy between a "contextual" approach, which would purport to give linguistic meaning little weight, and a methodology that is limited to determining the meaning ordinary speakers of English might give a statute. Consideration of context is appropriate and often necessary in determining the ordinary meaning of the textual language. To interpret acontextually is, often, to misinterpret. Furthermore, as explained above, even those who advocate a central role for linguistic meaning in legal interpretation must (and typically do) concede that the legal meaning of a text may sometimes differ from its linguistic meaning.

Properly viewed, debate regarding the *Train* case should focus on the methodology of textualism, which should not be conflated with linguistic analysis (or the insights offered by linguists). Manning (2010, 1288), a leading textualist, describes textualism as advocating that judges "should seek statutory meaning in the semantic import of the enacted text and, in so doing, should reject the longstanding practice of using unenacted legislative history as authoritative evidence of legislative intent or purpose." Although textualism discounts the legitimacy and relevance of legislative history, there is no linguistic principle forbidding an interpreter from consulting legislative history. Like other aspects of legal interpretation, the legitimacy of legislative history may depend on nonlinguistic considerations, such as insights from political science. Of course, linguists may be able to contribute to a proper understanding of the role of contextual evidence like legislative history in determining speakers' intent. Indeed, linguists like Solan (2005) have argued in favor of legislative history as a key determinate of legislative intent.

Putting to the side the conflation of textualism and linguistics, whether the *Train* case is a representative case is an empirical matter. If an archaeological-like dig through the legislative history of a statute, along with specialized principles of interpretation relevant only to legal interpretation (of which there are some, most of which relate to the resolution of textual ambiguity or uncertainty rather than the ascertainment of linguistic meaning), were always sufficient to discern the true intent of the legislature, it would be true that the linguistic meaning of the text would have little value to legal interpretation. Of course, the interpreter would still have to deal with the linguistic meaning of legislative history. Should the linguistic meaning of the various sources of legislative history control the interpretation of it, or should the intent of it be controlling? How would one find the intent of the intent (which, again, would require a decision about whether its linguistic meaning should control)?

Furthermore, a comprehensive critique of legislative history is beyond the scope of this chapter, but in general the legitimacy and usefulness of legislative history is now questioned in a way that was not true at the time of the *Train* decision.

Even if consideration of legislative history is in general a legitimate judicial practice, and conceding for the purposes of argument that it was directly on point in *Train*, the case is likely an outlier case in the sense that legislative history is typically not revealing regarding the many varied, and specific, issues that courts must decide. If this is true, the terms of the debate change. The context in which the legislation arose is often not particularly useful when slight nuances of meaning are at issue (which is typical in legal cases). In such situations, relying on broad general purpose, as a matter of general practice, requires some justification that goes beyond demonstrating that in some cases the legislative history is (allegedly) directly revealing of legislative intent.[31]

5. Problems with Legislative Intent

Whatever value the "little value" argument has as a normative matter (i.e., as a prescription of how interpretation should proceed), it does not represent the currently dominant approach to statutory interpretation. Manning (2013) indicates that the *American Trucking* interpretive approach was often used by the court in the five decades following the decision. The court now, however, generally has a different approach. In recent years, the Supreme Court has placed an increased emphasis on the linguistic meaning of the text in both statutory and constitutional cases (Scalia and Manning 2012). In Manning's view (2013, 456), the consensus is that while a court should consider anything that might cast light on a statute's objectives, including its legislative history, the linguistic meaning of a text "now sets a hard cap on the judge's discretion." The typical sequential process of statutory interpretation illustrates the importance of linguistic meaning. Courts first apply "general principles of statutory construction to the language of the statute in order to construe any ambiguous language to accurately reflect the intent of the legislature."[32] If the language is not ambiguous, however, "there is no room for further construction" and, with some exceptions, it is given its "ordinary and obvious meaning."[33] The sequence is standard, if not always followed. In a recent case, for instance, the Supreme Court indicated that it was "depart[ing] from a normal order of discussion, namely an order that first considers [the party's] statutory language argument[,]" in order to first consider the purpose and legislative history of the statute at issue.[34]

A core aspect of linguistic meaning is the principle that textual language should be given its ordinary meaning. The doctrine is perhaps the most widely cited axiom of legal interpretation. Scalia and Garner (2012, 6) refer to the ordinary meaning doctrine as "the most fundamental semantic rule of interpretation." Its use is both long-standing and widespread. The ordinary meaning doctrine's influence is not limited to statutory and constitutional cases, but rather is applied by judges when interpreting virtually every type of legal text, including contracts, trusts, wills, and even jury instructions. The presumption that language in legal texts (even technical ones) should be given its ordinary meaning is supported by various reasons, some of which are beyond the expertise of linguists and philosophers to evaluate. These reasons relate to issues such as notice to affected parties and the rule of law. This chapter will focus only on a couple of reasons that underscore the importance of ordinary meaning to legal interpretation, notwithstanding the validity of the notice and rule of law justifications. In general, the argument is that a presumption of ordinary meaning may offer a better approximation of legislative intent, as well as furthering important justificatory interests, than would methodologies that would give little or no weight to ordinary meaning.

Even for specialized statutes directed towards a relatively small, sophisticated audience, the principle that textual language should be interpreted in accordance with its ordinary meaning has salience. Courts, as well as various scholars, typically state that the words of the text (and the ordinary meaning of those words) are the surest, safest evidence of the author's actual intentions (Benson 2008). According to the Supreme Court, "[c]ourts assume that the ordinary meaning of statutory language accurately expresses the legislative purpose." This assertion is, of course, a generalization and does not acknowledge that many legislators do not read the language of the bills on which they vote, or may not have seriously considered the language. In any case, it seems uncontroversial that drafters of texts choose language (as do people generally) that reflects their purpose. Regardless of a court's method of giving meaning to statutory words, the legislature, if it is being at all careful, will have considered to some degree the meanings that courts could give to the statutory language. How could it not? With an ordinary meaning approach the legislature may be in a much better position to make predictions about meaning than with other approaches that depend on how well the interpreter draws inferences about meaning from contextual material that may be multivocal and conflicting.

Although a presumption that the ordinary meaning of a provision reflects legislative intent will be erroneous in some cases, a legislative history–centered approach must also address issues of legislative intent. In addition to the problem of multivocal and conflicting demonstrations of intent, a contextual approach that focuses on legislative history must also provide some persuasive theory for attributing the demonstrated intent of some subset of the legislature to the legislature at large. As Marmor (2005, 126) describes, "legislation in legislative assemblies is a complex and concerted action involving elaborate procedures." With statutes, any given clause or sentence may reflect various intentions, at different levels of generality, which reflect the many authors and their varied motivations. Some of the members of the legislature may vote for the bill in hopes that it will be interpreted in a broader or narrower manner than its terms would indicate. The identity of the speaker is thus a matter of dispute. Is it the legislature as a unit, all legislators considered collectively, the legislators who voted for the legislation or only those who read it, the drafter(s) of the legislation (even if not legislators themselves?), the sponsor(s) of the legislation, or some other possibility? Furthermore, what about the intentions of the president who signed the bill into law? The myriad of possibilities indicates that there is therefore no singular intention to which an appeal can easily be made, although some scholars have argued for various proxies for communicative intent. The proxies, though, must reflect some theory by which to attribute intent to some group representing the majority of the legislators based on the intent of a subset of that group.[35]

The proxies for collective legislative intent have various hurdles to overcome. Unlike the typical oral conversation, the legislative context is impersonal. Legislators and interpreters do not, generally, know each other personally, making clarification impossible (absent further legislation, of course, which nevertheless cannot be seen as the continuation of a conversation in any authentic sense). Contextual information regarding the legislators' intent is often either not available or is of questionable value. For statutes, as indicated above, "legislative history" has been widely attacked as being unreliable and subject to manipulation. Part of the reason is that the legislative process is a far less coopera-

tive one than is the typical communicative context. Due to strategic behavior, and other legislative practices, the legislative history may not accurately reflect the legislators' communicative intentions (at least with
respect to specific issues). Furthermore, like the text, the relevant interpreters, including judges, may have to interpret the legislative history
years after it was created.

A familiar response to the problems associated with an intentionalist
view of legislation, apart from arguing for a proxy for collective intent, is
to emphasize at a high level of generality the intentional aspects of legislation. Posner (1986, 196) makes the claim that a "document can mani-
fest a single purpose even though those who drafted and approved it had
a variety of private motives and expectations." Perhaps this is true, but
a general purpose is different than an actual intent regarding some specific issue, and different levels of generality regarding intent should not
be conflated. It may be true that at a very general level of intent a legislature had the intent to enact a statute, and did so in order to accomplish
some purpose. Such an observation, though, is not necessarily relevant
to any particular interpretive dispute (which often occurs at the margins
of the enacted law). One can still deny that specific aspects of the communicative intent of the legislature are discernible, if they can be said
to exist at all. An intentionalism that is based on something other than
generalized intent is not always (and maybe never) possible because the
author (or authors) does not always have a specific communicative intention regarding the interpretive dispute at issue. Rather, it is typical
that the author or authors failed to form any intent, or neglected to consider the issue at all. This is especially true with legislation because, as
mentioned above, due to the enormous volume of legislation and other
reasons, most legislators do not read most of the text of the statutes on
which they vote. Even if some proxy for legislative intent is used, such as
a committee report, the same problems remain.

An important justification for judicial reliance on linguistic meaning
is thus epistemic in nature. It is based on uncertainty regarding the ability of interpreters to accurately discern meaning apart from the linguistic meaning of the words in the text. This view is somewhat analogous
to the epistemic view of vagueness, closely identified with Williamson
(1996), which holds that the extensions (i.e., the referential range of application) of predicates are sharply defined but cannot be determined.
The actual intentions of the author(s) of a text may exist, but interpreters may not (or should not) have confidence in their ability to accurately

assess contextual evidence outside of that associated with the linguistic meaning of the textual language. This uncertainty may not preclude interpreters from considering extratextual evidence of meaning (and, indeed, some consideration may be necessary), but it may make them reluctant, at least explicitly if not implicitly, to dismiss linguistic meaning in favor of some other interpretation. Certainly, it requires interpretive resources to obtain nontextual evidence, such as legislative history or other indicia of intent, with uncertain increases in interpretive accuracy. Vermeule (1998, 2006) makes a similar point in arguing that any interpretive value added by the consideration of legislative history is not justified by the cost of doing so.

The problems associated with determining actual legislative intent have convinced some scholars that intent should be defined differently when a legal text is being interpreted than it would be with respect to a speaker's utterance in a typical conversation. Jori (1993, 2113, 2120) describes legal communication as focusing on impersonal, prescriptive, and linguistic-only signs and legal texts as being intrinsically impersonal in character with most of their features determined by the necessity of communicating messages out of context. Tiersma (2001, 440), a linguist, similarly argues that while "virtually any linguist would agree that the goal of interpretation is to determine what the speaker or author intends to communicate to his audience," an interpreter must recognize that an autonomous text must be interpreted as such. Thus, the interpreter determines the intent of the writer on the basis of what is contained in the text and must assume that the words have been used in an "ordinary" or "literal" sense. Jackson (1995) agrees that statutory language should normally be regarded as "unsponsored" language via a model of linguistic meaning rather than actual intent.

Treating legal texts as unsponsored should have various consequences, including underscoring the necessity of relying on linguistic meaning. Their unsponsored nature would seem to require that interpreters place sustained, if not exclusive, attention on textual rather than extratextual authorial evidence. More precisely, it requires that linguistic meaning, as opposed to authorial intent, be the primary determinant of the meaning of a legal text. In addition, it illustrates that the high level of generality at which inquiries into intent must be framed often results in the legislative intent being of a hypothetical, purposivist kind. An interpreter with a purposivist approach does not attempt to determine the actual intentions of the legislators, but rather may ask something along the lines of what a reasonable legislature wanted to achieve, or would have wanted to achieve if it had foreseen the issue, by enacting the legislation at issue (Marmor 2012). While such a methodology is defensible, it must be justified on grounds other than those that would support an intentionalist approach.

Notwithstanding the critique of intentionalism and legislative history given above, giving significant weight to linguistic meaning is consistent with an intentionalist methodology of interpretation, undermining the claims of skeptics that there is some fundamental tension between intentionalism and a concern with linguistic meaning. The linguistic meaning is the presumed meaning and can be overcome on whatever basis the court finds persuasive. If, for example, an intentionalist judge believes that the linguistic meaning of the relevant provision conflicts with legislative intent, the judge can simply find that some other meaning was nevertheless intended.[36] The court in *Flores-Figueroa v. United States*, for instance, indicated that the presumption created by rules of syntax (i.e., the ordinary meaning) can be rebutted where the "context" or "background circumstances" support a different interpretation.[37] Such a decision, though, requires an explanation, thereby illustrating the justificatory nature of legal interpretation. In general (and unlike ordinary conversations), courts do not simply announce or assume a particular interpretation but, rather, explain the process of reasoning. With regard to some objective of interpretation, such as the determination of linguistic meaning, courts explain how the evidence met the relevant standard for determining the meaning (often, but not always, defined as the "correct" interpretation). Determining the linguistic meaning therefore adds explicit structure to what might otherwise be a comparatively open-ended judicial explanation if such evidence were not explicitly considered and accepted or rejected.

Notwithstanding its defeasibility, the presumption of linguistic meaning thereby sets a useful default which requires that deviations from it be explained and justified, or that the indeterminate nature of the language be identified. Of course, courts might erroneously evaluate the relevant language, such as by exaggerating its definiteness. Judges are nevertheless accountable in the sense that they must give reasons for their decisions (Seidman 1988). Determining linguistic meaning enhances accountability by providing an anchoring point for deciding whether arguments about meaning are accepted or rejected. Certainly, courts frequently engage in statutory interpretation (or contract or constitutional interpretation) without carefully addressing linguistic meaning. Linguistic meaning is nonetheless fundamental to interpretation. In fact, it is likely that in most situations the linguistic meaning of the relevant textual language would be a primary consideration for courts implicitly, even if not explicitly. If a court takes the language of a legal text seriously, which it will invariably purport to do, it must give some linguistic meaning to the textual language. It would be odd for a court to immediately give the language some unordinary meaning. Even if done incorrectly, the necessity of considering linguistic meaning therefore cannot be avoided.

6. Erroneous Plain Meaning Interpretations and Linguistic Determinacy

Thus far, this chapter has argued that courts habitually focus on linguistic meaning, that claims that linguistic meaning is of "little value" to legal interpretation are unpersuasive, and that, to the contrary, the determination of linguistic meaning is essential to legal interpretation. Scholars skeptical of the centrality of linguistic meaning, though, often point to decisions where a court applied a "plain meaning" approach to interpretation, with unfortunate results, as evidence that the plain meaning approach is a flawed interpretive methodology. A plain meaning approach is not synonymous, though, with the judicial application of knowledge from linguists. Even if these criticisms are accurate they would not therefore establish that linguistic meaning, determined according to valid linguistic principles, is of little value to interpretation. Furthermore, as explained above, the application of linguistic knowledge to a provision does not preclude an interpretation made for legal reasons. Thus, even if the critics of specific cases were correct about a particular case or cases leading to "incorrect results," they would have to establish that this is an endemic aspect of giving weight to the linguistic meaning of the text.

In contrasting its "contextual" approach with a "plain meaning" approach, the court in *Train v. Colorado Public Interest Research Group*,[38] discussed earlier in this chapter, cited a 1975 *Columbia Law Review* article by Professor Arthur W. Murphy. In the article, Murphy argues that the Supreme Court's (infamous) decision in *Caminetti v. United States*[39] serves as an example of the court's occasional misguided reliance on the "plain meaning" doctrine. Caminetti was convicted under the Mann Act for transporting his mistress across state lines.[40] The Mann Act made it a felony to engage in interstate or foreign commerce transport of "any woman or girl for the purpose of prostitution or debauchery, or for any other immoral purpose."[41] The court indicated that if the language of the statute is "plain," "the sole function of the courts is to enforce it according to its terms."[42] In the court's view, the provision was not ambiguous, and it rejected the claim that the "immoral purpose" must be accompanied with an expectation of pecuniary gain.[43]

In determining that the language of the provision was unambiguous, the court rejected the notion that the *ejusdem generis* canon of interpretation required that a narrow meaning be given to the catchall, "or for any other immoral purpose." The *ejusdem generis* principle provides that "if a series of more than two items ends with a catch-all term that is broader than the category into which the proceeding items fall but which those items do not exhaust, the catch-all term is presumably intended to be no broader than that category" (Dickerson 1975, 234). The rationale for the *ejusdem generis* canon is straightforward and intuitive. Lists are pervasive in legal texts, and legislatures often use a general term at the end of a list of specifics in order to ensure that the provision has a broad scope (Tiersma 2005). Intuitively, though, the general term must be narrower in meaning than its literal meaning would suggest.

For instance, suppose that a man in California decides to visit his parents in Massachusetts. Knowing that his parents desperately want him to get married, the man pays a woman to travel with him to Massachusetts to pose as his girlfriend.[44] Under the literal meaning of the catchall, the man's actions fall within the scope of the Mann Act. Certainly, lying to one's parents, especially about something weighty such as marriage, can be deemed to be "immoral." Even so, it seems unlikely that a court would countenance a conviction for such activity. If this assertion is incorrect, surely another hypothetical with less serious facts can be created that would convince both reader and judge that conviction is unwarranted. The key issue in such a case would concern the theory by which the literal meaning of the catchall should be restricted. In *Caminetti*, the court reasoned that the catch-all term should not be interpreted narrowly, indicating that

It may be admitted that, in accordance with the familiar rule of *ejusdem generis*, the immoral purpose referred to by the words "any other immoral pur-

pose" must be one of the same general class or kind as the particular purpose of "prostitution" specified in the same clause of the statute. . . . But that
rule cannot avail the accused in this case; for the immoral purpose charged
in the indictment is of the same general class or kind as the one that controls
in the importation of an alien woman for the purpose strictly of prostitution.
The prostitute may, in the popular sense, be more degraded in character than
the concubine, but the latter none the less must be held to lead an immoral
life, if any regard whatever be had to the views that are almost universally held
in this country as to the relations which may rightfully, from the standpoint of
morality, exist between man and woman in the matter of sexual intercourse.[45]

In a dissenting opinion, Justice McKenna argued that the scope of
the statute should be limited to commercialized vice. Justice McKenna
focused on the catch-all phrase "any other immoral practice" but
only obliquely referenced the principle underlying *ejusdem generis*, as
follows:

Are [the words in the catch-all] controlled by those which precede them? If
not, they are broader in generalization and include those that precede them,
making them unnecessary and confusing. To what conclusion would this
lead us? "Immoral" is a very comprehensive word. It means a dereliction of
morals. In such sense it covers every form of vice, every form of conduct that
is contrary to good order. It will hardly be contended that in this sweeping
sense it is used in the statute. But, if not used in such sense, to what is it limited and by what limited? If it be admitted that it is limited at all, that ends
the imperative effect assigned to it in the opinion of the court. But not insisting quite on that, we ask again, By what is it limited? By its context, necessarily, and the purpose of the statute.[46]

Instead of relying on the *ejusdem generis* canon, and addressing the
common principle uniting the items on the list preceding the catchall,
Justice McKenna immediately considered the title of the statute, "White
Slave Traffic Act," and then discussed the legislative history of the act.
    The court's interpretation in *Caminetti* may well have been unper-
suasive, but the court's failure was due to mistakes in determining linguistic meaning and not to an overreliance on it. Chiefly, the court could
have properly considered contextual evidence and purpose through the
ejusdem generis canon, which is a valid determinate of linguistic meaning.[47] The catch-all phrase could not be given its literal meaning, which,

as explained above, would cover any immoral act no matter how serious. The issue was thus not whether the provision was "ambiguous" (any more than a catchall is ever ambiguous) but, rather, how the scope of the catchall should be restricted. As Justice McKenna explained in his dissent, consistent with legislative intent, the statute could have been limited to commercialized vice. Instead of tying his arguments to the language of the catch-all clause, and relying on the *ejusdem generis* canon, Justice McKenna focused on the title of the statute and its legislative history. Likely, Justice McKenna's opinion would have been more persuasive (at least to the majority) if it had reached the same interpretation but through a consideration of contextual evidence via the *ejusdem generis* canon. In any case, the linguistic meaning of the provision required that the interpreter consult the relevant context, making criticisms of an approach that would focus on linguistic meaning misplaced. Those critics who use the *Caminetti* case as an example of how the "plain meaning" doctrine leads to unfortunate results must therefore consider that the "correct" meaning could have been chosen even by relying on the linguistic meaning of the provision.

The above discussion illustrates that a supposed classic example of the dangers of "plain meaning" does not suffice to establish the argument, but it also hints at the underdeterminacy of language. The underdeterminacy associated with the *ejusdem generis* canon relates to the multiple ways in which the general catch-all term (usually an "other" phrase) can be given a limited meaning. The *ejusdem generis* canon may properly be part of linguistic meaning, but as with other determinants of meaning (such as legislative history), application of the interpretive principle leaves the interpreter with a core of ineliminable discretion. A determination via the *ejusdem generis* canon is, at its core, highly discretionary. The discretion is due to the issue of how broadly or narrowly to define the general class delineated by the specific items listed. The doctrine does not purport to guide whether the court should identify the genus at the lowest level of generality, highest level of generality, or some other level. Obviously a higher level of generality will give a broader scope to the "other" phrase. This determination is often crucial in deciding the outcome of the litigation. Thus, in the *Caminetti* case, should the catchall be defined as including only commercialized vice, only immoral sexual activity, immoral activity of any type, or should a different conceptualization be given? The majority never gave a specific answer to the question.

In response to claims that application of the *ejusdem generis* canon is highly discretionary, Scalia and Garner (2012, 208), two textualists, advocate that the interpreter should "consider the listed elements, as well as the broad term at the end, and ask what category would come into the reasonable person's mind." Often, in their opinion, the "evident purpose of the provision makes the choice clear," and the "difficulty of identifying the relevant genus should not be exaggerated." Of course, in general things should not be exaggerated, but advocating the reasonable person standard and the consideration of context does not foreclose the inherent discretion involved in selecting a general category that will account for the specific items listed. There are always multiple ways, at slight but legally significant degrees of difference, in which to define the general category, and often insufficient contextual evidence that makes one choice clearly superior to the others. Hence, like the other linguistic phenomena, the inherent discretion involved in the application of the interpretive principle cannot be negated by (bald) assertions that interpreters would invariably agree in their judgments.

7. Conclusion

The main argument of this chapter is relatively simple. The content of a legal text is not solely an instance of linguistic meaning. Rather, legal concerns sometimes trump the linguistic meaning of the text. Nevertheless, the linguistic meaning of a text is generally an important aspect of the text's legal meaning, and should be so. Especially because linguistic meaning is an important aspect of legal interpretation, knowledge of the ways in which language operates is important to the proper functioning of the law. Linguists are, by training, experts on language. Judges, in general, are experts on the law, and on principles of legal interpretation, but are not experts on language. It follows that judges can benefit from the expertise of linguists. One benefit is that linguists can demonstrate the contextual nature of language and the flaws of believing that linguistic meaning can accurately be determined without consideration of context. Another important benefit is that knowledge of language can reveal its indeterminacy. Contrary to the assumptions of some critics of the role of linguists in legal interpretation, adhering to the kind of analysis called for by linguists would underscore the underdetermined nature of some legal texts. Instead, by not adhering to valid principles of language usage, judges risk interpreting legal texts in ways that mask the inherently normative nature of interpretation. Counterintuitively, perhaps, a greater understanding of language can reveal the frequent necessity of nonlinguistic reasons for a given interpretation.

Notes

1. As indicated above, other disciplines, such as psychology, may also study how language is used and processed by humans. For purposes of brevity, this chapter will refer solely to linguistics, although the same arguments could be used to demonstrate the relevance of other disciplines to legal interpretation.

2. As noted in the introduction, other scholars, such as Poirier (1995), have argued that there is no reason to defer to the expertise of linguists on matters of language (i.e., the "native language users are themselves experts" argument).

3. In addition, the linguistic meaning (and ordinary meaning) of a text may differ from its literal meaning. This distinction is not central to the arguments made in this chapter and will not be explored. See Slocum (2015) for a discussion of the differences.

4. 513 U.S. 64 (1994).

5. *Id*. at 68.

6. 556 U.S. 646 (2009).

7. 18 U.S.C. § 1028A(a)(1) (2004).

8. 556 U.S. at 650.

9. *Id*. at 650–51.

10. *Id*. at 651–52.

11. *Id*. at 653.

12. Brief of Professors of Linguistics as Amici Curiae in Support of Neither Party at 1, Flores-Figueroa v. United States, 556 U.S. 646 (2009) (No. 08–108), 2008 WL 5394023.

13. 513 U.S. at 70.

14. See, e.g., State v. Hunter, No. 40275-I-II, 2011 WL 5825358 (Wash. App. Div. 2011).

15. See Slocum (2015) for an example of such a critique.

16. Chapter 8 provides an excellent example of such analysis.

17. If the "little value" argument is based entirely (or primarily) on the existence of precedents, the argument is correct but trivial. Unless one is interested in undermining the notion of stare decisis (which linguists and philosophers do not purport to do), which directs courts to not overrule the decisions of earlier courts, of course the linguistic meaning of a provision is of secondary importance to whatever the earlier court proclaimed to be its meaning. The

more interesting question, and the one with which linguists concern themselves, is whether the earlier court correctly determined the linguistic meaning of the text.

18. See Brudney (2013) for one discussion of the faithful agent view of interpretation.

19. 426 U.S. 1 (1976).

20. 33 U.S.C. § 1362(6) (1970).

21. *Train*, 426 U.S. at 9.

22. 310 U.S. 534 (1940).

23. *Train*, 426 U.S. at 10 (quoting United States v. American Trucking Ass'ns, 310 U.S. 534, 543–44 (1940)).

24. *Id*. at 23–24.

25. 143 U.S. 457, 459 (1892).

26. *Id*. In Zuni Public School Dist. No. 89 v. Department of Educ., 550 U.S. 81 (2007), Justices Stevens and Scalia debated the continuing vitality of *Holy Trinity*'s proposition that textual meaning should yield to legislative purpose.

27. It should be noted that this argument is meant to apply only to statutory interpretation (although it likely applies to the interpretation of various other legal documents, such as contracts), rather than constitutional interpretation. For various reasons, the Supreme Court has frequently expanded the meaning of constitutional provisions beyond their linguistic meanings.

28. See Hay and Spier (1997) for discussion.

29. 529 U.S. 694 (2000).

30. *Id*. at 707 n.9.

31. The linguistic meaning of the provision in such circumstances may also not be controlling if it is indeterminate. Determining the indeterminacy of the textual language, though, is consistent with the view that linguistic meaning is important to the interpretation.

32. Redco Const. v. Profile Properties, LLC, No. S-10–0255, 2012 WL 579415, at *7 (Wyo. Feb. 23, 2012). See also CSX Transp., Inc. v. Alabama Dept. of Revenue, 562 U.S. 277, 283 (2011) ("We begin, as in any case of statutory interpretation, with the language of the statute").

33. *Redco Const.*, 2012 WL 579415, at *7.

34. *Zuni*, 550 U.S. at 90.

35. See Solan (2005) for an excellent examination of such a theory. Raz (1996) makes a similar claim.

36. Of course, the ordinary meaning may not be definite, which is undoubtedly common, and precisification will result in a meaning that differs from the ordinary meaning of the language.

37. 556 U.S., at 652. See also United States v. Washington, 743 F.3d 938, 943 (4th Cir. 2014) (indicating that the special context is sufficient to rebut the

general presumption that a specified *mens rea* applies to all elements of the offense).

38. 426 U.S. 1 (1976).

39. 242 U.S. 470 (1917).

40. See *id.* at 482–83.

41. 18 U.S.C. § 397 (1910).

42. *Caminetti*, 242 U.S. at 485.

43. See *id.* at 486.

44. The reader skeptical of these facts is directed to the movie *The Wedding Date* where Kat Ellis, a single New Yorker, returns to her parents' house in London to be the maid of honor at her younger half sister's wedding. Anxious about the wedding, Kat hires escort Nick Mercer to pose as her boyfriend.

45. 242 U.S. at 487.

46. *Id.* at 496–97 (McKenna, J., dissenting).

47. See Slocum (2015) for an examination of the *ejusdem generis* canon as a determinant of ordinary meaning.

References

Ariel, Mira. 2010. *Defining Pragmatics.* Cambridge: Cambridge University Press.

Benson, Robert. 2008. *The Interpretation Game: How Judges and Lawyers Make the Law.* Durham, NC: Carolina Academic Press.

Brudney, James. 2013. "Faithful Agency versus Ordinary Meaning Advocacy." *Saint Louis University Law Journal* 57:975–96.

Dickerson, Reed. 1975. *The Interpretation and Application of Statutes.* Boston: Little, Brown and Company.

Eskridge, William, and Philip Frickey. 1995. *Cases and Materials on Legislation: Statutes and the Creation of Public Policy.* St. Paul, MN: Thomson/West.

Flanagan, Brian. 2010. "Revisiting the Contribution of Literal Meaning to Legal Meaning." *Oxford Journal of Legal Studies* 30 (2): 255–71.

Greenberg, Mark. 2011. "Legislation as Communication? Legal Interpretation and the Study of Linguistic Communication." In *Philosophical Foundations of Language in the Law,* edited by Andrei Marmor and Scott Soames, 217–64. Oxford: Oxford University Press.

Hart, H. L. A. 1958. "Positivism and the Separation of Law and Morals." *Harvard Law Review* 71: 593–629.

Hart, H .L. A., and Albert M. Sacks. 1994. *The Legal Process: Basic Problems in the Making and Application of Law,* edited by William Eskridge and Philip Frickey. New York: Foundation Press.

Hay, Bruce L., and Kathryn E. Spier. 1997. "Burdens of Proof in Civil Litigation: An Economic Perspective." *Journal of Legal Studies* 26 (2): 413–31.

Jackson, Bernard. 1995. *Making Sense in Law: Linguistic, Psychological and Semiotic Perspectives*. Liverpool: Deborah Charles Publications.

Jori, Mario. 1993. "Legal Semiotics." In *The Encyclopedia of Language and Linguistics*, edited by Robert E. Asher, and James M. Y. Simpson, 2113–22. Oxford: Pergamon Press.

Kaplan, Jeffrey, and Georgia Green. 1995. "Grammar and Inferences of Rationality in Interpreting the Child Pornography Statute." *Washington University Law Quarterly* 73:1223–51.

Manning, John. 2010. "Second-Generation Textualism." *California Law Review* 98:1287–318.

———. 2013. "Justice Ginsburg and the New Legal Process." *Harvard Law Review* 127:455–60.

Marmor, A. 2005. *Interpretation and Legal Theory*. Oxford: Hart Publishing.

———. 2012. "Textualism in Context." Unpublished manuscript. Accessed on February 14, 2016. http://papers.ssrn.com/sol3/papers.cfm?abstract_id=2112384.

Poirier, Marc R. 1995. "On Whose Authority: Linguistics' Claim of Expertise to Interpret Statutes." *Washington University Law Quarterly* 73:1025–42.

Posner, Richard A. 1986. "Legal Formalism, Legal Realism, and the Interpretation of Statutes and the Constitution." *Case Western Reserve Law Review* 37:179–217.

Raz, Joseph. 1996. "Intention in Interpretation." In *The Autonomy of Law: Essays on Legal Positivism*, edited by Robert P. George, 249–86. Oxford: Oxford University Press.

Ross, Stephen F. 1995. "The Limited Relevance of Plain Meaning." *Washington University Law Quarterly* 73:1057–67.

Scalia, Antonin, and Brian Garner. 2012. *Reading Law: The Interpretation of Legal Texts*. St. Paul, MN: Thomson/West.

Scalia, Antonin, and John F. Manning. 2012. "A Dialogue on Statutory and Constitutional Interpretation." *George Washington Law Review* 80:1610–19.

Seidman, Louis M. 1988. "Ambivalence and Accountability." *Southern California Law Review* 61:1571–600.

Shapiro, D. 1992. "Continuity and Change in Statutory Interpretation." *New York University Law Review* 67:921–48.

Slocum, Brian. 2015. *Ordinary Meaning: A Theory of the Most Fundamental Principle of Legal Interpretation*. Chicago: University of Chicago Press.

Solan, Lawrence M. 1995. "Judicial Decisions and Linguistic Analysis: Is There a Linguist in the Court?" *Washington University Law Quarterly* 73:1069–80.

———. 2005. "Private Language, Public Laws: The Central Role of Legislative Intent in Statutory Interpretation." *Georgetown Law Journal* 93:427–86.

Stanley, Jason. 2007. *Language in Context: Selected Essays.* Oxford: Oxford University Press.

Tiersma, Peter M. 1999. *Legal Language.* Chicago: University of Chicago Press.

———. 2001. "A Message in a Bottle: Text, Autonomy, and Statutory Interpretation." *Tulane Law Review* 76:431–82.

———. 2005. "Categorical Lists in the Law." In *Legal Discourse across Cultures and Systems*, edited by Vijay K. Bhatia, Jan Engberg, Maurizo Gotti, and Dorthee Heller, 109–30. Hong Kong: Hong Kong University Press.

Vermeule, Adrian. 1998. "Legislative History and the Limits of Judicial Competence: The Untold Story of *Holy Trinity Church*." *Stanford Law Review* 50:1833–96.

———. 2006. *Judging Under Uncertainty: An Institutional Theory of Legal Interpretation.* Cambridge: Harvard University Press.

Williamson, Timothy. 1996. *Vagueness.* London: Routledge.

CHAPTER TWO

Philosophy of Language, Linguistics, and Possible Lessons about Originalism

Kent Greenawalt

1. Introduction

This chapter first summarizes my general sense of the degree to which the philosophy of language and linguistics can enlighten our understanding of how legal interpretation does and should proceed. It then turns to the issue of originalism in statutory and constitutional interpretation, asking how far these disciplines can inform us about whether some form of originalism is warranted, and about what kind or kinds of original understanding should count. Since everyone agrees that in virtually all contexts the original sense of what a statutory or constitutional provision conveyed carries *some weight*, this latter question is important even for nonoriginalists. A central concern about what assistance philosophy of language can provide is the extent to which its limitations in resolving practical questions about the reading of authoritative directions curtail its help in resolving the debates between originalists and nonoriginalists, as well as the disagreements within both camps over the crucial elements of original content.

To summarize my conclusions at the outset, I believe the philosophy of language and linguistics can provide insights about how we understand language, including that in legal provisions, but cannot tell us exactly how legal interpretation by judges, other officials, and citizens should proceed. In respect to genuine debates over what kinds of original understanding should matter, and how much that should control if in tension with other considerations, philosophical perceptions about human communication can tell us that some approaches to original understanding do ignore key elements of ordinary uses of language. However, given the inability of those perceptions to resolve many practical issues about how interpretation should proceed, we must look elsewhere to reach most conclusions about original understanding and its role.

Two key aspects of this analysis are worth noting here. One is that most writing about the philosophy of language and linguistics concerns communications made by one person to an audience that receives the message immediately or very shortly thereafter. A crucial feature of statutes and especially constitutional provisions is that they are designed to last over time, even centuries. And they are adopted by a group with authority, not by any single person. These features bear significantly on how they are best interpreted.

In considering how official interpretation should proceed, one must recognize a basic distinction between what appears best as a matter of principle and what is needed to constrain judges (and perhaps executive officials). Roughly what I mean by this far from precise categorization is the difference between what highly competent judges would do if they faithfully carried out their proper role and what actual judges will often do when they lack clear and definite criteria of resolution. The latter concern, emphasized by Justice Scalia and other textualist originalists, is that without bright line standards, judges will end up interpreting in a way that fits their own ideas of justice and political desirability, a role it is claimed they should not possess in a liberal democracy with a separation of powers.[1]

Two respects in which "in principle" and "needed constraints" represent a distinction that is hardly precise are these. All human beings find some determinations about exactly what events happened, and precisely what language entails in certain contexts, as very difficult or even impossible. That reason for judges not to have to undertake such findings is grounded in essentially human fallibility, rather than any troublesome inclination of judges to implement their own ideas of desirable laws and outcomes when they interpret authoritative texts. A somewhat more subtle factor is the tendency we have, even when we seek to be guided by standards other than our own desires and sense of what is best, nevertheless to be subconsciously influenced by those elements when we make decisions.

Despite these line-drawing subtleties, it is nonetheless crucial to distinguish what a legal provision should be taken to mean if judges were highly competent and performed their function extremely well and what may be needed to restrain actual judges from effectively exercising powers not seen as within their proper roles. In some of these respects, it may matter whether the judges being considered are those of the highest court of a jurisdiction or of lower courts. Within the United States, a dominant focus is on how the Supreme Court should proceed. But we should not assume that the interpretive techniques that are best for those justices are also best for judges of trial and lower appellate courts.

2. The Philosophy of Language

Various perspectives among philosophers of language offer suggestions about what constitutes the meaning of what people say and write. Readers should understand that I am far from expert about either this field or linguistics, though I hope to grasp enough to genuinely support my conclusions in this essay.

We can perceive at least five ways in which the philosophy of language might relate to legal interpretation:[2] (1) By identifying the core features of language and communication, it may provide insight into what takes place when legal provisions are interpreted; (2) it may suggest possible approaches and provide analogies from nonlegal contexts; (3) it might suggest limits on what approaches are tenable or untenable; (4) it might indicate what approach is obviously correct, or at least provide strong reasons to favor one approach over all others, or, more modestly, provide bases that could count for or against certain approaches; (5) it might provide insights into why some forms of interpretation seem attractive apart from their actual merits.

My basic thesis is that neither the philosophy of language nor linguistics provides convincing bases to prefer one approach to statutory and constitutional interpretation over all its competitors; they can highlight reasons to question certain techniques but do not provide any overarching grounds to reject an approach that otherwise seems attractive.

Two important positions about the meaning of language are that it depends on speakers' intent or on convention. These are fairly seen as both relevant to meaning in most instances, but sometimes they do not fit. What carries the day if the speaker's intent deviates from conventional usage? The speakers' intent approach, defended over many years by Paul Grice,[3] definitely contains an important insight that matters for interpretation of many, or all, legal documents. In ordinary circumstances, those on the receiving end of language understand its import in accord with what they assume the speaker or writer is trying to convey. Suppose one person says to another, "You should arrive at two o'clock." Without specification, the listener will assume this means 2 p.m. unless he has a special reason to conclude otherwise. If the speaker is a teacher referring to her class, listening students will assume they should get there shortly before two. If the speaker is holding a party, an invitee will think that he should arrive at two or soon thereafter. If a person tells a child who has been naughty, "Go to your room and don't come out in the next half hour for any reason," the child will not assume he must stay in the room if a stroke of lightning somehow lights a fire within it. Often, apparently absolute language carries implicit exceptions, including ones that neither the speaker nor listener has actually thought of at the moment of communication. These are insights that can be relevant for some interpretations of legal provisions.

Language of instruction is not always understood to conform with its speaker's intention. A rather unusual situation is when an instruction is given by someone, but neither he nor the relevant listener wants or expects it to be fulfilled. A babysitter tells children to turn off their cell phones at 8:00 p.m., because he fears the parents will be angry that if he fails to say this; both he and the children understand that he does not expect them to actually do that. When such circumstances occur, it is hard to say that the instruction "means" what the speaker intended.

A more complicated, but much more common, situation is when the speaker gives an instruction he intends to be understood in one way, but which he has formulated inartfully. Suppose a rich American is in Europe and cannot attend an auction for a painting he would like to buy. He asks a personal servant to be his agent and says, "I want that portrait but I don't want to spend too many dollars. Don't bid more than 100,000." The painting is about to be sold for 95,000 euros, and the agent fails to bid more. When his principal says "You made a huge mistake; I said I bid up to 100,000," the agent responds, "Yes, but you had just referred to dollars, the bids were already above 100,000 dollars." According to the intention approach, the original communication *meant* what the speaker had in mind. But now the issue is whether the principal here has a good reason to criticize, perhaps even penalize, the listener, his agent. If he is reasonable, he must say to himself, "The mistake was mine. For purposes of any possible reprisal, my communication meant a limit on dollar value, not euros." Thus, a communication that means one thing for one purpose—how best to fulfill it—and means something else for another—how best to treat a different response. This is a very common problem for legal interpretation, since a primary issue often is how the communication would most plausibly have been understood by those directly subject to it. This presents a very powerful reason why speaker intentions, even if discernible after the fact, should not always be controlling.

With some documents it can be a genuine question how far speaker or writer intentions should control. Unless others are actually relying on what is contained in wills, one might think the intentions of the wills' writers should be the key. Thus, if a man who is heading abroad with his wife for a location in which they will be taking many risky trips on boats includes in his will that his relatives will receive his money if he and his wife suffer "coinciding" deaths, one may believe, contrary to what a British court actually decided,[4] that if they both died as a consequence of their boat sinking, the deaths should count as having "coincided" even if they probably occurred seconds or minutes apart. If the writer thought about such a situation, he almost certainly would have wanted it included. Competing with this conclusion is that courts and will writers need clear and consistent interpretations of similar language *and* that discerning after someone's death what was really intended is too difficult and subject to manipulation of evidence. Therefore, it is better to stick to the same content for the same terms.

Seeing the meaning of language as essentially conventional reflects the basic truth that when people communicate with each other, they ordinarily do so according to accepted standard uses of their language.[5] Of course, the relevance of conventions typically fits with the intent of the person communicating, but what should an interpreter do if in a particular instance, there seems to be a discrepancy between the two?

Conventional usage does not always provide a definite answer, since many important terms are rather vague, and various people using them may have slightly different senses of their meaning or their practical application, or both. Suppose a woman asks a man to show her "respect." Exactly what respect means is itself not very precise; acts like opening doors for another may seem respectful to one generation but not its successor, whereas using crude terms that once showed a lack of respect may now be taken as honest, lively conversation. Exactly how communications should be understood and applied when convention provides no clear answer *or* when others have substantial reasons to conclude that writers or speakers have through design, misunderstanding, or error departed from conventional usage cannot be resolved by acknowledgment of the general role of convention.

An illustration of assumed "error" within the law can arise when a straightforward application of language seems absurd. In one notable case, the Supreme Court had to decide whether a statute that gave "defendants" a privilege against testimony that would be prejudicial did or did not cover defendants in civil cases.[6] Clearly, a straightforward use of language embraced civil defendants, since the law could easily have referred to criminal defendants if it was meant to exclude others. Yet in civil cases, one can hardly imagine a reason why in this respect defendants should be given a significant privilege denied to plaintiffs, especially since it is often fortuitous in disputes over contracts who ends up as the plaintiff or defendant. The court read the statute as limited to criminal defendants, a result inexplicable in terms of conventional use of terms, unless one includes in this sense basic assumptions about what practical consequences would make good sense.

On the broad question of defining meaning, neither the speaker intent nor conventional usage is always determinative, although both play very important roles. While each approach gives some insight into how the language in legal documents, such as wills and contracts, as well as statutes and constitutional provisions, may be interpreted, neither conception yields any decisive resolution of what should be the guide for questions that are actually debatable.

3. Linguistics in Social Practice

When one turns to ideas of linguistics and its operation in pragmatic contexts, the degree of explanation of what legal provisions mean and how they are, and should be, interpreted become more inclusive. However, many circumstances still remain in which we have no decisive indication of what approach is preferable. The basic idea is that the meaning of what is communicated depends substantially on rules of grammar and other assumptions about how to say things, which are shared by writers and readers, or speakers and listeners. An example given by Lawrence

Solan (1993, 13) is that "He thought Fred convinced the jury" refers to a "he" that is other than Fred himself." An illustration that depends heavily on context is "You must be fourteen." If this language is used about driving automobiles, it means fourteen or older; if the reference is to eligibility for a youngsters' baseball team, it means fourteen or younger.

Sometimes, however, various components and the context of a communication can point in opposite directions. In the *Holy Trinity Church* case,[7] frequently referred to in debates about how to interpret, a statute had general language that seemed to refer (though only implicitly) to manual labor or service, barring contracts and payments made to those not yet in the country in order to bring them here. However, a range of exceptions included nonmanual forms of workers, such as singers and lecturers. A normal linguistic approach would yield the conclusion that if many exceptions are specified, other possible exceptions falling within the general wording are not granted. By this standard, contracts with foreign Christian ministers and priests were barred. Given the country's religious tradition, and the fact that many of our residents then worshipped in foreign languages, a barring of arrangements to hire clerics from abroad seemed in stark opposition to basic values of the society. The Supreme Court concluded that nonapplication was appropriate, a conclusion that did not rest exclusively on linguistics, unless one takes that to include more general social values.

In another case discussed by Professor Solan (1993, 34), which involved firing of a teacher, the court had to decide if a law allowing dismissal for "conviction of a felony or of any crime involving moral turpitude" applied to a teacher's growing of one marijuana plant. Normal linguistics would indicate that conviction for any felony would be enough, but the court reached the contrary conclusion and overturned the dismissal because that felony did not involve moral turpitude. With some frequency, judges are inclined to explain their resolution as one dependent on linguistic understanding, even when their actual basis is more complex.

As Geoffrey Miller (1990) has pointed out, and as both the cases just noted reflect, a pragmatic approach to interpretation gives weight to specific context and to overall purposes. On this approach, the court rightly concluded that a defendant's privilege to avoid prejudicial testimony did not reach defendants in civil cases. Just how much context and broad purposes should count for statutory and constitutional interpretation are central issues.[8]

Paul Grice (1989) developed interesting suggestions about natural communication that would ordinarily bear on meaning. One's communication should be as informative as required, but not more so; one should say what is true, not false; one should stick to what is relevant; and one should be brief and orderly. Given these guides, we can see that meaning often cannot be determined simply on the basis of the ordinary sense of words and structures of sentences. The conversational context and what is probably in the speakers' mind will also matter.

Insofar as speakers and listeners do actually share assumptions about how communications are to take place, those bear on how specific comments should be understood, and they can also matter for legal interpretation. But about Grice's specific ideas about rational communications, I think various qualifications are necessary. The first is that for ordinary conversation, what he says may fit typical assumptions of the well educated in England, but based on my limited experience with those from cultures beyond England and the United States, I do not think we have any universal practice of the sort. In some cultures, people are encouraged to express themselves freely without worrying much about relevance, coherence, and brevity. For ordinary conversation, we need to recognize that what one can infer may depend significantly on particular cultural practices. Of course, if the listener shares, or at least understands, the speaker's cultural assumptions, these variations do not affect Grice's basic theory about the control of speaker intentions.

For legal norms, cultural variations may rarely present a problem, but uncertainties can be created by the unsystematic way some laws are written, a difficulty that is much more common in the United States than in countries where a parliament selects the prime minister and the two are joined. Another obstacle is that on occasion language is intentionally chosen that is not clear in context precisely because of disagreements and compromises among legislators.

Two differences between legal texts and ordinary conversations are significant here. The first is that given compromises and stages of amendments, a statute may not have the coherence of most single conversations. Second, insofar as relevant conventions here depend partly on the respective roles of legislatures, administrative agencies, and courts, significant disagreements, such as now exist in the United States, can undermine assumptions about what shared conventions are and how far they actually exist.

My overall conclusion about insights into linguistic usage is similar to that of philosophic accounts of language. They can both help explain what is going on in standard exercises of legal interpretation, and they can sometimes provide a genuine basis for choosing one course rather than an alternative for a debatable issue. Nevertheless, they cannot, by themselves, resolve a great many questions about desirable interpretations, and these questions increase greatly when the crucial provisions are cast in general, open-ended terms, especially ones designed to last for centuries.

One particular disagreement among philosophic writers about language is whether vague terms do or do not have objectively determinate applications. For me, the answer depends on what sort of vague term one is talking about. If one asks exactly what the line between being tall or not tall is, or being bald or not bald, the answer is that we have no precise line, and people understand that. And, of course, what counts for these terms can also depend on context. Being 6′2″ is tall for ordinary women and short for male professional basketball players. In respect to whether a determinate application exists, if someone asks what the utmost respect he can give to a friend or spouse is, however vague this term may be and however uncertain it may be what constitutes the most possible respect, a single correct answer may still exist—at least for a particular relationship—and most people may believe in that.

When the law itself contains vague terms, people may or may not believe they always have correct applications. Stephen Schiffer (2001) has urged that since judges are often not going to be sure which are the correct applications, if they do exist, it will not matter for their interpretations whether they believe they exist. I am convinced that this somewhat oversimplifies reality. If judges have no solid basis to determine a correct answer, it is true that their belief that one exists will not determine their answer, but it can affect how they conceive their process of decision. A judge who thinks that the law does somehow provide the right answer to application of a vague term may focus on the law itself, including other provisions. A judge who thinks no correct answer exists within the law may be more comfortable looking elsewhere, for example to her own notions of justice and desirable outcomes. Or, feeling uncomfortable about reaching outside the law, she may decide she better look for an answer within the law that does not even depend on the vague term. In any event, whether one believes vague terms always or often have correct applications will not settle the vast majority of issues about legal interpretation.

4. Originalism, and the Relevance of Philosophical Insights

4.1 Introduction

A central modern debate about the interpretation of statutes and constitutional provisions concerns originalism. Among the central, and interrelated, questions are these: (1) How much does the original intent or understanding count in respect to other considerations? Should it be controlling or merely one factor that matters along with other considerations? Does it somehow incorporate what are actually portrayed as bases of decision different from it? Since no one claims the complete irrelevance of original understanding, I do not include an option of its being totally disregarded. (2) Should the basic inquiry be about reader understanding or enactor intent, or a combination of those? (3) Exactly which understandings or intents should matter, and what comparative importance should they carry? (4) Do crucial differences exist between typical statutory provisions and many parts of a constitution? (5) How far are various answers to these questions determined by principles about language or by premises of all or some liberal democracies, and how far are the difficulties of accurate assessments and the need to constrain judges and other officials crucial?

The insights provided by philosophy of language and linguistics can tell us a good deal about what makes sense as a matter of principle, but they definitely fail to provide simple answers about proper approaches. When it comes to concerns about untrustworthy assessments and needed constraints, they are even less help. Some assertions by originalists, such as Justice Scalia, can be defended only on the latter ground. In respect to critical factors and the weight of ordinary original understanding, many key constitutional provisions must be regarded differently from typical statutes. Always adhering to how the language of particular provisions was originally understood is not a workable judicial strategy.

Let me first say a word about the role of precedents, and then set that factor aside. Many originalists, perhaps virtually all, concede that established Supreme Court precedents should carry some power. The fundamental idea is that well-established law should not simply be cast overboard because it has not been built on appropriate standards of interpretation or rests on a misestimation by judges employing those standards. The underlying assumption is that even if justices who created the precedent had miscalculated or used mistaken techniques, the law they have established should not simply be abandoned. That makes practical sense. But presumably, if we have a new statute or constitutional amendment, courts should try to avoid falling into similar error, instead sticking faithfully to original understanding and trying *not* to create novel precedents that depart from that. If one actually approves of judges creating new precedents that are dictated by neither existing ones nor original understanding, one is not a strict originalist. The analysis that follows assumes that a true originalist thinks courts facing novel issues should seek to decide by original meaning, even if they accept already established specific legal outcomes and rules that have departed from that.

Of course, the tension between originalism and following precedents can be swallowed up if one posits that the original understanding about how judges should interpret not only the common law but statutes and constitutions included their relying on precedents. This view would also make it more easily defensible for judges to rely somewhat on precedents in related areas when new laws are adopted, even if those precedents were based on misguided interpretation. The status of ideas of interpretation is developed further in section 4.4.

4.2 Readers

The movement in recent decades has been away from enactor intent to reader understanding. One might defend this emphasis on the basis that, after all, it is the readers who must be guided by the law, so their sense should take priority. Alternatively, or additionally, one might claim that with laws, because the subjective intent of the lawmakers is not really important, we are simply left with original reader understanding of what those laws stand for.

Tied to these different rationales are questions about how one should conceive relevant readers, and what the consequence may be of an interpretation that departs from their understanding. If one focuses on how a law will affect those who actually read it, then concentrating on "ordinary readers" or "those readers subject to the legal requirement" makes sense. And as time passes, one may also need to ask how later readers would understand the law.

For the importance of reader understanding, exactly what kind of issue is involved should make a difference. Suppose an ordinary reader would perceive legal language as limiting the range of government action designed to benefit some people without harming others. Congress once adopted a statute that "consular officers" could provide financial support for stranded sailors to return to the United States. Since Alaska lacked consular officers, an attentive reader would have taken the language as failing to permit help for sailors stranded there. Since it is nearly impossible to see why those sailors should be denied the help given to those actually outside the country, and because no persons would be harmed by extending coverage beyond simple reader understanding, doing so in light of perceived congressional intent did not seem unfair to anyone.[9] Supported by continuing executive practice and repeated congressional financing, the Supreme Court did just that.[10] Granting aid like this is quite different from convicting a person that a reader would not perceive as having violated a criminal statute. In the latter circumstance, extending coverage beyond linguistic meaning is genuinely troubling.

If the relevant "reader" is taken in a more objective way, not to highlight people's actual responses to a law's terms but simply to discount legislative intent, then one might turn to extremely well informed, even hypothetical, readers who may perceive relevant factors that are beyond the capacities of the vast majority of human readers.

Two central questions about "readers" are how they will understand what is in a law and what judges making an inquiry about such readers may properly take into account. Here the insights of much of philosophy of language and linguistics provide, or, more accurately, support, an insight that is actually rather straightforward. Listeners and readers understand communications in terms of their context, and this can sometimes depart from a literal reading of the terms. An example provided earlier is the parent who says, "Do not leave your room in the next half hour for any reason whatsoever." A child of any intelligence will, if the circumstance arises, realize that the parent did not really mean to cover a fire breaking out or a bear somehow finding its way into the room. Absolute statements of the kind are often subject to unstated qualifications, ones that neither the speaker nor the listener may actually think about until the extreme situations arise. To take another illustration, suppose a coach at a time-out and with twenty seconds left in a basketball game tells his team, which has the ball and is ahead by two points, "Do not take any shots." The only tall member of the team finds seconds later he is under the basket with the ball and could perform a dunk, in which he succeeds over 99 percent of the time. He might well conclude that this is really an exception to what the coach was addressing.

On occasions, controlling legal language is somewhat vague, or ambiguous, and underlying purposes need to determine coverage. Suppose a local law forbids "sleeping in the railroad station." Does this cover ordinary passengers who fall asleep while waiting for a delayed train at midnight? Someone aware that the law was adopted to prevent homeless people from camping out in the station at night would assume not. On the other hand, if the penalty was only a small fine *and* a major concern had been that when passengers fall asleep, others are emboldened to commit thefts without being observed, a reader well might conclude that the law does reach ordinary passengers. Interestingly, Justice Scalia, the most prominent textualist, dissented in a case in which the court's majority concluded that a law that raised penalties when someone "uses" a firearm during a drug trafficking crime did apply when a "purchaser" turned over an unloaded weapon to acquire cocaine.[11] Scalia (1996, 23–24) employs the case in an article to explain why his approach is not a literalist one, explaining that "uses a firearm" generally means employing it as a weapon, firing it, or threatening to do so and does not cover trading it to obtain items. But, of course, as he recognizes, trading one thing for another is literally "using" it. More importantly, we can imagine situations in which a reader might assume this "use" is covered. Suppose, as has happened in some countries, inflation gets completely out of control, or many people actually lack cash and credit, and the trading of possessions in order to "purchase" has become common. In such a setting, legislators might be concerned that when people start trading weapons to acquire drugs, that puts in the hands of dangerous criminals weapons not registered to them. In that context, "uses" a weapon might sensibly be seen to include bartering one, loaded or not, for drugs.

If context matters considerably, in large part to show the purpose of the communicator, that can sometimes include a coverage that is broader than literal specific language rather than narrower. In a June 2014 decision, the Supreme Court considered whether the president's power to appoint higher officials without Senate consent when vacancies happened "during a Senate recess" allowed such appointments if the vacancies occurred prior to a recess but continued into the recess. By a five to four margin, the justices concluded that the answer was "yes," with the majority acknowledging that the language itself pointed in the contrary direction. The dissenters, including Justice Scalia, said the vacancy must actually occur during a recess.[12] Neither opinion needed to reach a narrower question on which I shall focus. Suppose that a relevant Senate recess is to begin at 9:00 a.m., August 15. Completely unexpectedly, official A dies at 10:00 a.m., on that day; official B dies at 5:00 a.m., but her death is not discovered until 10:00 a.m. Plainly the president has no actual ability to get prerecess approval of a new appointee for either position. Would not an actual reader be inclined to say, "Given the whole reason for the provision, which responds to the effective impossibility of Senate approval, should we not understand 'during' here to include *at least* those situations in which it is absolutely impossible to conceive of Senate approval before the recess?" A strict textualist might respond, "No, the language used here must be taken exactly according to its terms, because any latitude gives judges too much power to determine what the edges of coverage are." Although this argument is not completely implausible, it definitely moves from how an actual reader might understand matters to an argument that we need stricter constraints to curb judicial discretion.

A central point for many textualists, one on which Justice Scalia (1996, 29–32) has been explicit, is that courts should not take legislative history into account as authoritative. Except as designed to prevent successful manipulation by some legislators and to restrain judicial discretion, this restriction really does not make sense. Here are three reasons why. First, if readers will consider legal language in relation to its broader context and purposes, as revealed partly by social understandings and political concerns that precede legislation, why would they totally disregard actual communications by those involved that explain what they are trying to do? This restriction does not fit at all with how ordinary listeners would react to actual communications of purposes by real persons giving them instructions.

Second, for many decades courts were giving substantial weight to legislative history. A moderately well-informed reader, as well as legislators, would have assumed that laws were to be read in accord with legislative history and would have done so. What was then actual original reader understanding at the time of enactment did include legislative history.

Third, a textualist might respond that all that counts is how the reader would take the language by itself, but that does not explain why such a clear indication of purpose would be beyond consideration, and it also raises a troubling question of how the bar on reference to legislative history fits with what may be taken into account. Here, the recent *Hobby Lobby* case provides an interesting point of comparison.[13] Deciding that a closely held for-profit corporation qualifies under the Religious Free-

dom Restoration Act to be "a person exercising religion," Justice Alito
relied on the assumption in many laws that corporations count as persons and on a Dictionary Act that so provides unless "the context" indicates otherwise. Alito does not ask whether an ordinary reader would be
aware of all this, nor does he really face whether a well-informed, astute
reader might conclude that the objectives of RFRA and its particular
phrasing of "a person's exercise of religion" might reveal a context pointing in the opposite direction. But if justices are assuming "readers" who
are familiar with statutes and broad legal assumptions that are well beyond what an ordinary person reading a specific law like RFRA would
grasp, why should these astute, exceptionally informed readers *not* be
able also to take account of legislative history? No sensible answer exists, *unless* it depends on curbing legislators' manipulation and judicial
discretion.

4.3 Enactors

A crucial point made by insights into the nature of language and human communication is that a close relationship exists between enactor
intent, as revealed both by stated purposes and context, and how readers understand the coverage of language. Should it matter what enactors
were aiming to do, even apart from how original readers would generally
understand what they have done? No one supposes that reader understanding is irrelevant, and it matters especially for laws that restrict behavior and penalize violators. If judges and administrative officials can
discern what legislators were attempting to do, should they not also take
that into account? In ordinary life, if someone provides instructions to
last over time and those initially subject to them sensibly take them in
a certain way but subsequently discover that they were intended differently, would not a typical response be "Well, no one is to blame here, but
we should now try to conform to what these instructions were meant to
have us do"?

   If one thinks that enactor intentions properly matter, even to an extent that would not have been evident to actual readers at the time of
passage, which sort of enactors count when multiple persons perform the
formal act. One might think the intentions of all count equally, or that
more weight should be given to those who were better informed about
what was going on, or to those who were especially perceptive about objectives and influential in promoting adoption. A crucial issue here is

what one thinks about "delegation." Suppose we have strong reasons to suppose that most of the less informed members who are ignorant about details or broader purposes, and also some members who just lack strong convictions about proper understandings, self-consciously wish to delegate authority to those who are more central to passage. Surely in ordinary life, when members give one or more of their fellows authority to decide for their group about something, we take the decisions then reached as for the group. The notion of delegation is not one often addressed in the philosophy of language, but it is a natural ingredient of many decisions for groups. Justice Scalia (1996, 35–36) has written that delegation violates the separation of powers, attempting to confer on a subset of legislators what the whole legislature must do—adopt specific legislation—or leave it to the executive and judiciary to interpret. But it is hard to understand why delegation of special authority should be forbidden within group structures that have become increasingly complicated, given that most legislators are unaware of textual details of statutes they adopt.

4.4 Ideas about Interpretation

A central question about enactor intent, which also reaches reader understanding, is the status of how enactors believe the language they adopt *should* be interpreted. To take a kind of personal example, suppose that a man, who has spent years fighting racial discrimination and has had close contact with and great influence over a son, is reaching the end of his days; he says to the son, "I hope you will pledge to devote much of your life to working for human equality." The son says "Yes." We can imagine two sharply different contexts, as well as intermediate situations. If he father has made clear to his son his belief that within the United States, the only violations of genuine human equality were slavery for African Americans and the harsh treatment of Native Americans, when he speaks of human equality in this context, it could be clear that this is really what he means, nothing else. Suppose, in contrast, the father has conversed with the son at times about changing conceptions of what inequalities are unjust, noting that many people have begun to see differences in treatment of men and women and financial disparities as contrary to justice. Although he himself does not grasp future outlooks, he understands that basic perceptions about inequality can develop and thinks this is appropriate. If the father has clearly indicated the second view, the son would rightly think he was being faithful to his pledge if he devoted his efforts mainly to the equality of same-sex couples, which perhaps had never occurred to his father as a possible issue. What would be a legitimate carrying out of the father's general wording of "human equality" would include not only what he and his son thought was the linguistic meaning of the term; it would matter what the father conceived as its proper application over time. In other words, an instructor's understanding of the way his terms should be interpreted and applied would be central.

As a matter of principle, what enactors intended and what readers understood about how legal language was to be interpreted would be a core element of its context, especially as time passes. An original sense of somewhat flexible interpretation could take priority over specific applications then conceived and even over the narrower senses of what particular words meant. This presents yet another problem with any total exclusion of legislative history and delegation. If virtually all legislators believed that interpretation of statutes should give weight to legislative history—at least in part for reasons of delegation—*and* informed readers of the time possessed a similar view, especially given many Supreme Court decisions using this very approach, it is hard to see why in principle judges should never pay attention to legislative history, especially since legislators and informed readers may have been more aware of parts of that than of many statutory details and obscure statutes like the Dictionary Act.

Although in principle following conceived ideas about interpretation must be seen as a crucial element of original understanding, that approach carries two substantial difficulties. The first is that although enactors and readers of the time may have a rough idea about how interpretation of statutes and constitutional provisions should take place, none or almost none would have had a detailed and fully developed conception, and were different persons to try to be fairly precise, they would not agree on everything. Thus, the best judges could do is to follow general strategies that seemed to them to be prominent. The second, somewhat related point is that senses of proper interpretation have changed significantly over time, and we have no reason to suppose that they will stop doing so. Would it make sense for courts to try to figure out what approaches were accepted by legislators and readers when a particular statute was adopted? A conscientious and faithful execution of this

would lead to somewhat different techniques to interpret various statutes. We really cannot expect judges, or even Supreme Court justices,
to undertake this particular inquiry about each statute that has been
adopted and to fashion their interpretive approach in particular for that
statute. Rather, it makes sense for judges to adopt an approach that con-
forms with broad views over time when most presently applicable statutes were adopted.

On this point, the United States Constitution could be a bit less of
a problem. Justices might discern basic approaches accepted when the
original Constitution and Bill of Rights were adopted, and those used
at the time of the Fourteenth Amendment, and interpret in accord with
each, not attempting a similar effort for other individual amendments.
However, a basic problem here, one that exists with any strong version of
originalism, is that if judges *really* stuck to original understanding, the
main provisions of the Bill of Rights would have different applications
for the federal and state governments, since neither their conceived coverage nor the interpretive approaches were the same after the Civil War
as when the original Bill of Rights was adopted.

4.5 The Constitution as Compared with Statutes in the United States

Many strong reasons resist any notion that major constitutional texts
should be interpreted like most statutes. I shall simply sketch them here,
concentrating on the national constitution.[14] Its subject matter is almost
entirely about structures of government and the core rights of citizens.
The nature of these can affect desirable interpretation, especially since
the ways governmental organizations operate and the conceptions of
what is just and fair have shifted radically over time.

Many key constitutional provisions are cast in highly open-ended language; that in itself can greatly influence how far the text will provide
answers to specific circumstances. Although varieties of "balancing" are
needed for the application of various statutory provisions and common
law doctrines, some form of that is central for much of the Bill of Rights,
including "cruel and unusual punishment," "unreasonable searches and
seizures," and "prohibiting the free exercise" of religion.

It turns out that the United States Constitution has been very hard to
revise. Because amendments are not easily passed, one cannot expect
potential amenders to bring things up to date whenever social structure

and values change. Moreover, the Constitution carries heavy symbolic significance in our culture; frequent amendments and a lengthy detailed document would undercut that considerably.

The primary addressees for most parts of the Constitution are public officials, not private citizens, although citizens do act on the basis of rights they believe they are conferred. It can matter whether a document is primarily telling private persons and businesses how to act or is mainly directing the behavior of officials.

The Constitution, at least in some respects, may allocate responsibilities in a special way that affects how courts should respond. Most notably for the separation of powers between the Congress and president, and the division between federal and state authority, the primary responsibility for respecting and enforcing various limitations can lie with the political branches, and a key element of judicial interpretation may be deference to the decisions of political bodies, especially when those between whom power is divided seem to agree about what exercises are acceptable.

These various considerations are not ones addressed in any straightforward way by the philosophy of language and linguistics, but they are illustrations about how context affects how people do and should understand communications, especially directions that are lasting over centuries. This all fits with the chapter's general thesis. These other disciplines cannot provide determinative answers to whether, given all the complexities of laws and their enforcement, one contested approach is obviously better than a competitor, but they do help provide insights that tell us how far an approach does or does not tend to fit a natural understanding of communications. When we understand that an approach lacks such a fit, its defense must be based on some distinctive characteristic of legal rules, such as their adoptions by multiple persons, or on a claimed need to curb judicial forms of evaluation because correct answers are so hard to discern and because judges need to be constrained from implementing their own outlooks about desirable laws.

Notes

1. See, e.g., Scalia (1996).
2. These possibilities are explored in greater depth in Greenawalt (2010, 19–58).

3. See Grice (1957; 1968; 1969; 1989, 290–97).

4. In re Rowland [1963] Ch. 1 (Eng. C.A.).

5. See, e.g., Lewis (1969).

6. Green v. Bock Laundry Mach. Co., 490 U.S. 504 (1989).

7. Holy Trinity Church v. United States, 143 U.S. 457 (1892).

8. I explore these in some depth in Greenawalt (2013; 2015a).

9. Of course, the government would be paying more, and conceivably some employers in Alaska could benefit from having sailors stranded there.

10. Alaska S.S. Co. v. United States, 290 U.S. 256 (1933).

11. Smith v. United States, 508 U.S. 223 (1993).

12. Natural Labor Relations Board v. Noel Canning, 134 S. Ct. 2550 (2014).

13. Silvia Burwell, Secretary of Health and Human Services v. Hobby Lobby Stores, Inc., 134 S. Ct. 2751 (2014). Greenwalt (2015b) explores this case in some detail.

14. A much fuller account is in Greenawalt (2015a).

References

Greenawalt, Kent. 2010. Legal Interpretation: Perspectives from Other Disciplines and Private Texts. New York: Oxford University Press.

———. 2013. *Statutory and Common Law Interpretation*. New York: Oxford University Press.

———. 2015a. *Interpreting the Constitution*. New York: Oxford University Press.

———. 2015b. "*Hobby Lobby*: Its Flawed Interpretive Techniques and Standards of Application." *Columbia Law Review Sidebar* 115:153–27.

Grice, Paul. 1957. "Meaning." *Philosophical Review* 66:377–88.

———. 1968. "Utterer's Meaning, Sentence-Meaning, and Word-Meaning." *Foundations of Language: International Journal of Language and Philosophy* 4: 225–42.

———. 1969. "Utterer's Meaning and Intentions." *Philosophical Review* 78: 147–77.

———. 1989. *Studies in the Way of Words*. Cambridge: Harvard University Press.

Lewis, David. 1969. *Convention*. Cambridge: Harvard University Press.

Miller, Geoffrey. 1990. "Pragmatics and the Maxims of Interpretations." *Wisconsin Law Review* 1990 (5): 1179–227.

Scalia, Antonin. 1996. *A Matter of Interpretation: Federal Courts and the Law*. Princeton: Princeton University Press.

Schiffer, Stephen. 2001. "A Little Help from Your Friends." *Legal Theory* 7: 421–31.

Solan, Lawrence M. 1993. *The Language of Judges*. Chicago: University of Chicago Press.

CHAPTER THREE

Linguistic Knowledge and Legal Interpretation
What Goes Right, What Goes Wrong

Lawrence M. Solan

1. Introduction

As Frederick Schauer (2009, 18–20) writes, we routinely conceive of the law as rule-like and unproblematic. When the train has a "No Smoking" sign, we don't smoke, and if we do, we understand there will be consequences. For the most part, we go through life with a pretty good idea of what is expected of us and are able to stay out of trouble. Most "cases" of law are easy cases. In fact, they are so easy that we do not even notice that they are about law, and surely they are not brought before high courts. They are not brought before any court.

But this is not the whole story, of course. There are indeed plenty of borderline cases, uncertain inferences from context, and ambiguities that any legal system must confront. The effort to govern ourselves by written laws designed to apply generally makes law all about language. The more language is both "flexible and minute" in just the right ways, to use Benjamin Cardozo's (1922) terminology, the clearer a law's domain will be, and the better it will adjust to new circumstances as they surface. By studying the range of linguistic issues that arise in these disputes—and those that do not arise—we can come to some conclusions about how the architecture of our language faculty influences our ability to govern ourselves under a language-centric system of laws. Such research can tell us something about when we should put our faith in language as a means of organizing our rights and obligations toward one another, and when we should not.

Most of the literature on the interpretation of laws, constitutions, contracts, and other authoritative legal documents focuses on the problems that arise when the language does not yield an obvious answer. When a text appears to be ambiguous, what should the legal system examine in an effort to resolve the ambiguity in one direction or the other? What should the legal system do when a law or contractual provision seemingly applies to a given situation, but the law self-evidently was not intended to extend to such a situation? What should happen when the lawmakers err?

This focus is natural enough, given that its audience is itself typically embedded in the legal world. The person who breaks his arm does not marvel at the fact that humans are born with opposable thumbs, which permit the orthopedic patient to continue accomplishing some tasks while his arm heals. Yet directing so much attention to the problems we encounter (and now I'm back to legal interpretation) does paint a distorted picture of our everyday experience with laws and rules. In ordinary life, we generally seem to be able to comply with most of what is expected of us without a great deal of anxiety. If you decide that a traffic light has taken too long to turn green at 3:00 a.m., and carefully go through it only to find that the parked car on the right is occupied by a police officer who is patiently waiting for someone to do just what you have done, there is really little doubt that you will lose if you argue that you did nothing wrong. Similarly, absent a mistake, that same officer will *not* give you a citation if you do wait until the light turns green before you proceed. So much of our lives involve this latter experience that we do not notice that both we and the law are working as designed. After all, nothing has happened to make us think about it.

2. The Architecture of the Language Faculty

We use language to communicate. Yet our language faculty is not one big communication machine. Rather, it is comprised of a number of subsystems that interact with one another and with cognitive systems that are related to, but outside, the language faculty itself. How do the strengths and weaknesses of language as a multifaceted system of communication affect the ability to govern ourselves through legal institutions? We can address that question only if we first determine what these different subsystems of language actually are.

Different approaches to linguistics, naturally enough, focus on different systems and different interactions. Systemic functional linguistics, for example, focuses largely on how subsystems interact to produce and to understand the many subtle nuances in communicative intent (Halliday and Matthiessen 2014). The generative approach to linguistics, in contrast, focuses more on technical aspects of language, such as syntax, and aspects of semantics that follow from the structure of sentences. (See Jackendoff 2003 for a rich development of an architecture that includes these and other aspects of language, and Chomsky 2005 for focus on the interfaces among systems.)

Here, I use the taxonomy of contemporary generative grammar to discuss various legal indeterminacies. I believe that this framework best creates the opportunity to describe and discuss various forms of indeterminacy that plague legal interpretation. Readers are invited to analyze the examples presented later in this chapter in terms of other systems and to determine whether they can capture, or improve upon, the observations in this chapter.

At a minimum, language is comprised of the subsystems and interactions listed below. In each case, failures in the system produce interpretive dilemmas when the application of a legal text is at stake. While there is disagreement among linguists as to various aspects of the architecture of the language faculty, some of which are theoretically significant, for our purposes the following list should not be controversial and is sufficient to capture many of the recurrent problems of legal interpretation.

1. A computational system that generates well-formed structures (largely the syntax). When more than one syntactic structure can be assigned to the same string of words, the result is syntactic ambiguity. ("Visiting relatives can be annoying.")
2. A relationship between these structures and meaning. Semantic ambiguity arises when more than one set of semantic relations can be assigned to the same string of words even if those words are assigned only a single syntactic structure. ("James Bond believes the author of the letter is a spy.")
3. An interface between sound and meaning, mediated by the computational system, so that we can break the flow of speech up into words and phrases

and use this information to interpret what we hear. ("I am a rock, I am an island / in Ireland.")

4. An interface between (1) and (2) on the one hand, and a conceptual system on the other, so that we express in words and phrases the concepts we intend to express. When we fail at this, we either choose a word that is not entirely apt, or situations arise at the borderline of the concept and we argue about whether that situation should properly be considered as coming within the concept. (Should trading an unloaded gun for drugs be considered "using a gun" in a drug trafficking crime?)

5. Interfaces with various inferential systems that rapidly place the language we use in sufficient context to make sense of it (discourse, pragmatics, cultural assumptions, etc.). All kinds of inferences are the subject of legal dispute. (When a police officer asks a young man who's car he has stopped, "Does the trunk open?" is the officer requesting the man to open the trunk or ordering him to do so?) Here, I assume that (4) and (5) are separate systems, but nothing here depends upon that assumption.

My hypothesis is this: Most of the problems involving legal interpretation arise from the interfaces among the systems, rather than from the linguistic systems themselves. For example, we experience far more cases of vagueness—cases in which the events in the world are borderline cases of legal concepts—than of syntactic or semantic ambiguity, which are more purely linguistic phenomena. The reason for this is surely not that legal documents do not contain ambiguity. It is rather that the ambiguities generated by the syntax or semantics most often produce meanings that are so different from each other that we immediately resolve them in context without even noticing them. In contrast, vagueness is by definition a matter of closely related meanings, which is exactly what legal disputes are all about.

More specifically, we might expect to find more cases that focus on the fit between the concepts communicated in legal texts and the events in question than cases that need to resolve syntactic ambiguity. Similarly, there is great opportunity for people to speak in ways that will cause others to draw inferences that are licensed by the language but contrary to the hearers' interest. I begin by discussing instances of such cases and then turn to cases of pure linguistic ambiguity, which, as noted before, play less of a role in legal dispute than do problems resulting from the interface between language and other cognitive systems.

3. Legal Uncertainty in the Gaps between Language and Other Cognitive Systems

The classic failure in the interface between language and other systems is the inability to remember what was said. Some laws are hundreds of pages long, a typical length for complex contracts. Jury instruction in the United States can be too long to remember well. This is the most basic of performance errors, highlighted in Chomsky (1965). Writing, of course, ameliorates this problem. In the discussion that follows, all of the examples are examples of either written language or of short interactions in which there is no controversy about what was said. Memory limitations, though, reduce the flexibility of law by making writing a necessity and creating some safe harbors for dishonest conduct, and thus should be kept in mind as a serious problem in the interaction between language and other cognitive systems.

3.1. Pragmatic Inference When Language is Not Enough

To illustrate problems occurring at the interfaces between linguistic and other cognitive subsystems, consider the classic example of the right of the police under the US Constitution to search an automobile as long as the owner gives permission. Ordinarily, police officers need to obtain a warrant, or at least to have probable cause that a crime is being committed, before they may conduct a search. However, a driver may always consent to a search, which in essence waives her right to complain about there not having been probable cause. In the seminal case,[1] a police officer approached a car driven by a young Latino man in California and said: "Does the trunk open?" Apparently thinking he had no choice, the driver opened the trunk, and contraband (stolen checks) was discovered. The Supreme Court held that since the police officer asked permission, the search was legal, even though the officer did not have a warrant and even though there was no probable cause to conclude that a crime had been committed.

The legal issue was whether the young man had voluntarily consented to the search. If he had, then his rights were not violated, because he had waived them. If not, his rights had been violated and the evidence found in the trunk of the car would be suppressed, resulting in the case being dismissed. Resolving the legal question required that the court determine how "does the trunk open?" should be construed. It should certainly not be construed, the court rightly said, as a literal question about the spring mechanism in the back of the car. But the court never addressed the linguistic similarity of requests and commands and how to tell the difference. The words that the policeman uttered can be understood as either one of those speech acts, as it is ambiguous between them (see Searle 1969 for a seminal work on speech acts). Ordinarily, we decide whether it is one or the other based upon the relationship between the speaker and hearer, in particular their relative power. Moreover, in interpreting the police officer's question, people are likely to draw whatever inferences the context demands to make the utterance relevant (see Grice 1975; Horn 2004; Wilson and Sperber 2012).

The law books are full of problems that require pragmatic inference of this kind, engaging legal questions that range from how specific a person must be in order for an angry statement to be deemed a threat under criminal law, to whether a suspect's not answering questions asked him by the police constitutes his asserting his right to remain silent, to whether a hedged request, "maybe I should be talking to a lawyer," is good enough to assert the right to counsel.

Determining whether an utterance is a threat illustrates the problem. A 2015 US Supreme Court case, *Elonis v. United States*,[2] held that a man who posted poetry on his Facebook page suggesting both that his ex-wife should die and that he would like to kill her did not commit a criminal threat since he did not necessarily intend to threaten her personally, only to vent. Some of the language was very violent:

Fold up your [protection-from-abuse order] and put it in your pocket
Is it thick enough to stop a bullet? Try to enforce an Order
that was improperly granted in the first place
Me thinks the Judge needs an education
on true threat jurisprudence
And prison time'll add zeros to my settlement . . .[3]

The decision involves some interesting pragmatic questions. For one thing, it rejects defining threats solely in terms of the effect that the statement has on the hearer (the utterance's perlocutionary effect). Elonis's ex-wife was surely frightened, but that is not enough. Rather, the speaker has to have intended to frighten the hearer, according to the court. Recognizing that she is likely to be frightened merely as a side effect of some

other goal (perhaps writing bad rap music) is not good enough. Bruce
Fraser (1998) takes a similar position in his speech act analysis of threats
(see also Solan and Tiersma 2005).

It is not clear to me that people generally require this level of intent
before they would call an utterance a threat, and I know of no empirical studies on the issue. If a gang member says to someone, "I wouldn't
go out tonight if you want to be alive in the morning," how much should
it matter that his intent was only to impress his friends who overheard
the remarks and that he really had no interest one way or the other in
scaring the person to whom the remarks were addressed? The law, however, generally requires that an act be committed intentionally before it
will be deemed to be a crime, and the court applied that standard to this
case.

Interestingly, it is also not clear that a statement must actually succeed in intimidating the hearer for it to constitute a threat. Fraser (1998,
1620) does not believe this to be a necessary condition but does believe it
necessary that the hearer understand the speaker's intention. Consider a
criminal whose practice is to use a realistic-looking toy gun to hold people up at ATM machines. Most people are frightened and turn over their
money. But one person, Nick, was not frightened because he recognized
the gun as a toy. The perpetrator's act and state of mind were both identical to the successful threats. There is good reason to hold that the law
should treat the Nick incident as an unsuccessful, but nonetheless real,
threat. Such is the nature of the law governing attempted crimes.

Most significantly for purposes of the discussion here is that it is impossible to determine whether an utterance is a threat from the words
alone. Determining whether a speaker intends to intimidate by threatening an action that he believes the hearer to believe will have negative
consequences requires a sequence of inferences that are not expressed in
the language, but rather must be inferred from the context. In the *Elonis*
case, the Supreme Court made it clear that proving that Elonis intended
his wife to draw inferences that would cause her to be intimidated was
necessary to establishing that a crime has been committed. Until then,
the literal meaning of these verses would be taken at face value.

In the case of the right to remain silent, the US Supreme Court has
held that a person must clearly say that he plans to remain silent for the
assertion to have legal force.[4] The suspect, Thompkins, had been read
his rights, including the right to remain silent, and was asked to sign a

form saying that he understood them. He refused. Instead, he just sat there for about 2.75 hours, not responding as the police continued to question him. Then, the following exchange took place:

POLICE: "Do you believe in God?"
THOMPKINS: "Yes."
POLICE: "Do you pray to God?"
THOMPKINS: "Yes."
POLICE: "Do you pray to God to forgive you for shooting that boy down?"
THOMPKINS: "Yes."

Thompkins then looked away and later refused to make a written confession. The interrogation ended about fifteen minutes later.[5]

The Supreme Court held that being silent is not an adequate means for exercising the right to be silent. Rather, by failing to state with clarity that he was not going to answer any questions, Thompkins had decided on a question by question basis whether to answer. His refusal to sign the form indicating his having understood his rights was considered to be of no legal consequence either. Dissenting Supreme Court justices would have drawn the opposite conclusion: that there is no better way to assert one's right to silence than to be silent for a period that is long enough to make it a reasonable inference that the suspect has decided not to answer questions.

Whichever side one takes in this case, how we construe silence in legal contexts is a matter of pragmatic inference, as a number of scholars have convincingly argued (see, e.g., Ainsworth 2012; Tiersma 1995). Surely, the issue in this case can have nothing to do with an ambiguity in the literal meaning of an expression since there was no expression being analyzed, only the absence of an expression. Here again it is at the intersection of language and pragmatic inference that the interpretive problems in law arise.

There is a down side to this flexibility in drawing inferences from context in legal interpretation. It leaves space for a legal actor to convey the impression of a particular type of speech act when actually making another as sometimes happens in encounters between citizens and the police as we saw above. On other occasions, miscommunication can occur more innocently, as sometimes happens when people are engaged in contract negotiations, for example. Central to the issues raised here, the need for pragmatic inference creates a zone of uncertainty that permits judges to rule consistent with their personal values, as the distribution of votes by liberal and conservative judges in some of the cases discussed above illustrates.[6]

3.2. Concepts and Categories

The law encounters similar problems when the question is the interpretation of vague terms. Consistent with the terminology of linguists and philosophers of language, I use "vague" to refer to borderline cases in which it is not clear whether a particular event or thing should be considered as being a member of a category (Endicott 2000; Sorensen 2002; Wechsler 2015). How wide must a chair be before we call it a love seat? Or, in the classic *sorites* paradox, if taking away a single grain from a heap of sand would not cause you to say that there is no longer a heap, then how is it possible that if you remove the sand one grain at a time, at some point, you recognize that there really is no longer a heap? The fuzziness of conceptual boundaries in everyday speech is adaptive and efficient in that it leaves space for the flexibility to speak of new experiences and needs without creating new categories (Barsalou 1983).

In the realm of the law, the problem amounts to a mismatch between the flexibility of our concepts as expressed in words and the need for legal terms that are at once sufficiently flexible to cover their intended domain, while at the same time specific enough to reduce discretion in specific cases. Our concepts do not always meet both of these goals simultaneously, leading to perennial problems of interpreting vague laws. But the laws are not vague in some Platonic sense. Rather, they become situationally vague when the system is forced to make decisions about category membership at the margins, which happens every time an effort is made to apply a contract or a statute to an unusual situation. Thus, in the context of whether a fine is due for an overdue library book, there can be little question whether the hardcover library version of *War and Peace* is a book. In contrast, there can be serious doubt whether it should be considered a weapon if it was used to hit someone in the head during a robbery.

This problem of how to deal with borderline cases pervades legal interpretation. Commentators have observed that vagueness is a far bigger problem for legal interpretation than is ambiguity (Scalia and Garner 2012; Solan 2010; Waldron 1994). Again, consider a classic case from the US Supreme Court: When a law bans the payment of transportation into the United States for a person "performing labor . . . of any kind," does this include the payment of transportation for a Protestant minister hired from London to preach at a church in New York? The Supreme Court said no, in this 1892 case.[7] That is not what the legislature could have possibly intended, although the words of the statute seem to fit the facts of the case. The court held that the statute did not apply to the church and its new minister. To take another classic example, has a person "used a firearm" during a drug trafficking crime when the individual attempts to swap an unloaded machine gun for some illegal narcotics? In *Smith v. United States*,[8] the Supreme Court, decided a century later in 1993, answered affirmatively, with a powerful dissent to the contrary offered by Justice Scalia. The case provides an excellent example of the difference between interpreting legal concepts in terms of their outer boundaries and restricting them to how the words were most likely intended to be understood.

Whether to apply the most ordinary meaning of the concept, the meaning intended based on investigation of the surrounding legislative facts, or a broad meaning based upon the outer boundaries of a word's definition remains a matter of great debate in law (Scalia and Garner 2012; Slocum 2015; Poscher 2012; Solan 2010). Consider a case decided by a Massachusetts court that revolved around the question of whether a burrito should be considered a sandwich.[9] A fast food restaurant, Panera, had signed a lease with a shopping center that precluded the center from leasing to another tenant 10 percent of whose business would predictably come from the sale of sandwiches. When the shopping center leased space to a Mexican restaurant, Panera sued, claiming that their lease had been violated. The Mexican restaurant responded by demonstrating very little overlap in the menus, and it noted that Panera was aware of Mexican restaurants in the neighborhood before it signed the lease and did not seem to be bothered by them. The court ruled against Panera, partly based on the following definition of sandwich, taken from *The New Webster's Third International Dictionary*, a leading dictionary of American usage: "two thin pieces of bread, usually buttered, with a thin layer (as of meat, cheese, or savory mixture) spread between them." Scalia and Garner (2012) heaped praise on the judge who wrote a straightforward opinion relying on the dictionary, but Judge Richard Posner, a very prominent American jurist, thought otherwise (Posner 2012). Posner noted:

> A sandwich does not have to have two slices of bread; it can have more than two (a club sandwich) and it can have just one (an open-faced sandwich). The slices of bread do not have to be thin, and the layer between them does not have to be thin either. The slices do not have to be slices of bread: a hamburger is regarded as a sandwich, and also a hot dog—and some people regard tacos and burritos as sandwiches, and a quesadilla is even more sandwich-like. Dictionaries are mazes in which judges are soon lost.

Not only is the dictionary's prototype too narrow, as Posner points out, but what we call a sandwich is also culture-bound. The wrap, on the menus of many sandwich shops, is derived from the Mexican burrito. If a wrap is a forbidden sandwich, why should the burrito get off scot-free? The United States is not alone in its having difficulty determining the borderlines of legal concepts. In his illuminating book *Word Meaning and Legal Interpretation*, Christopher Hutton (2014) provides similar illustrations from England, India, and Hong Kong. The interface between language and our conceptual system is not a neat one.

* * *

The examples discussed above all involve the relationship between language and the world. In one set of cases the inferences we draw are between what we say and how we would like to be understood based on inferences we expect people to draw. In the other set of cases, the issue is the imperfect match between the words we use to express concepts and the ways we actually experience the things that the concepts are intended to denote.

4. Ambiguity: When the Computational System Produces Too Many Options

This section turns to problems that arise from the computational aspects of the language faculty itself. Legal writers use the word "ambiguity" loosely to refer to just about any way in which language underdetermines meaning. Thus, the cases of vagueness discussed earlier are likely to be referred to as ambiguous cases in the legal literature. As noted above, an expression is vague if it is at the borderline of a concept so that it is uncertain whether the expression fits within the concept or is outside of it. Ambiguity, in contrast, occurs when an expression can simultaneously have two different meanings.

In a sense, all ambiguity is semantic in that its diagnosis concerns meaning. Nonetheless, linguists and philosophers of language distinguish among different kinds of ambiguity, characterized by what aspect of the linguistic system has produced more than one possible interpretation. Focusing on those sources of ambiguity that might be legally relevant, we can distinguish among lexical ambiguity, syntactic ambiguity, and semantic ambiguity.

4.1. Lexical Ambiguity

Lexical ambiguity occurs when a word has more than one distinct sense (see Wechsler 2015 for discussion of "sense" in this context). A typical example is the word "bank," which can refer to a financial institution or to the side of a river or stream. Unlike the issue of when a chair becomes wide enough to be called a loveseat, there is no borderline between the two meanings of bank. It is one or the other, and they mean very different things. For the most part, ambiguity of this sort poses no problems in legal interpretation because the senses are sufficiently remote from each other that we resolve the ambiguity so quickly from the context that we do not even notice it. Although in using a word with multiple senses we convey only part of the information relevant to a situation, people are typically good contextualizers (Miller 1999) when it comes to distinguishing among disparate meanings of a word. Reporting on psycholinguistic literature addressing people's ability to disambiguate words from context, Rayner, Cook, Juhasz, and Frazier (2006, 469) note that when the context is clear, there is no difference in the time that individuals focus on an ambiguous word whose context suggests the preferred meaning and a control word that is not ambiguous at all. Unlike words whose conceptual boundaries are fuzzy, truly ambiguous words are not a significant problem in legal interpretation.

4.2. Syntactic Ambiguity

Syntactic ambiguity occurs when the same words can legitimately be assigned more than one syntactic structure. The meanings differ depending on how we do so. "Flying planes can be dangerous" is a classic example (Chomsky 1965). Although this kind of ambiguity indeed results in linguistic indeterminacy, most often the meanings are sufficiently distant from each other to cause the legal system no trouble. In all likelihood a hearer would know whether a speaker is talking about planes that are aloft, or the activity of piloting a plane.

In Solan (2010), I examined the US federal bribery statute to determine what linguistic problems led to the many cases decided in published opinions by the courts over a period of more than thirty years. Although the statute consisted of a single 199 word sentence, there was not a single case in which the syntactic relations within the statute were the grounds for dispute. In abridged form, the statute reads as follows:

> (b) Whoever—
>> (1) directly or indirectly, corruptly gives, offers or promises anything of value to any public official . . . ,
>>> (A) to influence any official act; or
>>> (B) to influence such public official or person who has been selected to be a public official to commit or aid in committing, or collude in, or allow, any fraud, or make opportunity for the commission of any fraud, on the United States; or
>>> (C) to induce such public official or such person who has been selected to be a public official to do or omit to do any act in violation of the lawful duty of such official or person;
> [Shall be punished . . .][10]

Just about every substantive word has been litigated: Who should count as a public official? What is an official act? Must the person taking the bribe be in the same government as the official act that the bribe is intended to influence? Do contractors performing governmental functions count as government officials?

In contrast, there are no reported cases in which syntactic ambiguity in this portion of the bribery law was the issue. There are syntactic ambiguities everywhere in such a long statute. But none of them was the subject of dispute because, in context, the available meanings are sufficiently distinct that no one would be confused. In fact, for the most part, the ambiguities go unnoticed. For example, the word "corruptly" may modify only the verb "gives," or it may modify all of the verbs in the list that begins with "gives." It makes no sense, however, for the legislature to have written a law in which the corrupt giving of a bribe is a crime, but in which the noncorrupt offering of a bribe is another way of committing the same crime. We quickly understand "corruptly" as modifying all of the verbs in the list and do not even notice the ambiguity.

Yet there are a few areas in which syntactic ambiguity causes problems of interpretation. Consider this law (once again, abridged): "Whoever knowingly transfers food stamps in any manner not authorized by the statutes or regulations shall be punished." Frank Liparota knowingly sold food stamps to another person, but he did not know (or at least claimed not to know) that he was not allowed to do so.[11] Did he violate the law? Here, the statute is ambiguous because we cannot tell whether "knowingly" modifies only the transfer or both the transfer and the failure of the transfer to be authorized under the law. The court applied the rule of lenity, which resolves uncertainty in meaning in favor of the defendant. This is a classic case of syntactic ambiguity in the scope of adverbs.

Consider similarly the more recent case *Flores-Figueroa v. United States*.[12] Ignacio Flores-Figueroa was an illegal immigrant who used a fake ID card to get work in California. A law that criminalizes identity theft calls for an enhanced sentence for certain other crimes—including immigration crimes—if the offender "knowingly transfers, possesses, or uses, without lawful authority, a means of identification of another person." Flores-Figueroa claimed that he knew he was using false identification but did not know that it contained the identification number (Social Security number) of an actual person. He had simply bought the card from someone who trades in such things. If *knowingly* modifies only the verbs, he was guilty of the crime and subject to a longer prison sentence for his immigration crime, since he did knowingly use the ID card. If *knowingly* also modifies *a means of identification of another person*, then he did not violate the statute and would be subject only to the prison sentence imposed by having violated the immigration law itself. The Supreme Court held that *knowingly* should be construed with broad scope and thus that Flores-Figueroa did not violate the identity theft statute that would have led to an enhancement of his sentence.

Such cases are not difficult to find. Many statutes, especially criminal statutes, contain state of mind adverbs. These frequently raise the twin questions of how much knowledge or willfulness is required (a matter of vagueness) and what the state of mind adverb modifies (a matter of ambiguity) (Poscher 2012). However, these cases make up a very small portion of the disputes over the interpretation of statutes, most of which involve conceptual vagueness, as discussed above.

Now consider another recurrent syntactic ambiguity, often discussed in law under the rubric, "the last antecedent rule." To illustrate, Avondale Lockhart was convicted under the US federal law that criminalizes the distribution of child pornography.[13] The statute calls for longer prison sentences when the offender had earlier been convicted of certain related crimes, "under the laws of any State relating to aggravated sexual abuse, sexual abuse, or abusive sexual conduct involving a minor or ward." The question was whether *involving a minor or ward* modifies all of the crimes that proceed it, or only the last one, *abusive sexual conduct*. Lockhart had earlier been convicted under New York law of sexually abusing his then-fifty-three-year-old girlfriend. That crime does not require that the victim be a minor. The Supreme Court held that only the last of the listed crimes need involve minors, and that therefore the sentence enhancement applies to Lockhart in light of his earlier conviction. The last antecedent rule is not applied evenly. Judges do not apply it when the context implies that the modifying clause was intended to receive a broader interpretation (see Kimble 2015 and Solan 1993 for discussion). Here, what is important is to note that the problem ambiguous scope of a modifying phrase is a recurrent one in law.

In some cases, the scope of an adverb and the last antecedent rule collide. Consider this nightmare of statutory drafting:

> Whoever **knowingly makes under oath** . . . any false statement with respect to a material fact in any application, affidavit, or other document required by the immigration laws or regulations prescribed thereunder, **or knowingly presents any such application, affidavit, or other document which contains any such false statement or which fails to contain any reasonable basis in law or fact** [. . . shall be punished.][14]

The statute defines two separate crimes: making a false statement under oath in an immigration document and presenting an immigration document that contains a false statement to the authorities. Zavkibeg Ashurov made false statements in his student visa application when he claimed that he would be devoting time to classroom study although he did not plan to do so. His statements were not made under oath, so he could be charged only with presenting a false document.[15]

The problem in construing the statute lies with both instances of the word *such*. The expression *any such application* in the definition of the second crime must refer back to the first crime. If *any such application* includes the statement having to have been made under oath, which is an element of the first crime, then Ashurov goes free, since he did not do that. But this makes no sense in context, as the court rightly noted. *Any such application* is better understood as referring only to the application's being false. By the same token, the court applied the last antecedent rule to the second *such*, which is in the phrase *any such false statement*, suggesting that the second *such* refers to the false statement of material fact and not to whether the application was sworn to under oath. Resolving both ambiguities in this way favors the government's case.

But there is a problem. If Ashurov can be convicted without having made a false statement under oath, what is the point of the oath requirement in the first place? The penalties for the two crimes are the same. Wouldn't this mean that the crime of making a false statement under oath is simply surplus language? A principle of legal interpretation instructs judges to avoid regarding statutory language as mere surplusage. The court had no answer to these questions and thus interpreted the law in favor of the defendant under the rule of lenity.

The cases discussed above are cases decided by appellate courts in the United States. But syntactic ambiguity is not merely a phenomenon of English, or of the US legal system. As Baaij (2012) has pointed out, many cases decided by the Court of Justice of the European Union concern laws that are ambiguous in one language version but not another. Thus, it is part of what it means to govern ourselves under a rule of law so highly dependent upon language that these cases illustrate.

4.3. Semantic Ambiguity: One Structure, More than One Meaning

Some cases involve semantic ambiguity. By "semantic ambiguity" I mean expressions in which a single syntactic structure yields more than one possible meaning because the semantic relations may differ even if the syntactic relations do not. Jill Anderson's work on a particular ambiguity that occurs in statutes—the *de dicto/de re* ambiguity—illustrates (see Anderson 2014). To take an example of the kind of ambiguity she discusses, when a person writes into her will, "I leave $100,000 to be divided equally among my grandchildren," does she mean this as shorthand for those grandchildren living at the time she signs her will (say four of them) or those grandchildren who are alive at the time of her death (perhaps five then)? The expression is ambiguous.

This same kind of ambiguity infects other areas of law. When we "agree to the terms of the user agreement" when we buy services such as cable television or internet or mobile phone service, have we consented to terms one through *n* as there listed, or do we agree that whatever the terms happen to be at any time, we agree to them, whether or not we know what they are and whether or not they change over time? The law has moved in the direction of understanding consent in this second, opaque manner.

Similarly, the US Constitution bans the use of "cruel and unusual punishment," a term that has produced great debate, especially in the context of the death penalty. Punishment, to pass constitutional muster, must be both noncruel and nonunusual. But how do we understand those terms? Let us assume that it matters to one extent or another what the framers of the Constitution understood in the late eighteenth century. Even accepting this proposition, we are confronted with a *de dicto/de re* problem. If we understand "cruel" as meaning "harsher than our norms accept as reasonable," then the concept has not changed very much over time, although the list of cruel punishments has. If we understand "cruel" as shorthand for a list of examples of the kinds of punishments that are unacceptable, then there has been great change over time, and a decision must be made as to how much attention to pay to the historical values and how much to pay to contemporary ones (see Solum 2011; Whittington 1999).

This is not to say that the *de dicto/de re* distinction dominates the landscape when it comes to semantic ambiguity. Interpretive issues as to the meanings of *and* and/or *in* in various contexts are prevalent, for example. Consider a contract (slightly paraphrased) that says, in part, "in the event that as of January 2010 Sycamore has not commenced and does not regularly distribute projects under the Sycamore trademark, its license shall be forfeited."[16] As for the relevant date, Sycamore had indeed commenced distribution but was not distributing regularly in relevant territories. The court applied de Morgan's law, the rule of logic that in the context of negation, *and* means *or*. Sycamore did not forfeit its rights since it did accomplish one of the two negated tasks.

Exactly how such semantic facts fit into the architecture of our linguistic faculty is a matter of significant debate. Some philosophers have taken the position that the different interpretations are a matter of pragmatics, in which case these examples illustrate our larger point that the interfaces between linguistic subsystems are far more problematic than are uncertainties emanating from the subsystems themselves. Others closely relate syntactic operations and semantic interpretation, leaving room for less purely semantic ambiguity (see Jacobson 2014). Here, I take a rather narrow view of semantics as including those aspects of meaning that arise from the formal relationships among the various words and phrases in language and separate that aspect of understanding from pragmatic inference and from vagueness (see Bach 2005).

Whatever the status, pure linguistic ambiguity, if not a rarity, does not predominate when it comes to legal disputes. That is because most of the time, ambiguity leads to a range of meanings that are sufficiently different from each other that the uncertainty is so quickly resolved from context that the ambiguity goes unnoticed. Researchers have shown that we construe language in terms of the question under discussion (QUD) that is presented to us either explicitly or tacitly (Clifton and Frazier 2012). When syntactic ambiguity yields one interpretation relevant to the QUD, we construe the expression accordingly. Yet instances of syntactic ambiguity in legal interpretation are significant because they illustrate that even the computational aspect of our linguistic faculty produces utterances that may be assigned more than one meaning, creating risk for a legal system so heavily dependent on the construal of authoritative language.

5. Conclusion

In our everyday lives we constantly are confronted with rule-like expectations, whether it is a matter of not smoking on a train, or getting to work or a class on time, or washing the dishes. For the most part, we do not have a great deal of difficulty understanding these expectations, which increases the obligation to take responsibility for not meeting them. Nonetheless, our language faculty has its limitations and these limitations establish a ceiling effect for governing ourselves under a rule of law in which language is paramount.

All of the subsystems and their interfaces, both with each other and with nonlinguistic cognitive systems, leave pockets of uncertainty in meaning. I have provided a few examples of these. There are more. However, the biggest problems for legal interpretation lie not in the syntax and semantics that linguists work so hard to describe. Rather, the bulk of the problems lie in the fact that our use of language relies heavily on our drawing pragmatic inferences and that our concepts are looser, and more flexible, than rule of law values require.

For the most part, we do not experience our encounters with rules and laws as a minefield that we can never walk through safely. This is because our computational system of language works quite well, and our inferential systems are sensitive enough to draw the right conclusions about intended meaning most of the time. Nonetheless, the examples presented here should serve as a caution that when our interpretive systems break down, we must look outside the language of the law for answers. To the extent that the legal system relies too heavily on the texts of authoritative legal documents in the name of fidelity to the words used, it risks undermining the goal of determining the communicative intent of the author.

Notes

1. Schneckloth v. Bustamonte, 412 U.S. 218 (1973).
2. 135 S. Ct. 2001 (2015).
3. *Id*. at 2006
4. Berghuis v. Thompkins, 560 U.S. 370 (2010).
5. *Id* at 376.
6. For example, in Berghuis v. Thompkins, the right to silence case, the decision was five-to-four in a politically predictable array.
7. Holy Trinity Church v. United States, 143 U.S. 457 (1892).
8. 507 U.S. 197 (1993).
9. White City Shopping Center, LP v. PR Restaurants LLC, 21 Mass. L. Rptr. 565 (2006).
10. 18 U.S.C. § 201(b)(1).
11. Liparota v. United States, 471 U.S. 419 (1985).
12. 556 U.S. 646 (2009). A group of linguists filed a brief to discuss the lan-

guage issues. It is available at http://www.americanbar.org/content/dam/aba/
publishing/preview/publiced_preview_briefs_pdfs_07_08_08_108_NeutralAm
CuProfsofLinguistics.authcheckdam.pdf.

13. Lockhart v. United States, 136 S. Ct. 958 (2016).

14. 18 U.S.C. § 1546(a); emphasis mine.

15. See United States v. Ashurov, 726 F.3d 395 (3rd Cir. 2013).

16. Earthgrains Baking Cos. v. Sycamore Family Bakery, Inc., 573 Fed.
App'x. 676 (10th Cir. 2014).

References

Ainsworth, Janet. 2012. "The Meaning of Silence in the Right to Remain Silent."
In *Oxford Handbook of Language and Law*, edited by Peter M. Tiersma and
Lawrence M. Solan, 287–98. Oxford: Oxford University Press.

Anderson, Jill C. 2014. "Misleading Like a Lawyer: Cognitive Bias in Statutory
Interpretation." *Harvard Law Review* 127:1521–92.

Baaij, Cornelius J. W. 2012. "Fifty Years of Multilingual Interpretation in the
European Union." In *Oxford Handbook of Language and Law*, edited by
Peter M. Tiersma and Lawrence M. Solan, 217–32. Oxford: Oxford Univer-
sity Press.

Bach, Kent. 2005. "Context *ex Machina*." In *Semantics versus Pragmatics*, edited by Zoltán Gendler Szabó, 15–44. Oxford: Oxford University Press.

Barsalou, Lawrence. 1983. "Ad Hoc Categories." *Memory and Cognition* 11:
211–27.

Cardozo, Benjamin N. 1922. *The Nature of the Judicial Process*. New Haven:
Yale University Press.

Chomsky, Noam, 1965. *Aspects of the Theory of Syntax*. Cambridge: MIT
Press.

———. 2005. "Three Factors in Language Design." *Linguistic Inquiry* 36:1–22.

Clifton, Charles C., Jr., and Lyn Frazier. 2012. "Discourse Integration Guided by
'The Question Under Discussion.'" *Cognitive Psychology* 65:352–79.

Endicott, Timothy A. O. 2000. *Vagueness in Law*. Oxford: Oxford University
Press.

Fraser, Bruce. 1998. "Threatening Revisited." *Forensic Linguistics* 5:159–73.

Grice, H. P. 1975. "Logic and Conversation." In *Syntax and Semantics 3: Speech
Acts*, edited by P. Cole and J. Morgan, 41–58. New York: Academic Press.

Halliday, M. A. K., and Matthiessen, Christian M. L. M. 2014. *Halliday's Introduction to Functional Grammar*. 4th ed. New York: Routledge.

Horn, Laurence. 2004. "Implicature." In *The Handbook of Pragmatics*, edited
by Laurence Horn and Gregory Ward, 3–28. Oxford: Blackwell.

Hutton, Christopher. 2014. *Word Meaning and Legal Interpretation: An Introductory Guide*. Hampshire: Palgrave Macmillan.

Jackendoff, Ray. 2003. *Foundations of Language: Brain, Meaning, Grammar, Evolution*. Oxford: Oxford University Press.

Jacobson, Pauline. 2014. *Compositional Semantics: An Introduction to the Syntax/Semantics Interface*. Oxford: Oxford University Press.

Kimble, Joseph. 2015. "The Doctrine of the Last Antecedent, the Example in *Barnhart*, Why Both are Weak, and How Textualism Postures." *Scribes Journal of Legal Writing* 16: 5–43.

Miller, George A. 1999. "On Knowing a Word." *Annual Review of Psychology* 50:1–19.

Poscher, Ralf. 2012. "Ambiguity and Vagueness in Legal Interpretation." In *The Oxford Handbook of Language and Law*, edited by Peter M. Tiersma and Lawrence M. Solan, 128–44. Oxford: Oxford University Press.

Posner, Richard A. 2012. "The Incoherence of Antonin Scalia." *New Republic*, August 24. http://www.newrepublic.com/article/magazine/books-and-arts/106441/scalia-garner-reading-the-law-textual-originalism.

Rayner, Keith, Anne E. Cook, Barbara J. Juhasz, and Lyn Frazier. 2006. "Immediate Disambiguation of Lexically Ambiguous Words During Reading: Evidence from Eye Movements." *British Journal of Psychology* 97:467–82.

Scalia, Antonin, and Bryan Garner. 2012. *Reading Law: The Interpretation of Legal Texts*. St. Paul, MN: Thomson/West.

Schauer, Frederick. 2009. *Thinking Like a Lawyer*. Cambridge: Harvard University Press.

Searle, John. 1969. *Speech Acts: An Essay in the Philosophy of Language*. Cambridge: Cambridge University Press.

Slocum, Brian G. 2015. *Ordinary Meaning: A Theory of the Most Fundamental Principle of Legal Interpretation*. Chicago: University of Chicago Press.

Solan, Lawrence M. 1993. *The Language of Judges*. Chicago: University of Chicago Press.

———. 2010. *The Language of Statutes: Laws and Their Interpretation*. Chicago: University of Chicago Press.

Solan, Lawrence M., and Peter M. Tiersma. 2005. *Speaking of Crime: The Language of Criminal Justice*. Chicago: University of Chicago Press.

Solum, Lawrence B. 2011. "We Are All Originalists Now." In *Constitutional Originalism: A Debate*, by Robert W. Bennett and Lawrence B. Solum, 1–77. Ithaca: Cornell University Press.

Sorensen, Roy. 2002. *Vagueness and Contradiction*. Oxford: Oxford University Press.

Tiersma, Peter. 1995. "The Language of Silence." *Rutgers Law Review* 48:1–99.

Waldron, Jeremy. 1994. "Vagueness in Law and Language: Some Philosophical Issues." *California Law Review* 82:509–40.

Wechsler, Stephen. 2015. *Word Meaning and Syntax: Approaches to the Interface*. Oxford: Oxford University Press.

Whittington, Keith E. 1999. *Constitutional Interpretation: Textual Meaning, Original Intent, and Judicial Review*. Lawrence: University Press of Kansas.

Wilson, Deirdre, and Dan Sperber. 2012. *Meaning and Relevance*. Cambridge: Cambridge University Press.

CHAPTER FOUR

The Continued Relevance of Philosophical Hermeneutics in Legal Thought

Frank S. Ravitch

I. Introduction

Philosophical hermeneutics has taken a strange path in legal scholarship. It was used by a few in the critical legal studies (CLS) movement to demonstrate the role traditions and preconceptions play in interpretation. Of course, many in the CLS movement eschewed philosophical hermeneutics in favor of deconstructionism.[1] The CLS scholars who did use philosophical hermeneutics took it into the realm of political theory and reform; areas well beyond the descriptive nature of philosophical hermeneutics. Other scholars, such as William Eskridge and Jay Mootz, understand the descriptive nature of philosophical hermeneutics and address philosophical hermeneutics in its more natural philosophical context.[2] Still others, like Michael Moore, reject philosophical hermeneutics because it gives no definitive basis upon which to decide what is a good or bad answer.[3]

This latter group, which consists heavily of natural law and positivist scholars, is most likely troubled by the very thing that attracted some members of the CLS movement to philosophical hermeneutics, namely, the concept of *dasein* (being in the world). *Dasein* is the notion that we exist within traditions that foster preconceptions and that these preconceptions affect our interpretive horizons. To the crits *dasein* suggested a basis for supporting the notion that power dynamics are embedded in lawmaking and legal interpretation (something one hardly needs philosophical hermeneutics to demonstrate). To natural law scholars, like Moore, *dasein* suggests that there is no Archimedean point from which any moral theory can be justified from outside of its own tradition, and therefore there can be no correct or best answer to any given legal question. Yet, both the critics and Moore read too much—or too little—into philosophical hermeneutics. Scholars like Eskridge and Mootz, who understand the potential benefits of the limited and descriptive qualities of philosophical hermeneutics, seem to best capture the nature of philosophical hermeneutics as applied to legal contexts. In fact, this chapter will demonstrate that it is precisely this limited, descriptive quality of philosophical hermeneutics that makes it valuable in understanding legal interpretation.

This chapter focuses on the relevance of the philosophical hermeneutics of Hans-Georg Gadamer (hereinafter "Gadamerian hermeneutics") to understanding legal interpretation. Concepts like *dasein*, horizons of interpretation, preconceptions, and fusion of horizons are descriptions of how people exist in the world and interpret everything from written texts to daily interactions. This chapter asserts that understanding philosophical hermeneutics dictates nothing normative. Any normative approach must be based on some other theoretical foundation. Understanding how people interpret, however, can help effectuate normative approaches. Unless we know how judges and other players in the legal system experience interpretation any normative approach will only succeed in the long run when there are closely shared horizons between those seeking to effectuate policy and those making and interpreting the law.

It is tempting to read about this sort of metaphysics tinted theory in the legal context and exclaim, "So what? Obviously people are affected by their traditions and culture." This chapter will provide an example that demonstrates Gadamer had valuable insights for legal interpretation all along. The example comes from my experience working on Japanese constitutional law as an American who has only learned the language and culture of Japan as an adult. This experience has been quite helpful in demonstrating the value of Gadamer's insights in the legal context as well as the limits of those insights.

2. A Brief Introduction to Gadamerian Hermeneutics

Interpretation is a necessary fact of life. We are always interpreting,[4] whether we know it or not. Every interaction we have, every program we watch, and every text we read is affected by our preconceptions. There is nothing mysterious or complex about much of this, and we usually do not realize we are interpreting when we engage with situations, people, or texts with whom we share a language and similar traditions.

A simple example of this arose when I watched a Mel Brooks movie with a friend who grew up in a small town in the Midwest. We both found the movie quite funny. Yet my friend did not pick up on the humor in a few scenes that I found hilarious. I grew up in a large metropolitan area on the East Coast and I am Jewish. Given where I grew up and the tradition I grew up in, I share certain understandings with Brooks that may seem alien to people who do not share that context. Much of Brooks's comedy transcended the traditions of the Jewish community in the Northeast, and my friend found those scenes to be hilarious, but the humor in some of the scenes only made sense from within the cultural and linguistic traditions of that community (or at least those who grew up with some exposure to that community).

Simply put, hermeneutics are an inescapable part of everyday life. The more complex the interpretive task, such as applying a text written in a different time and culture to a situation arising today, the more our preconceptions may impact the meaning of the text or situation we are interpreting.[5] Of course, there are many approaches to interpretation, and these often overlap on salient points. As I have written elsewhere, however, philosophical hermeneutics seems especially useful in the context of legal interpretation because of the potential time lag and cultural shifts between the drafting of laws and their application to a variety of fact scenarios.[6]

Gadamer explained that there is no absolute method of interpretation.[7] Each interpreter brings his or her own preconceptions into the act of interpreting a text (text can refer to more than just a written text).[8] These preconceptions are influenced by the tradition, including social context, in which the interpreter exists.[9] The interpreter's tradition(s) provides her with a horizon that includes her interpretive predispositions.[10] This horizon is the range of what the interpreter can see when engaging with a text.[11] The concept of *dasein*, or being in the world, captures this dynamic.[12] We exist in the world around us and that world influences how we view things.[13] Thus, our traditions and context are a part of our being.[14]

Still, the text has its own horizon of meaning.[15] That horizon is influenced by the context (or tradition) in which it was written, those influencing or interpreting it over the passage of time, the words used, and the context of the original author or authors.[16] Philosophical hermeneutics suggests that to understand a text a give-and-take must occur between text and interpreter, a dialogue between one's being and the object that one seeks to understand.[17] This conversation transforms both the text and interpreter as they engage in the give-and-take.[18]

The interpreter necessarily projects his or her horizon into the interpretive process but should also reflect upon it and the horizon of the text.[19] The horizon of the text has a binding quality in that if the interpreter openly enters into dialogue with the text, the horizon of the text will limit the range of preconceptions the interpreter can project consistently with the horizon of the text.[20] Since the text and interpreter are engaged in a dialogue to reach a common truth, neither text nor interpreter are the sole source of meaning.

Gadamer saw the quest for interpretive methodologies as interfering with the process of interpretation by obfuscating what is really going on. It is not that interpretive methodology is useless, but rather that it does not do what it purports to do—reach an objective meaning. The process of reaching meaning requires a constant dialogue between text and interpreter. This dialogue is mediated, however, by tradition (I prefer the term "context").[21]

Significantly, Gadamer did not believe that the lack of a clear interpretive method prevents one from reaching truth (understanding). It simply demonstrates that truth can be variable when different texts and interpreters engage in the hermeneutic dialogue, or when that dialogue is engaged in over time by the same interpreter. This is not a form of nihilism as some critics have suggested.[22] Through a dialogue between text and interpreter one can reach a better understanding of the horizon of the text than one who does not engage in such dialogue and simply assigns a reflexive meaning to the text. Thus, while there is no methodological approach to interpretation in Gadamerian hermeneutics, there is a way for text and interpreter to interact to reach a meaning that is both consistent with the text and cognizant of the role the interpreter plays in reaching that meaning.

If we are embedded creatures—embedded in our traditions and context—as the concept of *dasein* suggests, there is no Archimedean point
from which we can say that a given methodology is objective, at least
in contested interpretive contexts.[23] This does not mean nihilism must
reign. After all, as Gadamer points out, the dialogue between text and
interpreter can lead to meaning, and because the interpreter must throw
out preconceptions that are inconsistent with the horizon of the text in
order to fuse horizons and interpret, it seems obvious that the interpretive possibilities are limited to the range of what fits within both the horizon of the interpreter and the horizon of the text.[24] Legal interpreters
generally use a variety of interpretive modes from within the legal tradition when interpreting law.[25] The key question is whether claims that
these modes provide objective methods of interpretation are anything
more than illusion.[26]

It is essential to remember that philosophical hermeneutics is primarily a descriptive account of how interpretation—including legal interpretation—happens. There is nothing normative about it. A good example is
the concept of *dasein*, or being in the world. Judges are of course prod-
ucts of their context (Gadamer would say traditions). They thus exist in
the world as entities whose preconceptions influence their horizons. Pre-
modern and much modernist legal scholarship often ignored this dimension of legal interpretation or sometimes sought to deny its existence or
impact. Much of this may have stemmed from a fear that acknowledging or addressing the role of judicial preconceptions in the process of legal interpretation would undermine the legal system by undermining the
belief in its objectivity.

I wrote in *Masters of Illusion* that the "opposite" of objectivity is not
subjectivity, as many judges and legal scholars suggest, but rather context.[27] And acknowledging the role that various contexts, including
judges' contexts, play in law and legal interpretation is simply acknowledging the obvious. It is not dangerous nor will it undermine the legal
system because the texts legal actors must confront have their own horizons and most often a shared tradition that constrains the legal interpreter and thus prevents the spiral towards nihilism. For example, in a
case involving a breach of contract a long history of legal interpretation
exists to help the judge frame the legal principles that can guide the decision. This does not mean that the historical precedent will necessarily answer the specific questions in a given case, but it does usually con-

strain the modes of legal analysis because of the importance of concepts such as stare decisis.

Thus, the contribution Gadamer makes to legal scholarship is that there is a middle ground between the traditional legal obsession with having "a" correct answer or "best" answer, as Ronald Dworkin might have put it, and the potential for Derridian-like indeterminacy. Gadamer's contribution is that the dialogue between text and interpreter and the ultimate fusion of horizons, or coming to meaning between the two, lead to a range of potentially "correct" answers, but not an unlimited range.[28] Gadamer also teaches the importance of reflection in the interpretive process, which, as Justice Cardozo eloquently explained, may be a good judge's greatest asset.[29] Reflection may offer a way to expand one's horizon, at least where one's cultural embeddedness does not preclude this.

In the field of law and religion judges' and justices' preconceptions appear to play a major role in legal outcomes.[30] Interestingly, these preconceptions seem to be affected by more than simply a judge's or justice's religious background, although religious background does seem important at least in some cases.[31] Judges' political leanings, views on legal interpretation, and views regarding the proper role of government in our constitutional system, as well as the judge's authoritarian tendencies (or lack thereof), all seem to play a role. Of course, judges rarely acknowledge such preconceptions even when preconceptions are obviously operating to effect outcomes.

In *Reason in the Age of Science*,[32] Gadamer suggests that hermeneutics cannot be artificially separated from practice.[33] He argues for an inherent praxis between "theoretic awareness about the experience of understanding and the practice of understanding."[34] This is not an argument for a teleological approach or for any sort of normative approach, but rather an argument for a better understanding of understanding. In the legal academy this call can be heeded by people of all theoretical and political stripes, by those who accept philosophical hermeneutics as valid theory and those who do not. Nonfoundationalism should not be troubling to either mainstream or radical legal scholars, because a nonfoundationalist understands both the epistemological problems with claims to objectivity and the fact that people and systems perceive objectivity and thus perceptions of objectivity matter.

We all exist as beings in the world and we all perceive the world around us every day. For lawyers, law professors, judges, and law students there are numerous cases, statutes, and factual scenarios to consider. Thinking in the dualistic terms of objectivity and subjectivity has long hampered the understanding of legal interpretation. Gadamer has provided a way out of this morass by demonstrating that between the myth of objectivity in contested spaces and the nihilistic path of radical subjectivity lies a middle ground where context thrives and where interpretation happens through a dialogue between interpreter and text. The following example provides insight into how this works.

3. Japanese Law as an Example of the Role *Dasein* Plays in Legal Interpretation

One of the best ways to explore the role that tradition plays in interpretation is by interacting with a different cultural context. To do so in a manner that speaks to the many facets involved in interpreting as a being in the world, it is helpful to look at a field one is well versed in, but to do so in a different cultural context. This is not necessary to demonstrate the relevance of Gadamerian hermeneutics to interpretation, because we are always interpreting, whether within our fields and cultures or not. It is, however, eye opening.

I served as a Fulbright Scholar in Japan in 2001. At the time I spoke no Japanese other than a few words and was there primarily to share my expertise on US Constitutional law. At the time my understanding of Japanese law and culture was quite limited; although the experience was amazing and made me want to learn more. Years later I went back to Japan to give a talk and explore setting up a summer program. Before going I studied a bit of Japanese, but once there I quickly realized the significant limitations my poor Japanese language skills created for my ability to understand Japanese court opinions and to explain US law without requiring a translator. Over the next five years I became proficient, although not fluent, in Japanese and became extremely well versed in Japanese constitutional law and culture. Eventually, I began giving academic talks in Japanese and also writing a bit about Japanese law and religion.

Yet, even though I wanted to open my mind to Japanese legal culture, and even though the current Japanese constitution was imposed on Japan by the US and has many similarities to the US Constitution, I realized very quickly that understanding the Japanese legal system from out-side of Japanese traditions and culture was nearly impossible. One can learn the structure of a legal system, the outcome and reasoning of legal decisions, and even the application of law to culturally bound situations, and still fail utterly to understand why things were decided in a specific way, or even what a given legal principle means in a particular context.

It was hard for me as an American to understand many elements of the Japanese legal system without increasing my horizon to understand Japanese traditions and culture. In fact, in some cases, unless one be-comes versed in Japanese language and culture a give-and-take between the horizon of the text and the interpreter is transformed into the hori-zon of the interpreter overwhelming the horizon of the text. Because I am a lawyer, however, there were certain issues on which an adequate shared tradition existed to facilitate a fusion of horizons. Let's look at an example under articles 20 and 89 of the Constitution of Japan.[35]

Article 20 reads:

> 1. Freedom of Religion is Guaranteed to all. No religious organization shall receive any privileges from the state, nor exercise any political authority. 2. No person shall be compelled to take part in any religious acts, celebration, right or practice. 3. The State and its organs shall refrain from religious edu-cation or any other religious activity.

Article 89 reads:

> No public money or other property shall be expended or appropriated for the use, benefit or maintenance of any religious institution or association, or for any charitable, educational or benevolent enterprises not under the control of public authority.[36]

Articles 20 and 89 were designed by the American occupation govern-ment to end government support for state Shinto. State Shinto supported a system of "Emperor worship" (this term does not capture the exact meaning of the concept in Japanese but will suffice for present pur-poses). State Shinto supported many of the atrocities committed during the Meiji, Taisho, and early Showa periods (roughly the 1880s to 1946).[37] State Shinto itself was a serious distortion of traditional Shinto, which has been part of Japanese society since before written history in Ja-pan.[38] Of course, on their face, articles 20 and 89 appear to go well beyond a prohibition on government support for state Shinto. They prevent government support for any religion.

Yet, in a famous case known as the *Tsu City Groundbreaking Ceremony* case,[39] the Japanese Supreme Court essentially held that traditional Shinto, which is different from state Shinto, is part of Japanese culture rather than a purely religious practice. The facts are quite interesting. Shinto rites were performed at a city-sponsored groundbreaking for a municipal gym.[40] The ceremony and offerings were paid for by the city.[41] A case was brought by a local citizen alleging that the ceremony was a violation of articles 20 and 89.[42]

The trial court held that the ceremony was a folk custom and thus not religion for constitutional purposes.[43] The appellate court reversed, holding that government support for the ceremony violated the principle of separation of politics and state (Seiji to Shuukyou no Bunri).[44] The Japanese Supreme Court reversed.[45] It agreed with the appellate court that the state must be religiously neutral[46] but added that all state connection with religion is not prohibited.[47] State connection with religion that, *when considering Japanese social and cultural conditions* and the purpose and effect of the state action, exceeds a reasonable standard consonant with the objective of religious freedom is unconstitutional.[48] A violation of article 20, paragraph 3 occurs when government conduct has a purpose with religious significance or when the effect of the government conduct is to subsidize, promote, suppress, or interfere with religion.[49]

Here, the rites were obviously connected to religion,[50] but they were not unconstitutional when considering the totality of the circumstances, because the ceremony had the secular purpose of "marking the start of construction by a rite performed in accordance with general social custom to pray for a stable foundation for the building and accident-free construction work."[51] The effects of the ceremony did not subsidize or promote Shinto or suppress or interfere with other religions, according to the court.[52] Therefore, government support for, and involvement in, the ceremony was not a religious activity for purposes of article 20.[53]

My initial reaction to this case as an American law and religion scholar was that the Japanese Supreme Court must have been "wrong" given the language of articles 20 and 89. Even now that I understand the decision from a Japanese cultural and linguistic perspective I am still not a fan of the decision, but my reasons for this disagreement are no longer the knee-jerk response I had as someone embedded in US law and religion and US understandings of religion and culture.

For US legal scholars who read the opinion (assuming their Japanese is adequate or they have found the English translation), it is obvious the Japanese Supreme Court adopted a test very similar to the test adopted by the US Supreme Court in *Lemon v. Kurtzman*.[54] The Japanese Supreme Court, however, held that Shinto can be interpreted as a cultural practice and therefore government sponsorship and recognition of a Shinto ceremony was not unconstitutional.[55] This was perplexing.

The decision began to make sense as I came to understand Japanese culture better. Before that I was unable to see the nuances of the decision because my horizon was so heavily affected by American culture and American legal culture. In the United States those who advocate for and against government support or endorsement of religion do so from a perspective about culture and religion that would be completely alien to most Japanese. It was hard for me to escape the US experience of religious entities and individuals regularly trying to influence local, state, and federal government.

To truly understand the Court's opinion in *Tsu City*, even if you disagree with it, you have to understand the concepts of *wa* (roughly translated as "harmony"), *bunka* (roughly translated as "culture"), and ambiguity. Simply put, at first as an American unfamiliar with these concepts in Japanese culture, I was unable to understand the horizon of the text in its context. In fact, I was so influenced by my preconceptions that I even made assumptions about language—namely, I assumed that the term "separation of politics and religion" (*seiji to shuukyou no bunri*) had the same substantive meaning as "separation of church and state." As my horizon expanded, I came to see things in the opinion that I could not have seen earlier.

In order to avoid romanticizing the concepts of *wa*, *bunka*, and ambiguity, I will simply explain them as they are understood generally in Japanese culture. Of course, there are many understandings of these concepts and I can not capture this complexity in detail in this short chapter. The key is to give the reader a basic understanding of these concepts, how they affected the *Tsu City* opinion, and why someone from a Western tradition such as that of the United States can easily impose a view on that opinion that overpowers the horizon of the text.

Wa is roughly translated as "harmony," but it is an entire system of being that effects elements of everyday life, deeply effects *bunka* (culture), and explains the frequent use of ambiguity in Japanese culture and sometimes in legal decisions. Japanese culture has a heavy focus on avoiding confrontation within society. Getting along is important in Japan. Contrary to popular Western stereotypes this does not mean that everyone is always happy and warm on the inside. It means that people seek to interact in a way that minimizes conflict, and therefore at least in public, *tatamae* (the face, or outward presence) is more important than *hon'ne* (the person's inner feelings). People try to find consensus in daily life.

Bunka is roughly translated as "culture," but it can also mean cultural traditions or civilization. The key to the concept here is how religion is viewed by many Japanese. Numerous studies have shown that most Japanese, at least in recent times, engage in some Buddhist and/or Shinto religious traditions, but primarily as a matter of culture. These traditions are just part of the broader routines that people do every day. If an entity builds a building there is almost always a Shinto dedication ceremony, and even with the Shinto priest there, most people don't perceive it as having deep religious meaning. It's just what is done. Most Japanese are not practicing Shinto or Buddhists, and most do not have deeply held religious commitments to either but engage in many cultural practices that are connected to both.

Finally, ambiguity is a tool often used in Japan to avoid conflict. When a direct answer would be viewed as negative, inviting argument, or upsetting, an ambiguous answer will often be used. It is not too much of a stretch to say that in Japan yes means yes, maybe means maybe or no, and no is rarely heard directly. This confuses many Western businesspeople and lawyers unfamiliar with Japanese culture, but one can adapt to it if one can retrain oneself to think from the perspective of *wa*. As Gadamerian hermeneutics suggests, this may be hard or impossible for some Westerners who are unable to reflect adequately to question their own traditions in different cultural contexts. This is all well and good, but what does it mean for the *Tsu City* decision?

Wa, *bunka*, and ambiguity are all central to the *Tsu City* decision and to the Japanese Supreme Court's understanding and application of its version of the *Lemon* test in that case. Given the concept of *wa* it is not surprising that the Japanese Supreme Court avoided interfering with an ordinary cultural practice that had been happening in Japan for at least one thousand years. Additionally, because Japan does not generally share the American phenomenon of people and movements attempting to use government to support or impose their religion, and because the "line" between traditional Shinto as a religion and as a cultural practice is not well delineated in Japan, the court's use of what I have called *shuukyou no bunka* (religion as culture) is also not surprising. In fact, the court's decision was quite different in a later case, discussed below, which involved a nationalist Shinto shrine that is highly controversial and has repeatedly attempted to gain government endorsement and support (and through which some government officials have pandered to nationalists).

Until one understands the role of *wa* and *bunka*, the court's holding that a Shinto groundbreaking ceremony for the local gym is more a cultural tradition in purpose and effect *when considering Japanese social and cultural conditions* seems inconsistent with the language of article 20 and maybe article 89. It also seems inconsistent with application of the US Supreme Court's *Lemon* test. Ambiguity helps further support the decision. The court is quite ambiguous about the religious impact of the ceremony for those who are practicing Shinto and for those who do not partake even in the cultural elements of Shinto. From a US perspective, this might be viewed (as I initially viewed it) as intentional obfuscation, and the entire exercise as similar to the concept of ceremonial deism in the United States. But it is not. The social, religious, and political dynamics are different in Japan, and Western dualisms and categories are not easily applied without some adaptation. I should be clear that I, and many Japanese law scholars, still view *Tsu City* as wrongly decided. The reasons for this, however, are far more complex than my initial response as an American, which was something along the lines of shinto + religion = obvious violation of articles 20 and 89 because the city paid for and sponsored the groundbreaking ceremony.

In 1997, the Japanese Supreme Court issued an opinion that continued to follow, and augmented, the legal framework set forth in the *Tsu City* case but which drastically departed from that case's understanding of, and application of, that framework.[56] The *Ehime Tamagushi* case involved the use of public funds by government officials from Ehime Prefecture.[57] The funds were used for offerings given by government officials to the Yasakuni Shrine and the Gokoku Shrine at ceremonies held by those shrines.[58] The offerings cost relatively small sums of money and consisted of twigs from a specific type of tree, the sakiki tree, wrapped with folded white papers.[59] This sort of offering to a Shinto shrine is called *tamagushi*.[60] The offerings were paid for using government funds and given by representatives of the government at the behest of Haruki Shiraishi, the then-governor of Ehime Prefecture.[61]

The *Ehime Tamagushi* court applied the legal test from the *Tsu City* case,[62] but the court added endorsement of religion analysis similar to that used by the United States Supreme Court.[63] Significantly, the court held that "the Constitution should be interpreted as striving for a secular and religiously neutral state by regarding the total separation of state and religion as its ideal."[64] The court recognized, however, that total separation between politics and religion is impossible, because anytime government regulates social norms it can affect religion indirectly.[65] The test to determine whether religious neutrality is violated is the purpose and effects test used in the *Tsu City* case[66] but with an endorsement gloss—that is, considering whether the government action under review favors religion in the *eyes of the public*.[67] The court applied this analysis under both article 20 and article 89 and found that paying for and giving the offerings violated both the purpose and effect elements of the test and endorsed religion.[68] Applying that test, the court held that the offering of *tamagushi* (and *kumoturyo*, another kind of offering made to the shrines), in the name of the local government, directly supports the religious activity of the shrine.[69]

Yet, a key to the decision was the nature of the shrines involved. These were not traditional Shinto shrines but rather shrines connected to State Shinto by history and often to radical nationalists in practice. Visits to these shrines by government officials are quite controversial in Japan and these shrines are not part of daily culture. Therefore, the purpose and effect when viewed in the *eyes of the public* and *when considering Japanese social and cultural conditions* did favor religion.

These shrines do not obviously contribute to *wa*, and they are not a clear part of traditional and widely practiced *bunka*. In fact, the government action of traveling to and offering *tamagushi* at these controversial shrines caused a great deal of conflict and disturbed *wa*. Moreover, the choices the court was presented with were stark: either uphold this controversial government action or strike it down. There was not as much room for ambiguity because there was no way to couch these practices as culturally accepted by Japanese society as a whole. Thus, the context within the culture was quite different and the difference in results between the two cases makes some sense at least within Japanese society.

4. Conclusion

This chapter suggests that Gadamerian hermeneutics remains relevant to descriptive understandings of law and that the phenomena of *dasein* and interpretive horizons can be concretely demonstrated when we explore different legal and cultural systems. Of course, one need not learn a different legal system and culture to experience the impact of interpretive horizons and *dasein*. We experience these phenomena all the time whether we realize it or not. Yet my experience with Japanese culture and law has reconnected me with Gadamerian hermeneutics and fostered a better understanding of the need for a descriptive understanding of interpretation. Without a descriptive understanding of interpretation it is harder to effectuate normative approaches.

Notes

1. Stephen M. Feldman, "How to Be Critical," *Chicago-Kent Law Review* 76 (2000): 893 (unlike many scholars working with critical theory and philosophical hermeneutics, Feldman has a deep understanding of Gadamerian hermeneutics, and he has suggested that Gadamerian and Derridian theory are not inherently antithetical, although they are certainly in some tension with each other, as the dialogue between Gadamer and Derrida demonstrated).

2. William N. Eskridge, Jr., "Gadamer/Statutory Interpretation," *Columbia Law Review* 90 (1990): 609, 621–22; Francis J. Mootz, "The Ontological basis of Legal Hermeneutics: A Proposed Model of Inquiry Based on the Work of Gadamer, Habermas, and Ricoeur," *Boston University Law Review* 68 (1988): 523; see also *Legal Hermeneutics: History, Theory, and Practice* , ed. Gregory Leyh (Berkeley: University of California Press, 1992) (exploring legal hermeneutics generally).

3. Michael S. Moore, "The Interpretive Turn in Modern Theory: A Turn for the Worse?," *Stanford Law Review* 41 (1989): 871, 923–27.

4. Hans Georg Gadamer, *Truth and Method* trans. Joel Weinsheimer and Donald G. Marshall, 2nd rev. ed. (New York: Continuum, 1999).

5. Frank S. Ravitch, *Masters of Illusion: The Supreme Court and the Religion Clauses*, 2–6, 81–82 (New York: NYU Press, 2007).

6. *Id.* at 9–11.

7. This is a primary point in Gadamer, *Truth and Method*; see also Hans-

George Gadamer, *Reason in the Age of Science*, trans. Frederick G. Lawrence, 98–107 (Cambridge: MIT Press, 1981).

8. Gadamer, *Truth and Method*, 265–71.

9. *Id.*; Eskridge, "Gadamer/Statutory Interpretation."

10. Gadamer, *Truth and Method*.

11. *Id.*, 302–7, 374–75.

12. *Id.*, 257–64.

13. *Id.*

14. See generally *id.*

15. Gadamer, *Truth and Method*, 302–7.

16. *Id.*, 370, 374–75; Gadamer, *Reason in the Age of Science*, 98. This may actually be an underinclusive list.

17. The dialogue is central to Gadamer's theory of interpretation in *Truth and Method*.

18. *Id.*, 307.

19. *Id.*, 267–69.

20. *Id.*; Eskridge, "Gadamer/Statutory Interpretation," 627.

21. Gadamer, *Truth and Method*, 266–67, 276–77.

22. Jean Grondin, *Introduction to Philosophical Hermeneutics*, trans. Joel Weinsheimer, 141–42 (New Haven: Yale University Press, 1994).

23. Gadamer, *Truth and Method*.

24. See generally *id.*

25. Philip Bobbitt, *Constitutional Fate* (Oxford: Oxford University Press, 1984); Philip Bobbitt, *Constitutional Interpretation* (Oxford: Blackwell, 1991); Ravitch, *Masters of Illusion*, 6–8.

26. Ravitch, *Masters of Illusion*.

27. *Id.* (The term "opposite" is in quotes because context is not the literal opposite of objectivity but rather the thing that makes objectivity—at least at a metaphysical level—impossible).

28. The term "correct" in this context does not imply a singular right or wrong answer, but rather refers to answers that fit within the horizons of both text and interpreter.

29. Benjamin N. Cardozo, *The Growth of the Law* (New Haven: Yale University Press, 1924), 68.

30. Some of the most interesting research on the factors that affect judicial decisions in religion cases has been conducted by Michael Heise and Gregory Sisk. Their work does not address hermeneutics or preconceptions, but it provides a detailed empirical study of decisions on religion issued by lower court judges (Federal District Court and Court of Appeals). The studies show that a variety of factors, including judges' backgrounds and political affiliations, correlate with decisions favoring strict or less strict interpretations of the religion clauses. See, e.g., Michael Heise & Gregory C. Sisk, "Religion, Schools, and Ju-

dicial Decision Making: An Empirical Perspective," *University of Chicago Law Review* 79 (2012): 185; Gregory C. Sisk, "How Traditional and Minority Religions Fare in the Courts: Empirical Evidence from Religious Liberty Cases," *University of Colorado Law Review* 76 (2005): 1021; Gregory C. Sisk, Michael Heise, and Andrew P. Morris, "Searching for the Soul of Judicial Decision-Making: An Empirical Study of Religious Freedom Decisions," *Ohio State Law Journal* 65 (2004): 491.

31. *Id.*

32. Gadamer, *Reason in the Age of Science.*

33. Hans-Georg Gadamer, "Hermeneutics as Practical Philosophy," in *Reason in the Age of Science.*

34. *Id.*, 112.

35. Nihonkoku Kenpō [Constitution], art. 20 (1947).

36. *Id.*, art. 89 (1947).

37. *Ehime Tamagushi,* 51 Saikou Saibansho Minji Hanreishū [Minshū] 1673 (Grand Bench) (1997).

38. C. Scott Littleton, *Understanding Shinto: Origins, Beliefs, Practices, Festivals, Spirits, Sacred Places* (London: Watkins, 2011).

39. 31 Saikou Saibansho Minji Hanreishū [Minshū] No. 69 (Grand Bench) (1977).

40. *Id.*

41. *Id.*

42. *Id.*

43. *Id.*

44. *Id.*

45. *Id.*

46. *Id.*

47. *Id.*

48. *Id.*

49. *Id.*

50. *Id.*

51. *Id.* (Quote taken from the official English translation.)

52. *Id.*

53. *Id.*

54. 403 U.S. 602, 612–13 (1971).

55. See *id.* (the court held that article 89 was not violated because the money paid to the Shinto priests to conduct the ceremony was a fee for services, and for that reason did not violate article 89). That reasoning would not likely be followed under the post-1997 cases. See notes 57–70, this chapter, and accompanying text.

56. *Ehime Tamagushi,* 51 Saikou Saibansho Minji Hanreishū [Minshū] 1673 (Grand Bench) (1997).

57. *Id.*

58. *Id.*

59. *Id.*

60. Nobushige Hozumi, *Ancestor-Worship and Japanese Law* (2nd and Revised Ed. The Maruzen Kabushiki-Kaisha 1912), 59.

61. *Ehime Tamagushi*, 51 Saikou Saibansho Minji Hanreishū [Minshū] 1673 (Grand Bench) (1997).

62. *Id.*

63. *Id.*

64. *Id.* (Quote taken from the official English translation.)

65. *Id.*

66. *Id.*

67. *Id.*

68. *Id.*

69. *Id.*

CHAPTER FIVE

The Strange Fate of Holmes's Normal Speaker of English

Karen Petroski[1]

This chapter describes a puzzle and suggests some possible explanations for it. The puzzle concerns a passage from Oliver Wendell Holmes's well-known essay "The Theory of Legal Interpretation," published in the *Harvard Law Review* more than a century ago (Holmes 1899).[2] Judges following Holmes have used this essay as a kind of multipurpose tool. Their opinions have cited the essay to support different interpretive conclusions and apparently contrasting theoretical commitments. And yet one of the most frequently cited passages in the essay refers repeatedly to a figure about which neither judges nor scholars have had much to say: the figure Holmes calls the "normal speaker of English." Although judges sometimes mention this figure, they invoke it only about a third as often as they quote other material from the essay or simply cite the entire essay.[3] A few academics have suggested that the interpretation of legal texts either does or should involve the postulation of a figure like Holmes's "normal speaker," but these commentators have not subjected the figure to significant analysis or critique, either. This neglect is odd because Holmes explicitly likens the "normal speaker of English" to another legal figure that has received a great deal of scrutiny: the reasonable person (or as Holmes calls it, the "prudent man"). Thus the puzzle: Why have judges and commentators paid so little direct attention to the figure of the normal speaker of English, given the evident attractions of Holmes's essay as a resource for justification and analysis and given the analogy Holmes drew between the normal speaker and the reasonable person?

This chapter will suggest that neglect of the normal-speaker figure might stem partly from certain implicit attitudes toward the relationship between judicial discourse and everyday discourse and that not all of those attitudes are justified. In particular, the chapter suggests that objective figures like the normal speaker and the reasonable person are similar in some ways to fictional characters and that this similarity makes the normal speaker a particularly anxiety-provoking figure. As a foundation for this discussion, the chapter first describes the role that the normal speaker plays in Holmes's essay and in later important judicial opinions. The chapter then considers the implications of the analogy Holmes drew between the "normal speaker of English" and the reasonable person, as well as the analogies he did not explicitly draw between objective figures such as these and the kinds of fictional characters that novelists create and that some philosophers have written extensively about. Judicial treatment of these personifications of objectivity suggests that judges (and commentators) are, implicitly, "fictionalists" (Sainsbury 2010, 2) about some of the types of assertions conventionally used to justify legal conclusions.[4] That is, they accept that these assertions can be considered "true" in a special and limited sense, only within the context of legal activity and communication. In contrast, the prevailing view toward the assertions used to justify interpretive conclusions seems to be realist, rather than fictionalist. While the chapter does not offer a conclusive explanation of this contrast, it seems at least possible that judicial (and academic) anxiety about the legitimacy of interpretive conclusions has something to do with the different treatment of these figures. The concluding section of the chapter explores whether this anxiety is justified or not and argues that increased attention to the figure of the normal speaker might actually help to alleviate it.

1. A Biography of the Normal Speaker of English

The "normal speaker of English" plays an important role in Holmes's essay. Holmes refers to the figure five times in only four pages. The figure is closely related to Holmes's overall aim in the essay, which warns readers away from imprecise references to "intent" and advocates an interpretive stance oriented toward "external," public, and objective information and conclusions, rather than toward the internal, private, and subjective

(Holmes 1899, 418).[5] Holmes introduces the "normal speaker" toward the end of a much-quoted passage making these points:

> How is it when you admit evidence of circumstances and read the document in light of them? Is this trying to discover the particular intent of the individual [who created the document], to get into his mind and to bend what he said to what he wanted? . . . We are after a different thing. What happens is this. Even the whole document is found to have a certain play in the joints when its words are translated into things by parol evidence, as they have to be. It does not disclose one meaning conclusively according to the laws of language. Thereupon we ask, not what this man meant, but what those words would mean in the mouth of a normal speaker of English, using them in the circumstances in which they were used, and it is to the end of answering this last question that we let in evidence as to what the circumstances were. But the normal speaker of English is merely a special variety, a literary form, so to speak, of our old friend the prudent man. He is external to the particular writer, and a reference to him as the criterion is simply another instance of the externality of the law. (Holmes 1899, 418)

This passage appears at the end of the first page of the essay. Holmes refers to the "normal speaker of English" three more times in the essay, each time to make a similar point about the importance of the circumstances of utterance of legally operative statements (Holmes 1899, 418–19, 419, 420).[6] As the excerpt above indicates, Holmes's preference for an "external" approach to interpretation is aligned with his understanding of the function of law more generally. According to this essay, law is a system for adjusting interpersonal relations, rather than a system for effectuating individual exercises of will (Holmes 1899, 419).[7]

Within a few years of its publication, judges began citing Holmes's essay in their opinions.[8] Before the 1950s, judges cited the essay almost exclusively in cases concerning the interpretation of wills and contracts. Some references mentioned the normal speaker or an equivalent. In a 1922 opinion typical of this use of the essay, a federal judge cited Holmes as authority for the "elementary principle of judicial interpretation that the test to be applied is what the ordinary user of such language would understand the words under the circumstances to mean."[9]

Through the first half of the twentieth century, most judicial references to the essay were of this kind. Judges invoked Holmes's essay much as they might cite a Supreme Court opinion: as authority for a legal principle being used as a premise in support of a case-specific conclusion. These early references did not tie Holmes's normal speaker to any broader discussion of competing visions or theories of legal interpretation. Two more polemical judicial projects in the latter vein have contributed to continuing legal awareness of Holmes's essay. The first of these projects took shape in a series of opinions on contract interpretation written in the 1940s by Roger Traynor before he became chief justice of the California Supreme Court. The second appears in two highly influential statutory-interpretation opinions written by Judge Frank Easterbrook and Justice Antonin Scalia in the late 1980s and early 1990s. Although these more theoretical adoptions of Holmes's essay invoke the normal speaker or an equivalent figure, however, neither set of opinions further examines or explains the figure's attributes or significance.

Then-Justice Traynor's references to Holmes's essay track Traynor's development of his (controversial) approach to contract interpretation, according to which a judge may consult extrinsic evidence to determine whether a contract term is ambiguous in the first place, and not only after ambiguity has been detected. Traynor first referred to Holmes's essay in a 1942 concurring opinion in which Traynor began to articulate this position.[10] In a dissenting opinion from 1944, Traynor explicitly referred to the "reasonable man" in this connection, although not to the "normal speaker of English."[11] By the mid-1940s, Traynor's position had begun to influence judges in California's lower appellate courts; to justify their consideration of extrinsic evidence in contract disputes, these judges also cited Holmes.[12] By the 1960s, California appellate-court judges were citing Traynor's early separate opinions as a kind of alternative line of authoritative precedent.[13] Traynor himself had by this point become chief justice of the California Supreme Court and finally persuaded other justices to accept his theory.[14] Traynor's approach to the use of extrinsic evidence was largely faithful to Holmes's vision of legal meaning as "external" and interpersonal, rather than internal and subjective. But for all of Traynor's sustained effort in promoting his position, and despite his consistent references to normal-speaker-like figures, he never elaborated on the characteristics of that figure. His opinions suggest, but never explicitly state, that he understood the figure to be more akin to a "reasonable contracting party under the circumstances" than to a "reasonable user of language."

Judges have also used Holmes's essay to support methodological statements about statutory interpretation. Holmes addressed statutory interpretation as well as contract and will interpretation in the essay, but no judicial opinion concerning statutory interpretation cited the essay until 1953.[15] The second statute-related reference to Holmes's essay appeared in a 1972 Supreme Court opinion by Justice Douglas, who mentioned Holmes to justify skepticism about consulting legislative history: "In construing laws we have been extremely wary of testimony before committee hearings and of debates on the floor of Congress save for precise analyses of statutory phrases by the sponsors of the proposed laws. . . . The reason is the caveat of Mr. Justice Holmes, 'We do not inquire what the legislature meant; we ask only what the statute means.'"[16] (Note that Justice Douglas's doubts about the pertinence of "extrinsic evidence" to the statutory-interpretation task are nearly an inversion of Justice Traynor's view on the value of extrinsic evidence in contract interpretation.) This opinion laid a foundation for the development of textualist approaches to statutory interpretation in the following decades. The opinion was issued just when now-Judge Easterbrook and the late Justice Scalia were first working in Washington, DC, and coming into professional contact with one another.[17] A couple of decades later, these judges would write two defining statements of textualism that are probably the best-known recent judicial references to Holmes's essay.

The first of these references was in Judge Easterbrook's opinion in *In re Sinclair*, issued in 1989. The opinion describes what seems to be a direct conflict between statutory text and legislative history. Judge Easterbrook opts emphatically for the former, casting "legislative intent," in the sense of legislators' mental states and preferences, as irrelevant to the interpretive task and describing most uses of legislative history as attempts to divine that type of intent. To support this position, Judge Easterbrook quotes the entire passage in which Holmes introduces the "normal speaker of English," including the link between the "normal speaker" and the "prudent man." Holmes, according to Judge Easterbrook, "denounce[d the] . . . claim that judges should give weight to the intent of a document's authors."[18] Judge Easterbrook did acknowledge that statements by a statute's enactors might be useful as evidence of contemporary usage of legal terms.[19] This emphasis on the "external" meaning of statutory terms suggests a view of the normal speaker of English as an almost social-scientific construct, perhaps even a position that could be specified through survey data.

Justice Scalia did not pick up on this suggestion in his own founda-

tional reference to Holmes's essay. This reference appeared two years after *Sinclair*, in Justice Scalia's dissent in *Chisom v. Roemer*, a case turning on interpretation of a provision of the federal Voting Rights Act.
Justice Scalia notoriously opened this dissent by attributing to the Supreme Court an already-existing "regular method for interpreting the
meaning of language in a statute," namely, textualism. In fact, this dissenting opinion was the first explicit articulation by a modern Supreme
Court justice of that method, which starts and often ends by "find[ing]
the ordinary meaning of the language in its textual context."[20] Justice Scalia did not follow Judge Easterbrook in presenting the normal-
speaker perspective as one that might be described empirically; in fact,
Justice Scalia did not refer to the normal speaker of English at all but
only to "ordinary" variations on the figure. His first such reference supports Justice Scalia's demand that interpreters limit their inquiry to statutory text: "We are to read the words of that text as any ordinary Member of Congress would have read them."[21] The opinion does not contain
any further discussion of the "ordinary Member of Congress" or any explanation of how a judge or lawyer might figure out how an ordinary
member of Congress would read the words of a text. A later passage in
the opinion makes a similar casual reference to Holmes's figure. Justifying his conclusion about the meaning of "representatives," the statutory term at issue in the case, Justice Scalia again presents the "ordinary
speaker" as a position that a judge or lawyer can automatically and un-
problematically assume: "the ordinary speaker in 1982 would not have
applied the word to judges, see Holmes, The Theory of Legal Interpretation. . . ."[22] Justice Scalia does not elaborate further on this "ordinary"
language user at any point in the opinion.

As noted above, these articulations of textualist method use Holmes's
essay to support a position quite different from Justice Traynor's. Traynor had cited Holmes to stress the importance of examining not just the
language used in a legal instrument but also the circumstances in which
that language was used in giving the instrument legal effect. The textualists, in contrast, cite the essay in arguments that circumstances of use
are of limited, if any, significance. Both Justice Traynor and the textualists advocate a kind of "external" interpretation, but they seem to construe externality differently. For Justice Traynor, interpretation is external in that it as necessarily takes into account the circumstances of an
instance of human interaction—the pragmatics of a particular contractual commitment. The textualist conception of "external" interpretation

advocates a much more frugal focus on semantics and—at least in Justice Scalia's version—seems to equate circumstances of use with legislators' subjective, or "internal," intentions. Although both of these approaches might be said to be concerned with identifying "objective" meaning, Justice Traynor's vision of objectivity is more interpersonal (akin to what Matthew Kramer has called a "weakly mind-independent" view of objectivity), while Judge Easterbrook's and Justice Scalia's is impersonal (corresponding to a "strongly mind-independent" vision of objectivity; Kramer 2008, 243).

Both approaches, despite their differences, are thus logical extensions of Holmes's position. The essay has been a remarkably rich resource for justification. Judges have continued to cite it frequently in both contract- and statutory-interpretation decisions since the early 1990s.[23] None, however, have developed the normal-speaker figure any further than Traynor or the textualists did. Neither judges nor commentators have asked of this figure, for example, as they have asked of the reasonable person, whether it is a descriptive or normative construct. Is the normal speaker just a figure of speech (as some passages in Holmes's essay might suggest),[24] or is it, instead, a reference to a particular point of view that judges should try to assume (as other passages in the essay hint)?[25] If it is the latter, exactly what point of view does the normal speaker inhabit, and how does an actual lawyer or judge go about assuming it? The next section will further explain why it is puzzling and troubling that American lawyers have no tradition of asking these particular questions and will explore some initial explanations for the absence of any such tradition.

2. Normal Speakers and Fictional Figures

2.1 "Objective" Legal Figures and Fictional Characters

Holmes expressly described the normal speaker of English as "a special variety" or "literary form . . . of our old friend the prudent man." This reference to the "prudent man" (a figure this chapter calls the reasonable person) as "our old friend" suggests at least a superficial parallel between this figure and those we think of as more traditional fictional characters. Both can be discussed using the language normally reserved for actual people. Judges and lawyers routinely ascribe to the reasonable person dispositions and attributes, such as prudence and an ability to reason, that they also ascribe to actual people.[26] Of course no competent legal reader would be willing to say that the legal reasonable person actually exists in the sense that Justice Holmes, for example, did. Yet the "reasonable person" label seems to refer to something about which judges and lawyers can coherently argue and reason.[27] In all of these ways, the status of the legal reasonable person is analogous to that of a fictional character like Sherlock Holmes. The name "Sherlock Holmes" is meaningful to members of Anglo-American culture and seems to them to refer to something to which many characteristics typical of a person may be ascribed, even though we do not believe that Sherlock Holmes existed in our world as a person.[28] And just as we can intelligibly compare the fame or cleverness of an actual person to that of Sherlock Holmes, we (at least we lawyers) can intelligibly discuss how an actual person's conduct measures up against that of the reasonable person and often even agree on an answer to that question.

The reasonable person is not the only legal figure with these characteristics, but it is the most common, as well as perhaps the most controversial.[29] To be sure, these figures are not as robust as fictional characters like Sherlock Holmes. They do not have identifiable physical features or eccentric habits, and perhaps for this reason, disagreement about the characteristics of reasonable-person figures is probably more widespread than disagreement about the characteristics of well-known fictional characters. Even if reasonable-person figures are in some ways less stable than fictional characters, however, it does not follow that they are entirely unstable reference points. Classic cases featuring these figures, and the narratives in these cases, are part of the folklore of Anglo-American legal culture just as Sherlock Holmes's adventures are part of modern Anglo-American popular culture. We justifiably call these figures "objective" because they are part of this shared, public tradition. References to these constructs across fact patterns by different decision makers give the constructs at least weak mind-independence.

These legal personifications of objectivity also seem to both signify and require a kind of cognitive engagement that resembles a reader's engagement with fictional characters like Sherlock Holmes. Of course, reasonable-person figures are primarily instruments of justification, not storytelling. But their capacity to justify derives from their association with an impersonal perspective, not just from their conventionality. A lawyer providing legal advice on an issue as to which a reasonable-person standard applies must imagine the conduct of the figure in question. A lawyer engaged in advocacy on such an issue must be able to describe how the figure in question would perceive, infer, or act in the circumstances of the case, and that description must be consistent with the judge's understanding of the figure's likely behavior, or the lawyer's description will not be effective. Reasonable-person figures thus function very much like what the philosopher Kendall Walton has called "props" in games of "make-believe" (Walton 1990, 38–39). The reasonable person provides a focus for joint imagining and debate, and its features, fixed to some extent by precedent, "prescribe" certain imaginings by lawyers and judges about what the figure in question would and can do and think. Each judicial reference to the reasonable person contributes to construction of the figure's "character" while invoking a preexisting impersonal perspective.

The reasonable person in its various guises is, then, a symbol of "externality," but it is also a mind-independent reference point for lawyers and judges.[30] Holmes's 1899 references to the "prudent man" depended on both of these features of the figure. It seems plausible that Holmes's essay remains popular at least partly because of its development of these themes; since Holmes wrote, judges have continued to seek objective reference points for their interpretive decisions. Yet Holmes's normal speaker of English, introduced as another personification of objectivity, has never received the attention from judges or commentators that its objective cousins have.

This neglect can have unfortunate results. In a 2015 decision of the Supreme Court issued after the conference at which this essay was originally presented, the main point dividing the seven-justice majority and a dissenting Justice Thomas was the distinction, if any, between the reasonable person of tort law and the reasonable maker of statements.[31] The majority in this case, *Elonis v. United States*, saw no distinction; Justice Thomas insisted on a difference. (None of the justices—including Justice Scalia, who joined the majority opinion—cited Holmes's essay, but Justice Thomas's dissenting opinion advocated a position very similar to Holmes's.[32]) More troublingly, although the majority concluded that the trial court in the case had included an improper legal standard in its jury instructions, the majority was unable to specify exactly what legal standard trial courts should use, a failure that drew criticism not only from Justice Thomas but also from Justice Alito, writing separately. The majority opinion indicates that the seven justices joining that opinion were able to agree on only three propositions: first, the "reasonable speaker" is equivalent to the "reasonable person"; second, a "reasonable person" standard is a negligence standard; and third, criminal convictions generally require a mental state other than negligence. The first of these propositions might not have seemed so self-evident had more justices been accustomed to thinking of Holmes's "normal speaker" the way Holmes presented it: as a figure distinct from, although related to, the reasonable person.

As the concluding section of this chapter explains in more detail, it seems at least possible that the relative neglect of the normal-speaker figure contributed to the failure of the *Elonis* majority to recognize any distinction between this figure and the tort-law reasonable person, as well as to the majority's inability to reach agreement on the appropriate legal standard in the case. First, however, the next section of the chapter considers several potential explanations for the relative neglect of this figure, including the possibility that judges consider the fictional-character-like features of the normal speaker to be more problematic than those associated with other reasonable-person constructs.

2.2 Explaining the Strange Fate of the Normal Speaker of English

One explanation for judicial reluctance to dwell on the normal speaker as a prop or to flesh it out as a character might be that judges are aware of a real-life linguistic diversity that the "normal speaker" label seems to deny. Judges might find the "normal speaker" label useful as a kind of synonym for "ordinary meaning" but hesitate to conclude that they can assume a perspective identifiable with a singular normal speaker, given the dependence of linguistic meaning on context in general and on the context of different linguistic communities in particular. Careful readers of Holmes's essay, like Justice Traynor, would note its emphasis on the contribution of context to meaning and, if moderately self-aware, might hesitate to conclude that all linguistic contexts are equivalent. It is not at all clear that judges are consistently aware of linguistic diversity, however, and this explanation is also hard to reconcile with judges' treatment of other personifications of objectivity. In many other settings, judges seem perfectly comfortable assuming a perspective that is admittedly normative—demanding that members of different communities conform to a uniform standard—rather than descriptive.

Judge Easterbrook's social-scientific version of the figure suggests a related but distinct explanation for neglect of the normal speaker. Judges might be willing to accept, as Judge Easterbrook perhaps did, that a normal speaker is in theory empirically determinable and that an accurate description of that speaker's usage and intuitions would be pertinent to judicial assessments of legal meaning. But the same judges might be skeptical that they have or could obtain the information needed to construct such a description. This explanation, too, seems inconsistent with other judicial practices, especially the confidence many judges exhibit about "ordinary meaning" and other linguistic facts. Few judges seem interested in gathering information about linguistic usage beyond the information available in dictionaries. Judges could, but rarely do, receive expert testimony on how the normal speaker of English would understand statutory language, even though they regularly receive such testimony to understand, for example, how the "person having ordinary skill in the art" would understand the language of patent documents. Professor Solan has convincingly documented this phenomenon (Solan 1993, 17–28, 26); Justice Scalia's opinion in *Chisom* (discussed again in the concluding section of this chapter) is a prominent example of it.

A third explanation might be that judges have not developed the normal speaker figure because they do not see how such development could help them justify interpretive conclusions. Skepticism about the usefulness of the figure could be justified in several ways. Judges might, for example, more or less consciously sense a tension between developing the figure and maintaining an objective stance. A judge considering how to characterize a normal speaker would come face to face with his or her own power to shape this "character." Recognizing this power is a short step from fearing that it is utterly unconstrained, as much of the literature on reasonable-person standards reminds us.[33] If the normal speaker is reindividualized each time it is mentioned, it becomes less useful as support for conclusions about statutory or other legal meaning. This explanation, however, like others offered above, seems inconsistent with judges' willingness to consult their (often variable) intuitions about ordinary meaning, as well as with the long-established treatment of apparently analogous figures, like the reasonable person. After all, judges exercised their imaginations in developing other objective figures, yet those figures can still justifiably be called "objective." And despite the ease and familiarity of the inference from creativity to lack of constraint, that inference is not clearly valid.[34]

But there might be other reasons that closer attention to the normal-speaker figure would generate anxiety. Perhaps the risk judges sense, however obscurely, lies not in the problem of exercising their imaginations but in the prospect of understanding language, or conclusions about its meaning, as a matter of "make-believe." Understanding legal language and interpretive conclusions in this way would concede that they function as part of a specifically legal "game," that they are in some way less than fully authentic or sincere. This concession might affect conclusions about the meaning of legal texts differently than it would affect some other kinds of legal conclusions, such as conclusions about fault. To illustrate: One might paraphrase the sentence "The reasonable person would have engaged the safety catch before using the appliance" as "According to the law, a person should engage the safety catch before using the appliance." Each of these statements could be used in approximately the same way to justify a legal conclusion, with roughly the same rhetorical effect. This kind of paraphrase seems to work differently for judicial conclusions about meaning. Imagine paraphrasing "The normal speaker of English would understand 'representatives' not to include judges" as "According to the law, 'representatives' does not include judges." This paraphrase does not seem to state a legal standard; it seems to take an ordinary English word and arbitrarily provide it with specifically legal meaning. This move reintroduces the concerns about unconstrained decision mentioned above, in a slightly different guise. But this account of the strange fate of the normal speaker of English, unlike the others above, is consistent with the ways judges treat otherwise comparable figures like the reasonable person.

The use of paraphrase in the previous paragraph was inspired by an approach to the analysis of fictional discourse common to a number of philosophers. This view explains our intuition that sentences referring to fictional characters (such as "Sherlock Holmes lived at 221B Baker Street") can be true (as most of us would say that sentence is), even though they do not refer to any existing entity and thus do not truly refer to anything. When we take such sentences to be true, according to this approach, we are really conceiving of them as implicitly embedded in longer sentences beginning with suitable contextualizing tags (e.g., "In Conan Doyle's stories, Sherlock Holmes lived at 221B Baker Street").[35] Legal references to the reasonable person seem to work this way. Lawyers and judges write and read such references as if prefixed with a tag placing them in the context of legal discourse. But legal references to the normal speaker do not seem to work the same way. (There may be a chicken-and-egg dynamic at work here that keeps the normal-speaker figure from functioning like otherwise similar figures as long as it remains underdeveloped relative to them.) If this analysis is sound, it seems that lawyers and judges might be comfortable with a fictionalist attitude toward legal discourse when it is articulating specific legal standards or decisions about liability. That is, in such circumstances, legal language seems to legal professionals to be functioning properly even when it does not refer to any actual state of affairs. (Judges, especially appellate judges, might even see their discourse as operating most powerfully precisely when it does *not* refer to any actual state of affairs.) Lawyers and judges are less comfortable, however, regarding statements about the significance of language as fictional in the same way.

The final section of this chapter explores the reasons for this contrast in more detail. It also considers the possibility of a defensible fictionalist view of legal discourse about the meaning of legally significant language.

3. Another Way to Think of the Normal Speaker and Its Analogues

The previous section suggested that we might understand the strange fate of Holmes's normal speaker of English in terms of (perhaps implicit) judicial attitudes toward the fiction-like status of judicial discourse. With other objective figures, judges seem unafraid to be fictionalists or something similar. Those figures remain valuable tools for justifying legal conclusions even when they are acknowledged to be specifically legal constructs and to correspond to no actual person.[36] A fictionalist attitude toward the normal speaker of English, however, seems more problematic. This section further explores this difference and examines arguments for treating the normal speaker like other objective figures.

Judges do sometimes directly acknowledge the fictional status of figures like the reasonable person and the patent-law person of ordinary skill in the art. Doing the same with the normal speaker of English could have some possibly alarming implications.[37] Characterizing the normal speaker as a specifically legal construct would, for example, mean admitting that there may be a difference between the legal meaning of language and its nonlegal meaning. Judicial discourse could take a significant risk if it were to acknowledge that it is an insiders' game in this way. Judicial determinations are supposed to be grounded in and to respond to acts—including many linguistic acts—occurring outside the litigation process. If legal meaning is understood as distinct from nonlegal meaning, judicial conclusions about the meaning of nonjudicial language acts would be conceptually detached from those acts and from the world inhabited by the nonlegal audience for those applications. Engaging too seriously with a fictional normal speaker could thus threaten not just an apparent lack of constraint but also judicial solipsism, irrelevance, and illegitimacy.

Yet the current practices of avoiding direct confrontation with the fictional status of the normal speaker encounter many of the same problems. Most basically, as *Elonis* illustrates, the inability to discuss whether apparently ordinary terms (in that case, the term "threat") may be admitted to have a specifically legal meaning can force an analysis into something close to incoherence. On a more theoretical plane, the available alternative judicial understandings of the interpretive enterprise are also vulnerable to charges of solipsism. Although textualists and many proponents of ordinary-meaning interpretation argue that their approaches prevent judges from making statutory language mean whatever they want it to mean, it is far from clear that textualism as practiced achieves its stated goals of predictability and objectivity in interpretation (see, e.g., Fallon 2014, 695, 713). In fact, if we think judges should be striving for interpersonally acceptable interpretive conclusions, it might make sense for them to use the same kind of device for attaining mind-independent conclusions in this area that they use in others. In interpretation, as in the articulation of standards of conduct and decision, better-developed and self-aware use of a perspective like that of the normal speaker might prompt judges to step back from their own personal, prereflective understandings of the significance of legal texts. Perhaps some—or even all—judges already do interpret statutory and contractual language by imagining the intentions of hypothetical drafters or the comprehension of hypothetical readers (see Greenawalt 2000, 1664–68). There seems to be little reason for such judges to remain unaware of or silent about what they are doing. And as more judges acknowledge and embrace a normal-speaker perspective, the mind-independence of the figure would only increase.

The consequences of candor might also be no worse than those of silence. It is tempting to deny any difference between legal and nonlegal English, but legal English and nonlegal English are, in fact, different. Legally trained readers and readers without such training do not read and comprehend the same legally significant texts in the same way (for evidence, see "Proceedings" 1995, 924–26). Insisting that language functions identically inside and outside the legal context encourages the expectation that legal decisions will be immediately transparent to those subject to them, that legal acts will be comprehensible to nonlawyers in full without translation. When this transparency fails, as it often does, the legal outsider will regard the nontransparent legal decision as improper, and that reaction will be justifiable. Denying the difference between legal and ordinary English cannot help solve this problem. Judges willing to understand their opinions as written according to accepted "rules for imagining," in contrast, might be better positioned to think about exactly where those rules begin and end, and why, and to explain both the rules and the reasons for them to those unfamiliar with the game. (The same goes for lawyers in composing arguments, drafting briefs, and counseling clients.) If the legitimacy of interpretive conclusions is our concern, then, perhaps judges should develop a normal-speaker figure along the lines of the reasonable person, as Holmes originally suggested. Doing so would help judges strengthen the case for the mind-independence of their interpretive conclusions. It might also help them to be more articulate about the scope of the game they are playing, instead of presenting their conclusions in a way that suggests that their game board extends over the entire world.

What could judicial development of the "normal speaker" as a fictional character look like? This development would need to proceed case by case, like the development of other legal personifications of objectivity. Different cases will present different questions about the normal speaker's preexisting knowledge, familiarity with particular contexts, and so forth. But judges' interpretive vocabularies already contain protocharacterizations of this figure. Many of the canons of statutory interpretation, for example, are easily understood as presuppositions held by the legal normal speaker of English (see, e.g., Sinclair 1985), although they have rarely been described this way. To be sure, some judges might have to depart from current practice. They might need to develop more consistent and thoughtful approaches to consulting their own intuitions about word meaning (see Solan 1993; Fitzgerald 2009). And they might need to acknowledge that some expressions in English may have different legal and lay meanings. The normal speaker of English for purposes of legal interpretation will sometimes need to be understood as the normal speaker of legal English; judges might have to conclude that, in some cases, "ordinary meaning" in the sense of lay or everyday meaning either does not exist or is irrelevant to a legal decision.[38]

Some of these suggestions might seem counterintuitive or normatively undesirable. Two examples may demonstrate the importance and potential value of more self-conscious development of a normal-speaker figure: the opinions in *Elonis* and Justice Scalia's dissent in *Chisom*. The justices disagreed in *Elonis* about the instructions given to help jurors decide whether a defendant's communication counted as a "threat." The instructions had told jurors to ask themselves whether, if a reasonable person had made the defendant's communications (a series of Facebook rants addressed to the defendant's estranged wife and to law enforcement), that person would have foreseen that others would interpret the communications as threatening.[39] The instruction thus asked jurors to compare the defendant's actual communications with imagined equivalent communications made by a normal-speaker figure and to decide what this figure would have known about how others would take the communications. This instruction provided the jurors with a device or "prop" to guide their thinking about whether the defendant's communications qualified as "threat[s]" within the meaning of the relevant statute.

The Supreme Court majority did not analyze the instruction in this way, however. As noted above, the majority disapproved of the instruction on the ground that it would permit conviction even if the jury only found the defendant negligent with regard to the nature of his communications.[40] The authors of the majority opinion were, it seems, unable themselves to imagine the mental exercise described just above, unable to see the similarity of this exercise to the task of statutory interpretation, and unable to conceive of jurors using their imaginations in this way. By rejecting the instruction, moreover, the majority excused itself from the task of fleshing out a normal speaker's characteristics. As suggested earlier, the majority's distaste for the idea of a distinct normal-speaker figure—whether that distaste stemmed from unfamiliarity with the idea, distrust of jurors' ability to grasp it, uncertainty about whether it would be appropriate for jurors to apply it, or some other source— seems to have kept these seven justices from agreeing on anything more than the most minimal resolution of the case. Justice Alito wrote separately mainly to criticize the majority for failing to communicate any clear instructions to lower courts and lawyers dealing with prosecutions under the same statute.[41] In *Elonis*, then, the tradition of neglect of the normal-speaker figure might well have contributed to a remarkably dysfunctional disposition.

Justice Scalia's dissent in *Chisom* provides a second example of the potential benefits of greater attention to the normal speaker. As noted, Justice Scalia joined the *Elonis* majority and its rejection of a normal-speaker-like figure in an instruction to jurors. In his *Chisom* dissent, however, Justice Scalia invoked the figure to support his interpretation of statutory language, and he seemed to characterize the figure as a layperson, not a lawyer. The statutory text at issue in *Chisom* provided:

> A violation of [the Voting Rights Act] . . . is established if . . . it is shown that the political processes leading to nomination or election . . . are not equally open to participation by members of a class of citizens protected by [the statute] in that its members have less opportunity than other members of the electorate to participate in the political process and to elect representatives of their choice.[42]

The question presented by the case was whether this provision applied when the plaintiffs' showing concerned the ability of citizens to elect judges, rather than legislators, of their choice. The majority concluded that the provision did apply in this situation for a variety of reasons, including the history of amendments to the statute as well as the judicial decisions interpreting it before the most recent such amendment. Justice Scalia's dissent supported his contrary conclusion with a series of assertions about the ordinary meaning of "representatives":

> There is little doubt that the ordinary meaning of "representatives" does not include judges, see Webster's Second New International Dictionary 2114 (1950). The Court's feeble argument to the contrary is that "representatives" means those who "are chosen by popular election." On that hypothesis, the fan-elected members of the baseball all-star teams are "representatives"— hardly a common, if even a permissible, usage. Surely the word "representative" connotes one who is not only elected by the people, but who also, at a minimum, acts on behalf of the people. Judges do that in a sense—but not in the ordinary sense. As the captions of the pleadings in some States still display, it is the prosecutor who represents "the People"; the judge represents the Law—which often requires him to rule against the People. . . . The point is not that a State could not make judges in some senses representative, or

that all judges must be conceived of in the Article III mold, but rather, that giving "representatives" its ordinary meaning, the ordinary speaker in 1982 would not have applied the word to judges, see Holmes, The Theory of Legal Interpretation, 12 Harv. L. Rev. 417 (1899). It remains only to ask whether there is good indication that ordinary meaning does not apply.[43]

On its own, Justice Scalia's invocation of the permissible usage of "representatives" in the baseball context is appealing (although more than a few law students, at least, have intuitions differing from Justice Scalia's on this point). This reference suggests a genuine effort to speak to lay readers, consistent with the implication that a word should mean the same thing inside the law as it does outside the law. That proposition is attractive, even if Justice Scalia's intuitions do not match ours.

But the example is not the text at issue in this case, and the statutory passage in question does not self-evidently mean anything at all outside the law. Of course, each word in Section 2 of the Voting Rights Act does have a nonlegal meaning or set of meanings. But few would probably say that the provision as a whole has such a meaning, and it is not clear why we would want to insist that it does, any more than we would want judges to rule for "the People" in every case. Judges make decisions that bind us because we have agreed to have them do so, or perhaps because we do not have a choice in the matter—but very likely not because we believe that they decide the same way that anyone would in their position. They are players in a very serious game, operating according to a highly complex set of props and rules for imagining, to which they are able to devote most of their time. Why not admit it?

Notes

1. Thanks to Brian Slocum, Jay Mootz, and all participants at the conference at which this chapter was originally presented for their inspiring conversations and helpful feedback.

2. This article is among the most frequently cited law review articles on legal interpretation, and it is especially frequently cited by judges. As of 2012, only thirty-nine articles on legal interpretation (out of thousands) had been cited more often by other law review articles (Petroski 2012, 394). As of February 2016, Holmes's article had been cited by 106 judicial opinions (search run in the Westlaw "allcases" database on February 25, 2016). In contrast, the law re-

view article addressing legal interpretation that is most often cited by other legal scholars—Robert Cover's 1983 *Harvard Law Review* Supreme Court foreword (Cover 1983), cited 1,170 times by law review articles as of 2012—had been cited in judicial opinions only ten times as of February 2016 (search run in the West-law "allcases" database on February 25, 2016).

3. As of February 2016, the phrase "normal speaker of English" appeared in twenty-two of the 106 cases citing the essay.

4. R. M. Sainsbury offers this definition of fictionalism: "To be a fictionalist about some region of thought is to say that the things thought are of value (are in some sense to be esteemed, accepted, or commended), but this value does not consist in their being true" (Sainsbury 2010, 2).

5. The essay also argues for a certain understanding of what a "theory of interpretation" is. Holmes regards such a theory not as a set of laws or rules, but rather as a defensible description of the best interpretive practices, or perhaps just the most prevalent practices. Note, for example, how in the passage quoted in the text Holmes maintains that the consultation of extrinsic evidence in the construction of a legal document "does not disclose one meaning conclusively according to the laws of language" (Holmes 1899, 417).

6. The first of these references addresses the context of property transfer: "If the donor, instead of saying 'Blackacre,' had said 'my gold watch' and had owned more than one, inasmuch as the words, though singular, purport to describe any such watch belonging to the speaker, I suppose no evidence of intention would be admitted. But I dare say that evidence of circumstances sufficient to show that the normal speaker of English would have meant a particular watch by the same words would be let in" (Holmes 1899, 418–19). The second addresses contractual language: "For each party to a contract has notice that the other will understand his words according to the usage of the normal speaker of English under the circumstances, and therefore cannot complain if his words are taken in this sense" (ibid., 419). The third addresses the interpretation of wills: "It is true that the testator is a despot, within limits, over his property, but he is required by statute to express his commands in writing, and that means that his words must be sufficient for the purpose when taken in the sense in which they would be used by the normal speaker of English under his circumstances" (Holmes 1899, 420).

7. Holmes writes: "Of course, the purpose of written instruments is to express some intention or state of mind of those who write them, and it is desirable to make that purpose effectual, so far as may be, if instruments are to be used. The question is how far the law ought to go in aid of the writers" (ibid., 419).

8. The first citation in a judicial opinion dates from 1903. It does not quote or discuss the passage this chapter focuses on, but rather describes Holmes's essay as supporting judicial recourse to "a natural, unaided first impression" of a document's meaning: "In the oral discussion some one said that the court below had not given adequate consideration to the canons of construction, the princi-

ples of interpretation and the rules of law to which its attention had been called, but had brushed them all aside, saying that this will was too clear for argument. In sympathy with and defense of the court below, we want to say that in a case of this kind there is nothing so mind satisfying as a natural, unaided first impression. . . . The value of these natural impressions in the interpretation of documents, and especially of a will not drawn by a lawyer, is shown in an article on 'The Theory of Legal Interpretation,' by Professor Oliver Wendell Holmes. . . .". Robbins v. Smith, 27 Ohio C.C. 91, 95 (Ohio Cir. Ct. 1903).

9. Western Petroleum Co. v. Tidal Gasoline Co., 284 F. 82, 84 (7th Cir. 1922).

10. Universal Sales Corp. v. California Press Mfg. Co., 20 Cal. 2d 751, 776 (Cal. 1942) (Traynor, J., concurring) ("The exclusion of parol evidence regarding . . . circumstances merely because the words do not appear ambiguous to the reader can easily lead to the attribution to a written instrument of a meaning that was never intended. . . . [S]ee Wigmore on Evidence, 3rd ed., §§ 2458–2478; 'The Theory of Legal Interpretation,' 12 Harv. L. Rev. 417, by Oliver Wendell Holmes (then Chief Justice of Massachusetts.)").

11. In re Rule's Estate, 25 Cal. 2d 1, 22 (Cal. 1944) (Traynor, J., dissenting) ("The statement sometimes found in the cases that the extrinsic facts are admissible only when a written instrument is ambiguous, simply means that the language used by the parties must be susceptible to the meaning claimed to have been intended by the parties. . . . Holmes, The Theory of Legal Interpretation, 12 Harv. L. Rev. 417, 420. If the evidence offered would not persuade a reasonable man that the instrument meant anything other than the ordinary meaning of its words, it is useless.").

12. Wells v. Wells, 74 Cal. App. 2d 449, 456 (Cal. App. 1946) ("The appellant . . . argues that where a contract is clear on its face it is error to admit parol evidence for the purpose of ascertaining the intent of the parties. There has been much written on this subject and it is quite apparent that there is some difference of opinion among the members of the Supreme Court of this state on this issue."); Jegen v. Berger, 77 Cal. App. 2d 1, 7 (Cal. App. 1946) (citing this passage from Wells v. Wells).

13. Roberts v. Reynolds, 212 Cal. App. 2d 818, 826 n.4 (Cal. App. 1963) ("It should also be noted that the determination of the trial court is sound when viewed in the light of the reasoning of the concurring opinion in *Universal Sales Corp* . . . . .").

14. Chief Justice Traynor's efforts culminated in his opinion in Pacific Gas & Elec. Co. v. G.W. Thomas Drayage & Rigging Co., 69 Cal. 2d 33, 37–38 (1968) ("The test of admissibility of extrinsic evidence to explain the meaning of a written instrument is not whether it appears to the court to be plain and unambiguous on its face, but whether the offered evidence is relevant to prove a meaning to which the language of the instrument is reasonably susceptible. . . . A rule that would limit the determination of the meaning of a written instrument to its

four-corners merely because it seems to the court to be clear and unambiguous, would either deny the relevance of the intention of the parties or presuppose a degree of verbal precision and stability our language has not attained."). Chief Justice Traynor did not cite Holmes in this opinion, perhaps because of the emphasis the opinion places on the contracting parties' intent.

15. Claim of Berson, 126 N.Y.S. 2d 579, 582 (N.Y. App. Div. 1953) ("Our inquiry is not in the abstract what the legislature intended but rather what meaning we can reasonably give to the words which the legislature used. 'Thereupon we ask, not what this man meant, but what those words would mean in the mouth of a normal speaker of English, using them in the circumstances in which they were used.'") (citing Holmes).

16. S & E Contractors, Inc. v. United States, 406 U.S. 1, 13 n.9 (1972) (citing Holmes).

17. Antonin Scalia, who graduated from Harvard Law School in 1960, began working as general counsel for the Office of Telecommunications Policy in 1971 and became chairman of the Administrative Conference of the United States in 1972. Two years later, in 1974, he was appointed assistant attorney general for the Office of Legal Counsel; in the same year, Frank Easterbrook, who graduated from the law school at the University of Chicago in 1973, began working as an assistant to the solicitor general. This convergence suggests a bigger political-institutional story about the genesis of contemporary textualism (and originalism) in Washington, DC, during the first half of the 1970s. This chapter focuses more narrowly on how Judge Easterbrook and Justice Scalia used Holmes's essay to support their respective statements of textualist method.

18. In re Sinclair, 870 F.2d 1340, 1343 (7th Cir. 1989) (citing Holmes).

19. Judge Easterbrook writes: "Legislative history may be invaluable in revealing the setting of the enactment and the assumptions its authors entertained about how their words would be understood. It may show, too, that words with a denotation 'clear' to an outsider are terms of art, with an equally 'clear' but different meaning to an insider. It may show too that the words leave gaps, for short phrases cannot address all human experience; understood in context, the words may leave to the executive and judicial branches the task of adding flesh to bones. These we take to be the points of cases . . . holding that judges may learn from the legislative history even when the text is 'clear.' Clarity depends on context, which legislative history may illuminate. The process is objective; the search is not for the contents of the authors' heads but for the rules of language they used." In re Sinclair, 870 F.2d at 1343.

20. Chisom v. Roemer, 501 U.S. 380, 405 (1991) (Scalia, J., dissenting) (quoting Holmes).

21. *Id*. at 405.

22. *Id*. at 411.

23. Eleven contract-interpretation opinions cited the essay between 1991 and

2014. Thirty-three statutory-interpretation opinions cited it during that same period.

24. Holmes writes, for example, that "a reference to [the normal speaker] as the criterion [of meaning] is simply another instance of the externality of the law" (Holmes 1899, 418). This passage suggests that the "normal speaker" might be simply a personification of the value of externality or objectivity.

25. See, for example, the second reference to the normal speaker cited in note 6 above. This passage suggests that a judge construing a contract "externally" should seek to assume a particular perspective, one not identical with that of either the parties to the contract or the judge him- or herself.

26. Gregory Keating summarized the reasonable person's characteristics this way: "Reasonable persons . . . assign substantial weight to security; they cooperate on fair terms with others who are prepared to reciprocate their cooperation; they do not prefer their interests to those of others; and they restrain the intensity of their preferences so that they do not make demands upon others that they would not be prepared to honor themselves" (Keating 1994, 373–74).

27. To be sure, there is debate over the understanding of the reasonable person construct within specific areas of law, such as the law of negligence, as well as across different legal areas, such as criminal procedure, sexual harassment law, and the criminal-law doctrines of provocation and self-defense. Some commentators, for example, have argued that the reasonable person of tort law is necessarily a normative construct (Miller and Perry 2012, 326), while others describe the construct as a more descriptive reference to the "average" person (Gilles 1994, 1032). Other commentators have explored the varying attributes of "reasonableness" found in different legal contexts, such as tort, criminal, and sexual-harassment law (Moran 2003); establishment clause doctrine (Hill 2014); criminal procedure (Mandiberg 2010); and contract law (Sourgens 2014). And as discussed in the text, the lack of consensus about the scope and purposes of the reasonable person, and its differences, if any, from a normal-speaker figure, were the principal reasons for the disagreement between the seven-justice majority and Justice Thomas in Elonis v. United States, 135 S. Ct. 2001 (2015). Despite all the disagreement, none of this work, nor any of the many other efforts in the same vein not mentioned here, would exist in the absence of prior judicial and scholarly references to the reasonable person as an identifiable perspective or standard of conduct.

28. Sherlock Holmes is a favorite example for philosophers interested in the operation of apparent references to fictional entities and the metaphysics of such entities (e.g., Lewis 1978, 37; Currie 1990).

29. Other such legal characters include the "reasonable jury" of several procedural doctrines, the "person having ordinary skill in the art" of patent law, and the "ordinary observer" of copyright and design patent law. To varying de-

grees in each of the relevant legal areas, these figures have been assigned certain fixed characteristics, which judges occasionally acknowledge not to be realistic. The reasonable juror, for example, disregards evidence that he or she was instructed to disregard. See, e.g., United States v. Downing, 297 F.3d 52, 59 (2d Cir. 2002); United States v. Salameh, 152 F.3d 88, 116 (2d Cir. 1998). The person having ordinary skill in the art has knowledge of all pertinent prior art and also has "ordinary creativity." See, e.g., KSR Int'l Co. v. Teleflex, Inc., 550 U.S. 398, 421 (2007).

30. The figure may deserve the "objective" label for other reasons, too. Gregory Keating has argued that the canonical reasonable person of tort law is "impartial (or objective) in two senses. First, the reasonable person 'gives an impartial consideration to the harm likely to be done the interests of others as compared with the advantages likely to accrue to his own interests. . . .' Second, the reasonable person also 'give[s] to the respective interests concerned the value which the law attaches to them'" (Keating 1994, 337–38 (citing Rest. (2d) Torts § 283 cmt. e)). Nicole Negowetti has made a similar argument drawing on ideas from social psychology (Negowetti 2014, 704, 736–37).

31. *Elonis*, 135 S. Ct. 2001 (2015).

32. *Id*. (Thomas, J., dissenting) (slip op. at 8–11, 17–19).

33. Much, but not all, of this work considers the application of reasonable-person standards by jurors, but the concerns about subjectivity in the application of such standards are not limited to that context (e.g., Braman 2010, 1459; Burke 2005, 1052; Hill 2014, 1422; Mandiberg 2010, 1488–89; Nourse 2008, 36–37). A few commentators have considered this problem in the context of interpretive decisions by judges (e.g., Fallon 2014, 695; Greenawalt 2000, 1661).

34. Walton, for example, notes: "Imaginings are constrained also; some are proper, appropriate in certain contexts, and others not" (Walton 1990, 39).

35. This operator-prefixing understanding is one of several approaches philosophers take to examining the potential truth value of statements about fictional characters (Lewis 1978; Currie 1990). John Searle proposed a different approach, according to which saying "Sherlock Holmes lived on Baker Street" should be taken to be equivalent to pretending to say that "Sherlock Holmes lived on Baker Street" (Searle 1975, 324). This approach fits judicial discourse less well because judges' pronouncements do not seem to be feigned pronouncements, and Searle's position seems to have fewer contemporary proponents than Lewis's. Another possibility would be an understanding along the lines of Walton's theory (Walton 1990). In this view, saying "Sherlock Holmes lived on Baker Street" would be equivalent to creating a prop for use in a game of make-believe about Sherlock Holmes. Section 3 of this chapter suggests that this is a legitimate approach for judges to take.

36. To be sure, much of the commentary and controversy surrounding

reasonable-person standards stems from their lack of correspondence to actual people and their stylized characteristics (see, e.g., Moran 2003 for an extended argument along these lines).

37. Commentators have been more willing to make this acknowledgment (e.g., Fallon 2014, 695, 705, 713; Greenawalt 2000, 1657, 1660 n.118, 1661, 1664–68)—but for the reasons presented in the text, they might see it as easy to do this in ways that judges do not afford to do so in ways that judges cannot.

38. It might also require judges to acknowledge that in some circumstances, dictionaries should not carry the weight they currently do, despite their connotations of objectivity.

39. *Elonis*, 135 S. Ct. 2001 (2015) (slip op. at 7).

40. *Id.* (slip op. at 13).

41. *Id.* (Alito, J., concurring in part and dissenting in part).

42. *Chisom*, 501 U.S. 380, 394 (1991) (quoting 2 U.S.C. § 1973).

43. *Id.* at 410–11 (Scalia, J., dissenting) (some citations omitted).

References

Braman, Donald. 2010. "Cultural Cognition and the Reasonable Person." *Lewis & Clark Law Review* 14:1455–80.

Burke, Alafair S. 2005. "Equality, Objectivity, and Neutrality: Review of Cynthia Lee, *Murder and the Reasonable Man: Passion and Fear in the Criminal Courtroom* (2003)." *Michigan Law Review* 103:1043–80.

Cover, Robert. 1983. "*Nomos* and Narrative." *Harvard Law Review* 97:4–68.

Currie, Gregory. 1990. *The Nature of Fiction*. Cambridge: Cambridge University Press.

Fallon, Richard H., Jr. 2014. "Three Symmetries Between Textualist and Purposivist Theories of Statutory Interpretation—and the Irreducible Roles of Value and Judgment Within Both." *Cornell Law Review* 99:685–734.

Fitzgerald, Gareth. 2009. "Linguistic Intuitions." *British Journal for the Philosophy of Science* 60:1–38.

Gilles, Stephen C. 1994. "The Invisible Hand Formula." *Virginia Law Review* 80:1015–54.

Greenawalt, Kent. 2000. "Are Mental States Relevant for Statutory and Constitutional Interpretation?" *Cornell Law Review* 85:1609–72.

Hill, B. Jessie. 2014. "Anatomy of the Reasonable Observer." *Brooklyn Law Review* 79:1407–53.

Holmes, Oliver Wendell. 1899. "The Theory of Legal Interpretation." *Harvard Law Review* 12:417–20.

Keating, Gregory C. 1994. "Reasonableness and Rationality in Negligence Theory." *Stanford Law Review* 48:311–84.

Kramer, Matthew H. 2008. "Is Law's Conventionality Consistent with Law's Objectivity?" *Res Publica* 14:241–52.

Lewis, David. 1978. "Truth in Fiction." *American Philosophical Quarterly* 15: 37–46.

Mandiberg, Susan S. 2010. "Reasonable Officers vs. Lay Persons in the Supreme Court's *Miranda* and Fourth Amendment Cases." *Lewis & Clark Law Review* 14:1481–1536.

Miller, Alan D. and Ronen Perry. 2012. "The Reasonable Person." *New York University Law Review* 87:323–92.

Moran, Mayo. 2003. *Rethinking the Reasonable Person: An Egalitarian Reconstruction of the Objective Standard*. Oxford: Oxford University Press.

Negowetti, Nicole. 2014. "Judicial Decisionmaking, Empathy, and the Limits of Perception." *Akron Law Review* 47:693–751.

Nourse, Victoria. 2008. "After the Reasonable Man: Getting Over the Subjectivity/Objectivity Question." *New Criminal Law Review* 11:33–50.

Petroski, Karen. 2012. "Does It Matter What We Say About Legal Interpretation?" *McGeorge Law Review* 43:359–402.

"Proceedings, Northwestern University/Washington University Law and Linguistics Conference." 1995. *Washington University Law Quarterly* 73:800–970.

Sainsbury, R. M. 2010. *Fiction and Fictionalism*. Abingdon and New York: Routledge.

Searle, John. 1975. "The Logical Status of Fictional Discourse." *New Literary History* 6:319–32.

Sinclair, M. B. W. 1985. "Law and Language: The Role of Pragmatics in Statutory Interpretation." *University of Pittsburgh Law Review* 46:373–420.

Solan, Lawrence. 1993. *The Language of Judges*. Chicago: University of Chicago Press.

Sourgens, Frédéric G. 2014. "Reason and Reasonableness: The Necessary Diversity of the Common Law." *Maine Law Review* 67:73–130.

Walton, Kendall L. 1990. *Mimesis as Make-Believe: On the Foundations of the Representational Arts*. Cambridge: Harvard University Press.

CHAPTER SIX

Originalism, Hermeneutics, and the Fixation Thesis

Lawrence B. Solum

Originalism is certainly controversial.[1] Almost every version of originalism claims that the communicative content of the constitutional text is fixed at the time each provision is framed and ratified and that contemporary constitutional practice should be constrained by this fixed original meaning (unless the text is amended). In this chapter, I will develop a case for the claim that meaning is fixed and respond to an objection raised by Francis J. Mootz in "Getting Over the Originalist Fixation" (chapter 7, this volume). Mootz's objection draws on the wonderful and elegant account of hermeneutics developed by Hans-Georg Gadamer in his magnum opus, *Truth and Method* (Gadamer 2004). My reply will draw on Gadamer as well, arguing that his views are broadly consistent with the idea of fixation—although taking his views into account may contribute to the enterprise of clarifying originalist claims about the nature of the original meaning of the constitutional text. We can begin by investigating the nature of originalism itself.

1. The Role of the Fixation Thesis in Originalist Constitutional Theory

What does the word "originalism" mean and from whence does it come? Once we have an understanding of originalism in place, we can formulate a preliminary version of the fixation thesis and explain the role it plays in the constitutional theories of the originalist family.

"Originalism," the word, was coined by Paul Brest in 1980, in a law review article entitled "The Misconceived Quest for the Original Understanding" (Brest 1980). Brest stipulated the following definition: "By 'originalism' I mean the familiar approach to constitutional adjudication that accords binding authority to the text of the Constitution or the intentions of its adopters" (Brest 1980, 204). So the word "originalism" is a technical term, used in academic and political discourse about constitutional law and theory. Like many technical terms, the meaning of "originalism" is a function of both stipulated definitions (like Brest's) and patterns of usage among linguistic subcommunities (e.g., judges, lawyers, and constitutional theorists).

The meaning of the word "originalism" and the phrase "living constitutionalism" are contested. For the purposes of this chapter, I will simply stipulate working definitions, recognizing that the definitions offered here could be challenged and reserving my arguments in the metalinguistic dispute over the word for future work. Here are the stipulations:

- *Originalism*: The word "originalism" is stipulated to refer to the family of constitutional theories that claim that the communicative content of the constitutional text is fixed at the time each provision is framed and ratified and that constitutional practice should be constrained by that communicative content.
- *Nonoriginalism*: The word "nonoriginalism" is stipulated to refer to the set of constitutional theories that deny that communicative content is fixed at the time each constitutional provision is framed and ratified and/or that deny that constitutional practice should be constrained by that communicative content.
- *Living constitutionalism*: The phrase "living constitutionalism" is stipulated to refer to the family of constitutional theories that affirm that the content of constitutional doctrine should change (in some substantial way) in response to changing circumstances and values.

Given these stipulated definitions, there are two possible relationships between living constitutionalism and originalism. Some forms of living constitutionalism may be compatible with some forms of originalism: so long as changes in constitutional doctrine are constrained by the original meaning of the constitutional text, a living constitutionalist can also be an originalist. Jack Balkin affirms a form of compatibilist living constitutionalism in his book *Living Originalism* (Balkin 2011). Other forms of living constitutionalism are incompatible with originalism: for example, Ronald Dworkin's theory of "law as integrity" sanctions departures from the communicative content of the text (Dworkin 1997, 1259–60). Originalists who believe that the original meaning of the constitutional text fully determines the content of constitutional doctrine will reject all forms of living constitutionalism.

Contemporary originalism is a family of constitutional theories united by two core ideas: fixation and constraint. The fixation thesis claims the original meaning ("communicative content") of the constitutional text is fixed at the time each provision is framed and ratified. The constraint principle claims that constitutional actors (e.g., judges, officials, and citizens) ought to be constrained by the original meaning when they engage in constitutional practice (paradigmatically, deciding constitutional cases).

The originalist family converges on these two core ideas, but particular versions of originalism differ in many other respects. For example, some originalists focus on the original public meaning of the text, while others believe that original meaning is determined by the original intentions of the framers or the original methods of constitutional interpretation.

Despite their differences, these originalist theories agree that the communicative content of the constitutional text was fixed at the time each provision was framed and ratified. There may be slight differences in the way that different originalists view fixation. "Original intentions originalism" (or "intentionalism" for short) maintains that meaning is fixed by the intentions of the framers of the text: thus, the moment of fixation is the moment the relevant intentions are formed, roughly the moment drafting occurs. Originalists who focus on the understanding of the ratifiers might place the crucial moment at a slightly later time period—the period during which ratification occurs. As a practical matter, these differences are likely to be minor: framing and ratification are likely to be proximate in time, separated by a few years at most.[2]

Originalists also agree on the constraint principle—the notion that the communicative content of the Constitution should constrain constitutional practice, including decisions by courts and the actions of officials such as the president and institutions such as Congress. Most constitutional theorists would agree that the linguistic meaning of the Constitution should make some contribution to the legal content of constitutional doctrine. For example, Stephen Griffin (Griffin 1994) and

Phillip Bobbitt (Bobbitt 1991) have suggested that constitutional practice includes multiple modalities or a plurality of methods of constitutional argument. Bobbitt's list of modalities includes text, history, structure, precedent, "ethos" of the American social order, and prudence.
Pluralists can accept that the original meaning of the constitutional text
should be (or even must be) considered by judges who decide constitutional cases (and other officials when they engage in constitutional interpretation and construction). Characteristically, originalists argue that
the role of original meaning is not simply that of one factor among many;
originalists typically believe that original meaning should *constrain* constitutional practice. Another way of putting this is to say that originalists
characteristically believe that the original meaning is lexically prior to
other modalities of constitutional interpretation and construction.

For the purposes of this chapter, let us stipulate that a theory should
count as "originalist" only if it affirms a form of constraint that meets or
exceeds what we can call "the minimalist version of the constraint principle." The minimalist version can be formulated as the conjunction of
the following two requirements:

(1) Constitutional practice, including the content of constitutional doctrine and
    the conduct of officials (including judges), should not be inconsistent with the
    communicative content of the constitutional text.
(2) The content of constitutional doctrine should include rules that fairly capture
    the communicative content of all of the portions of the text that are in force
    (not repealed).

The minimalist version of the constraint principle allows for constitutional doctrines that supplement the constitutional text in various ways—
so long as these doctrines are consistent with the communicative content
of the constitutional text. For example, the minimalist version would allow for gap filling, precisification of vague or open-textured provisions,
and implementation rules.

Even if originalists agree that original meaning should have a con-
straining role in constitutional practice, they might disagree on the precise form that constraint should take. We can imagine a spectrum of
constraint, ranging from the minimalist version to a maximalist formulation that requires that every doctrine of constitutional law be derived
directly from the constitutional text. Because the maximalist form of
the constraint principle includes the minimalist form, we might think of

constraint as consistency as a least common denominator, the form of constraint upon which all originalists could agree; disagreement with the minimalist version is sufficient to render a constitutional theory nonoriginalist in the sense stipulated in this chapter.

For the purposes of this chapter, I will use the words "interpretation" and "construction" in the stipulated technical senses, as follows:

- *Constitutional interpretation*: The phrase "constitutional interpretation" is stipulated to refer to the activity that discerns the communicative content (linguistic meaning) of the constitutional text.
- *Constitutional construction*: The phrase "constitutional construction" is stipulated to refer to the activity that determines the content of constitutional doctrine and the legal effect of the constitutional text (including the decision of constitutional cases by the courts).

There is one more important point to be made about the interpretation–construction distinction. Interpretation is an empirical inquiry. The communicative content of a text is determined by linguistic facts (about conventional semantic meanings and syntax) and by contextual facts (about the context in which the text was written). Interpretations are either true or false in theory—although in practice there may be some cases in which we lack sufficient evidence to show that a particular interpretation is true or false. Constructions are justified by normative considerations. This is true even in cases where the constructions seem compelled by the meaning of the text. Article 1 of the Constitution provides that each state is represented by two senators: this is a case where interpretation of the text is easy and hence the construction (legal effect) to be given to the text seems obvious and intuitive. But if we ask why we ought to give the constitutional text the effect that follows naturally from the meaning of the word "two," our answer must be some normative consideration. For example, we might believe that we are obligated to follow the clear directives of the constitutional text, because the United States Constitution was adopted by "We the People" and hence has democratic legitimacy that constitutional constructions by unelected judges do not possess. In the construction zone, we will need some theory of constitutional construction to give legal effect to the underdeterminate constitutional text. That theory might provide a general default rule (resolve underdeterminacy in favor of actions by elected officials), or it might require consideration of first-order normative concerns (resolve underdeterminacy so as to achieve justice).

2. Formulating the Fixation Thesis

Given our understanding of originalism as a family of constitutional theories and the interpretation–construction distinction, we are now in a position to formulate a more precise version of the fixation thesis. We can begin with a statement of the fully elaborated version and then proceed to analysis of its elements:

> *the fixation thesis*: The object of constitutional interpretation is the communicative content of the constitutional text as that content was fixed when each provision was framed and/or ratified.

The thesis can be unpacked by providing an explanation for each of its major elements:

> *the object of constitutional nterpretation*: The fixation thesis is a claim about constitutional interpretation—in the sense of "interpretation" specified by the interpretation–construction distinction. That is, the fixation thesis is a thesis about the activity of discovering the communicative content of the constitutional text. By itself, the fixation thesis does not make a claim about the legal content of constitutional doctrine or the decision of constitutional cases. Such claims require some version of the constraint principle and information about the communicative content of particular constitutional provisions. Thus, the fixation thesis itself does not claim that the communicative content of the constitutional text ought to be decisive in constitutional construction.

> *the communicative content of the constitutional text*: The fixation thesis is a claim about the communicative content of the authoritative version of the constitutional text. The phrase "communicative content" is used to provide a more precise formulation than "meaning" or "linguistic meaning." The use of the phrase "communicative content" is intended to be neutral between various theories of that content, for example, original public meaning versus original intentions (and other theories). The

authoritative version of the text is the particular instance of the writing that was officially promulgated.

as that content was fixed: It is the communicative content that is fixed at the time of origination. Communicative content is not legal content or legal effect. Therefore, the fixation thesis is not a claim about the fixation of constitutional doctrine or the fixation of constitutional practice. Different accounts of meaning in the philosophy of language may produce slightly different accounts of how fixation occurs and what fixation means. For example, original intentions originalism ties fixation to the intent of the framers, whereas public meaning originalism conceives fixation as a function of the content communicated to the public. For each such account, there will be a theory of fixation, but the fixation thesis itself is neutral between such accounts.

when each provision was framed and/or ratified: The fixation thesis claims that fixation occurs during a time frame: "when each provision of the Constitution was framed and/or ratified." The use of "and/or" is intended to reflect theoretical disagreement about the precise moment of fixation, with some originalists endorsing the moment at which the text was created (framing) and others endorsing the moment at which the text became legally operative (ratification).

The precise formulation of the fixation thesis and the explanation of its elements reveal an important characteristic of the defense of the fixation thesis offered here. Just as originalism is a family of constitutional theories united by the fixation thesis and the constraint principle, originalists could affirm a of variety slightly different views about fixation. The formulation of the fixation thesis offered here is intended to be ecumenical; it is formulated to be as neutral as possible with respect to the variations between these views.

3. The Case for the Fixation Thesis

The affirmative case for the fixation thesis can be articulated via intuitive and commonsense observations about the nature of written communication. If we want to know what a text means and the text was not written very recently, we need to be aware of the possibility that it uses language somewhat differently than we do now. Moreover, meaning is in part a function of context—and context is time-bound. So if we want to know what a text means, we need to investigate the context at the time when the text was produced. In this section, these simple and intuitive ideas are elaborated.

Informally stated, the fixation thesis claims that the meaning of the constitutional text is fixed at the time of framing and ratification. But what does the word "meaning" mean? In the legal context, the word "meaning" is ambiguous, and it can be used in at least three distinct (but related) senses.

Sometimes when we ask about the meaning of a legal text, we are asking about the implications it will have, usually in a particular context. For example, we might ask, "What does First Amendment freedom of speech mean for my defamation suit? Does it provide me a defense?" When "meaning" is used in this sense in the context of a legal text, we are concerned with the application of the text to a particular case or to some set of cases. We can call this *meaning in the applicative sense.*

"Meaning" is also used to refer to the purpose or motive that produced a particular legal text. For example, we might ask about the aim of a constitutional provision by saying, "What did the drafters mean to accomplish through the privileges or immunities clause of the Fourteenth Amendment?" We can call this *meaning in the purposive sense.*

Finally, "meaning" can be used in the sense of the communicative content of a legal text. We sometimes call this "linguistic meaning." For example, we might ask what the framers meant by using the phrase "arms" in the Second Amendment: Were they referring to weapons or to the upper limbs of the human body? We can call this *meaning in the communicative sense.*

The fixation thesis is a claim about meaning in the communicative sense: what is fixed is communicative content. It is not a claim about the purposes for which the text was adopted—although those purposes are time-bound (since the purpose for an action is set when the action is performed). And the fixation thesis is not a claim about the correct applications of the constitutional text to particular fact patterns or to general types of fact patterns—although the fixed communicative content may be given legal effect that determines or partially determines such applications.

Because the meaning of "meaning" is ambiguous in the way we have just specified, the fixation thesis can easily be misunderstood. If the fixation thesis were a claim about meaning in the applicative sense, it might be understood as the claim that all future applications of the constitutional text are fixed at the time the text is framed and ratified. This claim seems implausible for a variety of reasons. Constitutionally relevant facts may change over time. Do the freedoms of speech and press apply to the Internet? If the application of these provisions had been fixed at the time they were framed and ratified, the implication would seem to be that somehow a text written in 1791 had the future of communication technology baked in. Does infrared surveillance constitute a search? It seems implausible to believe that the answer to this question was fixed when the Fourth Amendment was framed and ratified.

Of course, the fixed communicative content of the constitutional text can, when combined with facts about the world, determine (or partially determine) the outcome of particular cases. But the facts about the world to which the constitutional text can be applied are not themselves fixed at the time the text is written. We might summarize this idea in the following way: *the communicative content of the constitutional text is fixed at the time of framing and ratification, but the facts to which the text can be applied change over time.*

The best way to understand the fixation thesis is to consider the role of fixation in communication, considered as a general phenomenon. The generalized version of the fixation thesis might be stated as follows:

> *generalized fixation thesis*: The communicative content of a communication (oral or written, verbal or nonverbal) is fixed at the time the communication occurs.

The generalized fixation thesis expresses our commonsense understanding of how meaning works. When I give a lecture, the communicative content of my lecture comes into being then—and not at some later time. It would be strange to think that the content of my lecture changes after the lecture ends and even more strange to think that a lecture that I gave in 2014 would acquire a new meaning (in the communicative sense) if linguistic practices were to change gradually over the decades so that words I used then have totally difference senses in 2264—250 years later.

One of the difficulties with thinking about the fixation thesis in the constitutional context is that the examples are all normatively charged. The generalized fixation thesis can be illustrated and supported with more prosaic examples, where fixation is intuitively obvious and unlikely to be controversial. Thus, if you are reading a thirteenth-century letter that uses the word "deer" and you learn that "deer" meant four-legged mammal at the time the letter was written, (Steinmetz 2008, 49–50) you are very likely to accept this linguistic fact as crucially important to understanding the letter.

Just to be clear, the fixation thesis claims that meaning itself is fixed and not our beliefs about meaning. So it might well be the case that someone would read an old letter that used the word "deer" and form the belief that it refers only to the species specified by the modern usage. And then they might learn of their mistake, and their belief about the meaning of the letter might change. Communicative content itself is fixed; beliefs about communicative content can change.

The generalized fixation thesis is a function of two distinct mechanisms by which communication occurs. First, when authors or speakers attempt to convey meaning to readers or listeners, they can take advantage of conventional semantic meanings and the rules (or regularities) of syntax and grammar. Second, the contextual enrichment of semantic content is determined by the context at the time communication occurs. Each of these two mechanisms requires further explanation.

The first mechanism is the fixation of conventional semantic meaning by linguistic facts at the time a communication occurs. Thus, as I write this sentence, I rely on the conventional semantic meanings of the words and phrases comprised by the sentence and the grammatical relationships between these units of meaning. Conventional semantic meanings are time-bound: because of the phenomenon of linguistic drift, the words that I am using now could change—as could the syntactic regularities that we sometimes call "rules of grammar." The relevant linguistic facts upon which I rely are facts about patterns of usage as of the time of writing. It is difficult to even imagine how I could communicate on the basis of conventional semantic meanings that do not yet exist—setting science-fiction scenarios aside. To the extent that meaning is conveyed using conventional semantic meanings and regularities of syntax, meaning is fixed by linguistic facts as they exist at the time a text is written (or a speech is made).

A few examples of linguistic drift, drawn from Sol Steinmetz (Steinmetz 2008) may illuminate these ideas. In the thirteenth century, "abode" meant the act of staying, whereas it now refers to homes or dwellings. We now use the word "average" to refer to what mathematicians call the "mean" or "arithmetic mean," but in the fifteenth century it referred to a tax or duty leveled on the shipment of goods. Linguistic drift is one of the reasons that the fixation is important. The generalized fixation thesis properly directs us to read a text using the linguistic information that was available to the author and readers at the time the text was written.

The phenomenon of linguistic drift can be illuminated by considering some of the mechanisms that are responsible for changes in the meanings of words and phrases—again drawing the examples from Sol Steinmetz. Linguistic drift frequently occurs as the result of a mistaken usage that "takes off" and eventually becomes standard, but it might occur as the result of deliberate repurposing of a word. For example, the word "satellite" originally meant a bodyguard, but Johannes Kepler adapted this word to refer to the moons of Jupiter and then Jules Verne tweaked Kepler's usage to refer to imaginary man-made devices orbiting the earth. Verne's usage was then applied to Sputnik, an actual version of Verne's fictional device. That usage of satellite eventually became standard. Today, no one uses the word "satellite" to refer to bodyguards.

To the extent that meaning is conveyed by the conventional semantic meanings of words and phrases, the relevant meanings are fixed by linguistic facts at the time the words or phrases are employed. If you wanted the correct interpretation of a ship's log from the fifteenth century, you would translate "average" as a tax or duty and not as a reference to an arithmetic mean. If you were reading a historical account of the security measures for the king of France written in the sixteenth century, you would understand that "satellites" were bodyguards and not some early version of the Death Star ready to fry English assassins with high-energy particle beams (or even extremely long-range crossbow bolts launched from near-earth orbit).

In sum, the first mechanism of fixation is semantic. The semantic content of a writing is fixed by linguistic facts about patterns of usage at the time the text is authored. Subsequent linguistic drift does not change the meaning of a prior writing, although it could result in changing beliefs about that meaning.

The second mechanism by which meaning is produced is context. Conventional semantic meaning is a powerful tool for communication, but its power is not unlimited. We can illustrate this idea by considering the second independent clause of the sentence immediately prior to this one: "its power is not unlimited." The semantic content of this clause is ambiguous—it could mean many different things. That ambiguity is brought out by imbedding the same clause in a different sentence: "The

Tesla Model S has a powerful battery, but *its power is not unlimited*." The clause means two different things in the two contexts. The original occurrence of the clause refers to the capacity of conventional semantic meanings to convey communicative content; the second occurrence of the clause is about the capacity of the electrical batteries of the Tesla Model S to propel the automobile at high speeds for long distances. The context in which a writing occurs is time-bound. Thus, the communicative content of the first occurrence of the clause I have been discussing ("its power is not unlimited") is in part determined by contextual facts that are fixed once I have completed the writing of this chapter.

The generalized fixation thesis follows from the fact that conventional semantic meanings and contextual facts are time-bound. The meaning of language changes over time, and as a consequence, the meaning of a communication depends in part on the way language is used at the time the communication occurs. The meaning of a writing or saying is in part a function of the context in which the communication occurs; the relevant context is the context at the time of writing or saying.

Legal communication is distinctive in various ways, but it is still communication. If we want to understand a judicial decision from the sixteenth century, we will need to know about sixteenth-century linguistic facts and the sixteenth-century context in which the decision was written. If we want to understand a contract written in 2013, we should pay attention to the conventional meanings that contract terms have in the twenty-first century and the contemporary context in which the contract was written. If we want to understand the communicative content of Warren Court cases, we will need to know how language was used in the fifties and sixties and understand the legal and political context in which the Warren Court's opinions were written. Legal communication uses conventional semantics and syntax and context to produce meaning—and for this reason, the generalized fixation thesis holds for legal communications.

Constitutional communication is simply a form of communication and a particular subspecies of legal communication. If the fixation thesis holds for communication generally and for legal communication in particular, then it would be somewhat mysterious if it did not hold for constitutional communication. Conventional semantic meanings and regularities of syntax and grammar, when combined with context, provide an account of how communication is possible. We can convey meaning because words and phrases are used in regular ways and can be combined using regular patterns of syntax and grammar. We can deliver more content still by relying on our readers' knowledge of the communicative context. But once we understand these mechanisms, they imply fixation. Anyone who accepts the generalized fixation thesis but denies that the communicative content of the constitutional text is fixed owes us several explanations. How does constitutional communication occur? How do we understand the words and phrases and combine them into meaningful clauses? What is the context of constitutional communication if it isn't time-bound?

The fixation thesis is a claim about communicative content—meaning in the communicative sense, or, roughly, linguistic meaning. It is not a claim about legal content. The communicative content of the constitutional text is fixed at the time each provision is framed and ratified, but this does not (logically) entail that the legal content of constitutional doctrine is fixed as well. The fixation thesis is a thesis about constitutional interpretation; it is not a claim about constitutional construction.

Consider the oft-made observation that originalism does not account for the obvious need to adapt the Constitution to changing circumstances. We will also consider a related objection that uses the metaphor of a "dead hand" (Samaha 2008). If the original meaning of the text is fixed, how can we apply the freedom of speech to the Internet or the Fourth Amendment to overflight of private homes by drones with infrared sensors? Let us call this point the "novel applications objection." The assumption of the novel applications objection is that fixed meaning entails fixed legal effect. If the meaning of the Fourth Amendment is fixed, then so too must be the content of Fourth Amendment doctrine and the set of situations to which the Fourth Amendment does, and does not, apply. But the assumption that fixed communicative content entails static doctrines and a frozen set of applications is false—for two reasons.

First, the argument that fixation of linguistic meaning entails fixed legal effect is conceptually confused. Communicative content is simply the meaning of the text: you need more than meaning to get legal effect. Compare the communicative meaning of the Constitution of the Confederate States of America to the legal effect of that document, if you have any doubt on this score. For the fixation thesis to have any logical implications for legal practice, it must be combined with some other premise (such as the constraint principle).

Second, to the extent that the fixation thesis does have implications for constitutional practice when it is combined with the constraint principle, this does not imply that either doctrine or applications are frozen. This point can be illustrated by considering the case of nonlegal commands generally. Suppose that a college dormitory adopts a regulation that prohibits residents from placing their own furniture in the common areas: "No resident may position furniture in common areas, except temporarily for the purpose of moving the furniture either in or out of the resident's own room." At the time the regulation was written, there were tables, chairs, and many other types of furniture, but no beanbags or futons. New types of furniture are invented from time to time—presumably, love seats and chaise lounges have not existed since prehistoric times. The semantic content of the term "furniture" can be fixed, even though new kinds of furniture are invented. This commonsense point about general terms in ordinary language use extends to the Constitution: even if the semantic content of "search" is fixed, that does not entail that there cannot be novel methods by which searches are conducted.

Notice that this answer to the novel applications objection is ecumenical: it can be embraced by new originalists who accept the existence of construction zones and by originalists who believe that the communicative content of the constitutional text is thick enough to provide determinant (or nearly determinant) constitutional doctrine.

To be clear, our analysis of the novel applications objection does not answer a related objection—that the communicative content of the text may need to be changed to keep up with the times. Let us call this objection the "dead hand objection." Imagine that the world changes in a way that renders some provision of the Constitution obsolete. The Constitution assumes that there is a plentiful supply of humans over the age of thirty-five—the constitutional minimum for becoming president. What if that were to change because of a disease that killed everyone over the age of thirty? Obviously, we would amend the Constitution if we could, but what if we couldn't? (The plague has disrupted so many state legislatures that it is simply not possible to enact an amendment for a two- or three-year period, and we need a president right away.) This is a case where the dead hand of fixed communicative content would prevent us from doing something we need to do. This would be a reason to suspend or disregard the Constitution (to act contrary to the constraint principle), but it is not an objection to the fixation thesis. Indeed, the dead hand objection *assumes that the fixation thesis is true!* The dead

144 LAWRENCE B. SOLUM

hand objection is a challenge to the constraint principle—and the case for and against constraint is simply outside the scope of this chapter.

There is one more implication of this clarification. The fixation thesis claims that the communicative content of the constitutional text is *fixed*, but it does not claim that this content is fully *determinate*. It may well be the case that the fixed communicative content of the constitutional text would underdetermine the content of constitutional doctrine and the decision of some constitutional cases. For example, the communicative content of some constitutional provisions may be vague or open texts. Other provisions may be irreducibly ambiguous, have gaps, or even be contradictory. Some new originalists explicitly affirm the fact of constitutional underdeterminacy and hence the existence of "construction zones" in which the communicative content of the constitutional text will have to be supplemented in some way.

The core of the affirmative case for the fixation thesis is rooted in commonsense intuitions about the meaning of old texts of all kinds. When we encounter an older text, we run into two interpretive problems. First, the language may be unfamiliar, or familiar words may seem to be used in unfamiliar ways. When we read a contemporary text, we rely on our knowledge of conventional semantic meanings and contemporary syntax. When we read an old text, we may need to access the semantic and syntactic conventions of the time during which the text was written. Second, the text may be ambiguous or misunderstood because we lack knowledge of the context in which the text was written. This same problem can occur with a contemporary text. When we read a text (old or new), we may need to learn about the context in which the text was produced—this will enable us to "read between the lines" and resolve ambiguities.

These commonsense principles apply to legal texts in general and the Constitution in particular. If we want to glean the communicative content of the provisions of the Constitution that were drafted in 1787, we need to know something about the way words were used at that time and about the circumstances in which the Constitution was produced. Similarly, if we want to discern the meaning of the Reconstruction amendments, we will need to look to mid-nineteenth-century linguistic practice and the context in which the Thirteenth, Fourteenth, and Fifteenth Amendments were framed and ratified.

4. The Hermeneutic Critique of the Fixation Thesis

Hans-Georg Gadamer produced a powerful and influential theory of hermeneutics in his magnum opus, *Truth and Method*. A deep engagement with Gadamer's theory is beyond the scope of this chapter, but we can investigate his views of legal hermeneutics and their relationship to the fixation thesis. We can begin with Gadamer's critique of the view that the task of legal historians and jurists is fundamentally different. Gadamer writes:

> In my view it would not be enough to say that the task of the historian was simply to "reconstruct the original meaning of the legal formula" and that of jurist to "harmonize the meaning with the present living actuality." This kind of division would mean that the definition of the jurist is more comprehensive and includes the task of the legal historian. Someone who is seeking to understand the correct meaning of a law must first know the original one. Thus he must think in terms of legal history—but here historical understanding serves merely as a means to an end. (Gadamer 2004, 335)

Earlier in *Truth and Method*, he wrote:

> [A]s late as 1840, Savigny in his *System des römischen Rechts*, regarded the task of legal hermeneutics as purely historical. Just as Schleiermacher saw no problem with the interpreter having to identify himself with the original reader, so Savigny ignores the tension between the original and the present legal sense.
>
> It has emerged clearly enough in the course of time that this is a legally untenable fiction. Ernst Forsthoff has shown in a valuable study that for purely legal reasons it was necessary for an awareness of historical change to develop, which involved distinguishing between the original meaning of a law and that applied in current legal practice. (Gadamer 2004, 225–26)

Up to this point, Gadamer's description of legal hermeneutics seems broadly consistent with the fixation thesis. Original meaning can diverge from the current meaning because of historical change. But Gadamer's analysis takes a turn toward what we call "living constitutionalism" in the immediately following passage:

> It is true that the jurist is always concerned with the law itself, but he determines its normative content in regard to a given case to which it is applied. In order to determine this content exactly, it is necessary to have historical knowledge of the original meaning, and only for this reason does the judge concern himself with the historical value that the law has through the act of legislation. But he cannot let himself be found by what, say, an account of the parliamentary proceedings tells him about the intentions of those who first passed the law. Rather, he has to take account of the change in circumstances and hence define afresh the normative function of the law. (Gadamer 2004, 336)

This passage might be read as an endorsement of judicial creativity, reflecting the antiformalism of contemporary constitutional theory that sometimes frankly acknowledges the legislative role of the Supreme Court when it engages in constitutional construction (Leiter 2015). But it becomes clear that Gadamer's view more closely resembles legal formalism (in its contemporary forms) than it does American legal realism:

> The work of interpretation is *to concretize* the law in each specific case—i.e., it is a work of *application*. The creative supplementing of the law that is involved is a task reserved to the judge, but he is subject to the law in the same way as is every other member of the community. It is part of the idea of a rule of law that the judge's judgment does not proceed from an arbitrary and unpredictable decision, but from the just weighing up of the whole. Anyone who has immersed himself in the particular situation is capable of this just weighing up. That is why in a state governed by law, there is legal certainty—i.e., it is in principle possible to know what the exact situation is. Every lawyer is able, in principle, to give correct advice—i.e., he can accurately predict the judge's decision on the basis of existing laws. (Gadamer 2004, 338–39)

The things that Gadamer says in this passage may strike some contemporary American legal scholars as inconsistent, odd, or naive, combining as they do the belief that law is determinate and certain with the acknowledgement that the judicial function is creative.

Notice that the English word used by the translators, "interpretation," is used to express the concept that I have represented by the word "construction." Gadamer's text seems to presuppose the interpretation–construction distinction as a conceptual matter: he clearly distinguishes between the recovery of original meaning ("interpretation") and the application of the text to a particular case ("construction"). And because his account of interpretation (in the sense stipulated here) focuses on original meaning, it would seem that he accepts the fixation thesis. Creativity occurs in construction (in the stipulated sense), but such creativity must operate within the bounds of the rule of law. Using the vocabulary developed here, we might say that Gadamer accepts something like the minimalist version of the constraint principle. Given our stipulated definition, Gadamer is an originalist and a living constitutionalist, because he believes that the judge can "take account of the change in circumstances" and "define afresh the normative function of the law" while simultaneously respecting "original meaning of a law" and remaining "subject to the law."

But this is not the end of the story. As Francis J. Mootz correctly emphasizes, Gadamer argues that understanding a historical text requires a "fusion of horizons" (chapter 7, this volume). Our understanding of a text from the past is always mediated by our own horizon, constituted in part by our "prejudices" understood in a nonpejorative way as the set of beliefs that necessarily condition our understanding of the past. Thus Gadamer writes, "[A] hermeneutical situation is determined by the prejudices that we bring with us. They constitute, then, the horizon of a particular present, for they represent that beyond which it is impossible to see" (Gadamer 2004, 316). This might be read to suggest that historical understanding is impossible, but that is not Gadamer's point.

> Rather, understanding is always the fusion of these horizons supposedly existing by themselves.
>
> [. . .]
>
> Every encounter with tradition that takes place within historical consciousness involves the experience of a tension between the text and the present. The hermeneutic task consists in not covering up this tension by attempting a naïve assimilation of the two but in consciously bringing it out. (Gadamer 2004, 317)

To those unfamiliar with Gadamer's language and the philosophical tradition in which he wrote, these passages may seem obscure. What follows is my understanding of Gadamer, informed by both study of his work and its intellectual context but offered on this occasion as a reconstruction of his point and not as exegesis. The reconstruction is presented in the language of debates about contemporary constitutional theory, but

these points could be translated into a variety of other technical vocabularies, both legal and nonlegal.

When we attempt to reconstruct the original meaning of the constitutional text, we necessarily do so from our own perspective in the here
and now. That perspective includes a variety of assumptions (or "prejudices" in the sense that Gadamer's translators assign to that word).
We have assumptions about the conventional semantic meanings of the
words used in the constitutional text. If the words are ambiguous, our
understanding of the context in which the Constitution was written is
necessarily conditioned by our assumptions about the purposes or aims
of the particular provision and the Constitution as a whole.

For these reasons, our interpretation of the constitutional text may
fail to capture the original meaning. We may assume that the word "unusual" in the Eighth Amendment has the contemporary conventional semantic meaning that is closely related to meaning of the word "rare" and
the phrase "out of the ordinary," but it might be the case that in the late
eighteenth century the conventional semantic meaning was closer to the
contemporary meaning of the word "novel" and the phrase "contrary
to longstanding practice" (Stinneford 2008). And our understanding of
what the word "cruel" means is necessarily influenced by contemporary
practices of punishment, including long periods of incarceration, that
did not exist at the time the Eighth Amendment was framed and ratified.
We may not overcome our assumptions about the meaning of the words
"cruel" and "unusual," and hence it is always possible that we will mis-
understand the late-eighteenth-century meaning of those words.

Our beliefs about the meaning of the constitutional text are therefore
subject to change both in response to changing circumstances and values and (importantly) in response to new information about the past. We
lack access to an Archimedean point from which we would have direct
access to the original meaning of the constitutional text, and as our hermeneutic situation evolves, so will our understanding of original meaning. For this reason, our *understanding of* original meaning (as opposed
to the original meaning itself) is always subject to change; it cannot be
"fixed" if fixation requires an understanding that is somehow guaranteed to remain the same for all time.

Let us stipulate for the sake of argument that my presentation of Gadamer's point is correct. Does this entail that the fixation thesis is false?
Recall that the fixation thesis is consistent with the fact that beliefs about
meaning change. Indeed, one of the points of originalism in general and

the fixation thesis in particular is to produce changes in beliefs about the meaning of the constitutional text through engagement with linguistic facts (about the conventional semantic meanings of words) and contextual facts (about the public context of constitutional communication). Originalists do not believe that our understanding of the constitutional text will never change; the practical point of originalism is to change at least some of our understandings.

But changes in beliefs about meaning are not identical to changes in meaning itself. The fact that our knowledge of original meaning is imperfect does not entail that there is no original meaning. And these observations are consistent with the possibility that our beliefs about original meaning are necessarily conditioned by and filtered through our other beliefs. That kind of preconditioning applies to all of our beliefs, including beliefs about science, engineering, and the marital status of our next-door neighbors. If this analysis is correct, then there is nothing in Gadamer's hermeneutics that undermines the fixation thesis—once that thesis is properly articulated and understood.

It seems clear that Mootz would not accept my interpretation of Gadamer's argument. Why not? One possible answer to this question begins with the fact that Mootz believes that Gadamer's claims are ontological and not epistemic. After presenting Gadamer's argument, he concludes, "There are no objective facts about the past existing independent of our inquiries; rather, history is our mode of being; as finite beings who can never rise out of our historical situation" (chapter 7, this volume). This is a radical claim. Mootz claims there are *no objective facts about the past* that are independent of inquiries. Put the other way around, Mootz is claiming that every fact about the past is dependent on human inquiries into those facts.

If there are no objective facts about the past that are independent of our inquiries, then there are no objective facts at all—as the present continually recedes into the past. And this means that there is no fact of the matter about such mundane and insignificant questions as whether this paragraph was first composed on July 17, 2015. Nor could there be an objective fact of the matter about the occurrence of the Holocaust or indeed whether the Allied forces invaded Normandy beginning on June 6, 1944.

But surely most readers will agree that there is a fact of the matter about the date upon which this paragraph was first composed—even if they do not themselves have sufficient evidence to confirm or deny that fact. And surely almost every reader will agree that D-day did occur on the sixth day of June in 1944—certainly they will agree if they do some research about the topic. And I suspect that most readers will agree that these facts are properly described as objective in the sense that their existence does not depend on our beliefs or inquiries. If a future global totalitarian regime successfully collected all the evidence that D-day occurred and locked it away in an impregnable vault and then threw away the key, that would not change the historical fact that the invasion did in fact occur. Even if every living human came to believe that the D-day invasion was a myth created by Allied propaganda, the events of June 6, 1944, would still have occurred.

I do not know how Mootz would respond to this point. One possibility is that he would distinguish between historical facts about events (such as D-day) and historical facts about meaning (such as the original meaning of the word "unusual" in the Eighth Amendment). But even if his claim were limited in this way, its implications are still radical and implausible. The Constitution provides that each state shall have two representatives in the Senate. Is there any doubt that there is an objective fact of the matter about the conventional semantic meaning of the word "two" in 1787 when article 1 of the Constitution was drafted? Surely "two" meant two and not three or lasagna. And if there is an objective fact of the matter about the meaning of the word "two," then the ontology of human understanding is not inconsistent with the existence of historical linguistic facts. Linguistic facts are facts about patterns of human behavior in the world; they are not facts about some mystical realm that cannot be the subject of empirical investigation. Indeed, a whole subfield of linguistics, called "semantics," is devoted to empirical investigation of linguistic facts about the semantic meaning.

Perhaps Mootz's criticism is based on his assumption that "original meaning" is a function of a counterfactual "reasonable person" and that these imaginary beings (and the original meanings produced by thought experiments involving them) cannot give rise to objective facts. There is some reason to attribute this assumption to Mootz. Consider the following passage:

> It bears emphasis that the "communicative content" is not really an empirical fact that is the result of actual persons understanding the texts in question at the time of the enactment. Most new originalists concede that the "communicative content" of a text must be retrieved through a hypothetical construc-

tion of how reasonable persons at the time of enactment would have understood the text. (chapter 7, this volume)

It is true that some originalists have used a hypothetical "reasonable
person" in their versions of originalist theory, but this is not my position.
The notion of a "reasonable person" is best viewed as playing a purely
heuristic or expository role in originalist theory. Mootz seems to realize
this as he notes that the source he cites for the proposition that originalists generally employ a hypothetical original person, Stephen M. Feldman (2014, 285–86), noted that I ("Solum") have not expressly adopted
this view (chapter 7, this volume).

The fixation thesis is embedded in a view that affirms that communicative content is an empirical fact. Thus, conventional semantic meanings are determined by patterns of usage—and not by the hypothetical
understandings of a counterfactual reasonable person. There is nothing wrong with using the notion of a reasonable person as a heuristic
device to represent the complex processes by which we determine conventional semantic meanings. Actual persons discover conventional semantic meanings by observing patterns of usage. And particular actual
persons sometimes make mistakes—often by guessing incorrectly about
the meaning of a rarely used word in a context where the meaning is not
apparent. Indeed, it is possible (even likely) that almost every speaker
of a native language has at least a few false beliefs about conventional
semantic meanings. The hypothetical reasonable person can be used to
represent the fact that no single actual individual is correct about communicative content all of the time. Conventional semantic meanings are
conventions among linguistic communities and subcommunities and are
not the psychological states of particular individuals.

Mootz may make another move that might avoid the radical and implausible implications of denying the objectivity of meaning. The move
is to equate objectivity with certainty. I'm not sure whether Mootz intends to make this move, but it is suggested by the following passage:

> This ontological account of the historicity of understanding, as exemplified
> in legal practice, is not a relativist or skeptical philosophy. We can achieve
> knowledge of the law, and of history, but this knowledge is not to be mea-
> sured according to the standards of mathematics. The rhetorical knowledge
> that girds law is a social activity under conditions of probability rather than a
> cognitive achievement regarding certainties. (chapter 7, this volume)

Mootz is correct that our knowledge of communicative content and linguistic facts is not measured by the standards of mathematics—at least not if by "mathematics" we mean the hypothetico-deductive methods associated with geometry. There are no fixed linguistic axioms from which we can deduce the original meaning of the constitutional text. Once again, consider the example of semantics. When we seek to determine the meaning of the words of our natural language our method is usually abductive—inference to the best explanation of the linguistic facts. Sometimes we are able to infer the conventional semantic meaning of a word or phrase from a single instance of usage; sometimes several instances are required. As the number of instances grows, we may become progressively more certain that we have correctly identified the semantic content of a word or phrase, but we may never achieve perfect certainty, because new facts about usage might require us to revise our hypothesis about the conventional semantic meaning of the word or phrase. At some stage, we may become convinced that further refinements are very unlikely and that any revisions in our understanding of the conventional semantic meaning of a word or phrase will be extremely subtle with an effect on a very narrow range of cases. At this stage, we might call our knowledge of semantic meanings certain for all practical purpose but acknowledge that it falls short of apodictic or absolute certainty.

Take the example of the word "two" as used in article 1 of the Constitution. It is theoretically possible that we would discover evidence that would require us to revise our understanding of the meaning of "two." It is difficult to imagine what such evidence would be. The word "two" was clearly used in the late eighteenth century in the same way the word "two" is used now. The criteria for application of the word two are very clear. Chuck Schumer is one senator; Kirsten Gillibrand is also one senator. Together they make two senators. Is it theoretically possible that we would discover new linguistic facts about eighteenth-century usage that would cause us to revise our opinion about this matter? There is no absolute guarantee that such facts cannot emerge. Perhaps one day we will discover that Chuck Schumer's personality is so large that given eighteenth-century linguistic practices, he counts as two senators and that Kirsten Gillibrand is therefore not entitled to her current office. But this possibility seems just as remote as the possibility that we would discover that the D-day invasion was a hoax or that gold is not really an element and should be removed from the periodic table. These are skeptical possibilities and not practical ones.

Nothing much hangs on the question whether we can be *certain* about the original meaning of the older provisions of the constitutional text. The law deals with uncertainty all the time. In civil trials, the burden of persuasion is preponderance of the evidence; in criminal trials, it is proof beyond reasonable doubt. No one thinks that our inability to find facts with absolute certainty entails the conclusion that there are no objective facts of the matter about causation in a civil case or whether the defendant fired the deadly bullet in a criminal trial. Uncertainty does not imply a lack of objectivity—in the sense of "objectivity" that I am using when I assert that there are objective facts about original meaning. Nor does the fact that our beliefs about the law are the product of a social activity imply that they are nonobjective. The hard sciences are social activities, but that does not entail the conclusion that the objects of scientific investigation are not objective facts.

In sum, there is no good reason to believe that Gadamer's hermeneutics casts doubt on the fixation thesis, and there are many good reasons to believe that Gadamerian hermeneutics should embrace the conclusion that the communicative content of the constitutional text is fixed by objective facts about linguistic practices and the context of constitutional communication.

5. Conclusion: Focusing on the Constraint Principle

Francis J. Mootz's "Getting Over the Originalist Fixation" is a splendid example of the role that metatheoretical disagreement about the nature of interpretation can play in the evolution of constitutional theory. Mootz's objections to the fixation thesis have provided the opportunity to clarify the thesis itself and to explore its relationship to Gadamer's hermeneutics. But in my opinion, it is unlikely that contemporary nonoriginalism is motivated to a significant degree by Mootz's metatheoretical concerns. Rather, the crux of the debate between originalists and nonoriginalists is more likely to be a disagreement over the constraint principle. If one rejects the constraint principle in in the minimalist version, then one believes that constitutional actors (judges and other officials) should have the legitimate authority to adopt constitutional constructions that override the communicative content of the constitutional text. Originalists argue that judges and officials should not have this power for a variety of reasons; among the reasons they advance are arguments from popular sovereignty and the rule of law.

There are good reasons for some constitutional theorists to believe that judges should have a power to override the original meaning of the constitutional text. Depending on one's political preferences, there may be some very attractive doctrines of constitutional law that are inconsistent with the original meaning of the constitutional text. Nonoriginalists can argue for these doctrines, but originalists cannot. This is a normative disagreement about constitutional practice and not a metatheoretical disagreement about the nature of interpretation. Indeed, I find it hard to imagine that any significant number of nonoriginalist judges, lawyers, or scholars would throw in the towel and convert to originalism if they were convinced that originalists had won the debate over fixation.

If this diagnosis is correct, then the debate between originalists and nonoriginalists is likely to be clarified if the disputants set the fixation thesis to the side and focus their attention on the constraint principle. The aim of this chapter has been to facilitate the transition to this more illuminating and productive debate.

Notes

1. The account of the Fixation Thesis in this article draws on a more extended discussion (Solum 2015).

2. The Twenty-Seventh Amendment is an exception, having been submitted to the states for ratification in 1789 and achieving ratification in 1992 (Bernstein 1992).

References

Balkin, Jack M. 2011. *Living Originalism*. Cambridge: Harvard University Press.
Bernstein, Richard B. 1992. "The Sleeper Wakes: The History and Legacy of the Twenty-Seventh Amendment." *Fordham Law Review* 61:497–557.
Bobbitt, Philip. 1991. *Constitutional Interpretation*. Oxford: Blackwell.
Brest, Paul. 1980. "The Misconceived Quest for the Original Understanding." *Boston University Law Review* 60:204–38.

Dworkin, Ronald. 1997. "The Arduous Virtue of Fidelity: Originalism, Scalia, Tribe, and Nerve." *Fordham Law Review.* 83:1249–68.

Feldman, Stephen M. 2014. "Constitutional Interpretation and History: New Originalism or Eclecticism." *Brigham Young University Journal of Public Law* 28:284–350.

Gadamer, Hans-Georg. 2004. *Truth and Method.* Translated by Joel Weinsheimer and Donald G. Marshall. Revised second edition. Continuum: London and New York.

Griffin, Stephen M. 1994. "Pluralism in Constitutional Interpretation." *Texas Law Review* 72:1753–69.

Leiter, Brian. 2015. "Constitutional Law, Moral Judgment, and the Supreme Court as Super-Legislature." *Hastings Law Journal* 66:1601–16.

Lieber, Francis. [1839] 1970. *Legal and Political Hermeneutics.* Edited by Roy M. Mersky and J. Myron Jacobstein, 43–44, 111n2. Getzville, NY: Wm. S. Hein & Co

Samaha, Adam. 2008. "Dead Hand Arguments and Constitutional Interpretation." *Columbia Law Review* 108:606–80.

Solum, Lawrence. 2015. "The Fixation Thesis: The Role of Historical Fact in Original Meaning." *Notre Dame Law Review* 91:1–78.

Steinmetz, Sol. 2008. *Semantic Antics: How and Why Words Change Meaning.* New York: Random House.

Stinneford, John. 2008. "The Original Meaning of 'Unusual': The Eighth Amendment as a Bar to Cruel Innovation." *Northwestern University Law Review* 102: 1739–825.

CHAPTER SEVEN

Getting Over the Originalist Fixation

Francis J. Mootz III[1]

Sigmund Freud famously argued that one's psychological well-being could be impaired as a consequence of not progressing through a necessary series of psychosexual stages of development. Freud characterized the failure to achieve full psychological maturity and autonomy as a "fixation" on one of the stages. For example, a person might experience an "oral fixation" as a result of atypical breast feeding, generating obsessive oral behavior leading to problems such as smoking, drinking to excess, or eating disorders as manifestations of the fixation. In this theoretical universe, fixations are maladaptive and should be treated and overcome.

Unfortunately for Freud, there is very little scientific evidence to back many of his claims, including his theory of fixation (see, e.g., Cioffi 1998). However, his theory does provide an apt metaphor for my critique of the new originalist scholarship and its "Freudian slip" of championing the "fixation thesis." I shall argue that the fixation thesis represents a stunted inability to move beyond a certain stage of development in legal theory and that we are best counseled to overcome the fixation thesis therapeutically. The desire for certainty is a powerful motivating force in our lives, giving rise to all manner of confused self-understandings that cloak our nature and provide some measure of psychological comfort in the face of our human condition. As painful as it may be, though, it is time to wean ourselves of the fixation thesis in law.

Larry Solum has done more careful and extensive work to promote the fixation thesis than any other legal theorist, and so I will attend to his recent comprehensive defense of the thesis (Solum 2015).[2] I have utmost respect for Solum's effort to defend the fixation thesis with precision and integrity. Nevertheless, Solum's defense fails. I use the word "fails" advisedly. I will not argue, as most opponents might, that the fixation thesis is a trivial truth without important normative implications. Instead, I will argue that the fixation thesis is false. By failing to challenge the plausibility of the fixation thesis directly, theorists have been unable to respond effectively to new originalism.

I. The Fixation Thesis

I begin with Solum's articulation of the fixation thesis. The central features of "fixation" are the singularity and immutability of meaning. Solum claims "that *the* meaning of the constitutional text is *fixed* when each provision is framed and ratified" (Solum 2015, 1; emphasis added). He then provides the following definition of the fixation thesis: "*The object of constitutional interpretation* is the *communicative content* of the constitutional text as that content was fixed when each provision was framed and/or ratified" (Solum 2015, 13; emphasis added). This definition adds a layer of assumptions: first, that there is a singular object of constitutional interpretation; and, second, that this object is just the singular and immutable communicative content of the text at the time of framing/ratification.

Solum quickly assures us that the fixed meaning that is the object of constitutional interpretation does not generate a specific result in any particular case. "By itself, the fixation thesis does not make a claim about the legal content of constitutional doctrine or the decision of constitutional cases . . . [and it] does not claim that the communicated content of the constitutional text ought to be decisive in constitutional construction" (Solum 2015, 13). He distinguishes "interpreting" the textual meaning from "constructing" the legal effect of the text for the case at hand.[3] For example, understanding the fixed communicative content of the Eighth Amendment ban on "cruel and unusual punishments" holds no significance without a normative argument that the legal result in a case should follow the communicative content, followed by a construction of the communicative meaning to address the particular question in issue (Solum 2015, 75). He stresses the necessity of acknowledging a "fundamental conceptual distinction between 'communicative content' (the linguistic meaning communicated by the legal text in context) and 'legal content' (the doctrines of the legal rules associated with a text)" (Solum 2013a, 479). And so, despite establishing that every con-stitutional provision has a singular and immutable meaning, the fixation thesis by itself has no determinate effect on legal practice because ulti-mately there must be a defensible normative judgment whether, and how, to follow the meaning of the text in a particular instance.[4]

We may summarize Solum's approach by highlighting the key terms he uses in describing the implications of the fixation thesis:

> The affirmative case for the Fixation Thesis can be articulated via intuitive and commonsense observations about the *nature of written communication.* If we want to know what a text means and the text was not written very re-cently, we need to be aware of the *possibility that it uses language somewhat differently* than we do now. (Solum 2015, 18; emphasis added)

> Interpretation is an *empirical inquiry.* The communicative content of a text is determined by *linguistic facts* (facts about conventional semantic meanings and syntax) and by *facts about the context in which the text was written.* Inter-pretations are *either true or false*—although in *some* cases we may not have *sufficient evidence* to show that a particular interpretation is true or false. *Constructions are justified by normative considerations.* This is true even in the cases where the constructions seem compelled by the meaning of the text. (Solum 2015, 12; emphasis added)

Under this view, interpretation is subject to the scientific measure of truth rather than the rhetorical measure of appropriateness to the sit-uation,[5] although the construction of the text is a separate undertaking that does not necessarily follow directly from the singular and immuta-ble meaning of the text.

Solum is engaging in a very clever and alluring rhetorical strategy. He argues in favor of the fixation thesis as a very narrow claim that the communicative content of a text can be regarded as a historical fact. Be-cause this claim lacks normative effects it can and should be accepted as a (perhaps trivial) truth by all theorists before turning later to the nor-mative contest. Of course, when the contestants arrive at the battlefield they will find that they have been outflanked. The normative value of "constraint" will be posited as a powerful and nearly undeniable prem-ise of the rule of law, and the value of constraint can be realized only by hewing to a singular and unitary meaning of the text except in the most egregious situations when doing so will offend fundamental standards of justice. As Solum notes, almost in an offhand manner, if "originalists are right about the Constraint Principle, then the truth of the Fixation Thesis should have important implications for constitutional practice" (Solum 2015, 78). Truer words have never been spoken. It is imperative that we confront the fixation thesis at the outset of the argument. Once one accepts in principle that the communicative content of the text is singular and immutable at the time of drafting, one has already wheeled the Trojan horse inside the city's walls. Solum's appeal is generous: just follow me for a short way down the path of a theoretical argument, and we will get to the real debates later. We should not be seduced by this generosity. "[Theorists], never trust that horse. Whatever it is, I fear the [new originalists], especially bearing gifts."[6]

2. The Fixation Thesis is False

My critique of the fixation thesis unfolds in three parts. First, I reject the fixation thesis on ontological grounds, drawing from Hans-Georg Gadamer's contemporary hermeneutical philosophy. Solum hews to nineteenth-century hermeneutics in an unsuccessful effort to maintain singular and immutable meanings in a world of interpretive vertigo. I explore the differences and similarities between the work of a legal historian and the work of a judge to illuminate the philosophical foundations of interpretive practice. Second, I consider Solum's refutations of the "contemporary reader" theory of meaning and demonstrate that he has erected a straw man who does not embody the philosophical critique of fixed meaning. In short, Solum has not responded to his strongest critics in developing his argument. Third, I consider the bizarre implications for legal practice even if we assume that the fixation thesis both is true and has nontrivial consequences for practice. One must carefully question the utility of a theory that undermines the longstanding core of legal practice, even if the theory is psychologically appealing and initially plausible. I conclude that the fixation thesis is a beguiling distraction from the hard work that must be done to better understand the historically grounded hermeneutical and rhetorical practices that comprise our legal system.

2.1 The Ontological Basis of Legal Hermeneutics[7]

The fixation thesis is a theory of textual meaning that contradicts the way in which texts have meaning for us. Meaning always is the result of interpretive activity and is never a historical fact that exists independent of an interpreter. Because we unreflectively assume that meaning sometimes can be immediately apparent and therefore does not require an active "interpretive" effort, I will use the less common term, "hermeneutical activity," to refer to the source of meaning. Hermeneutical activity should not be confused with conscious efforts to decode a vague or ambiguous text. Hermeneutical activity is our interpretive disposition toward the world that opens the possibility for meaning. It grounds all later expressly interpretive activities. This is not a radical claim. Perception is a hermeneutical activity. For example, color is not an independent quality of objects in the world but rather is part of the perceptual activity we bring to bear with our eyesight. The color red does not exist independently of the viewer, but neither does the viewer create the color red as a subjective act.[8] We may acknowledge that this is the case intellectually, but it is difficult to remember that color is not a characteristic of a world that exists separate from the viewer, just as it is difficult to remember that meaning is not a feature of a world that exists separate from the interpreter. We intuitively regard our hermeneutical activity as the neutral apprehension of a world of empirical realities: an apple is red even if we are not looking at it, and a text has meaning even if we are not reading it. This intuition is false.[9]

2.1.1 GADAMER'S PHILOSOPHICAL HERMENEUTICS.   Hans-Georg Gadamer reshaped hermeneutical philosophy fifty-five years ago with his wide-ranging book *Truth and Method* (Gadamer 1989). After canvassing the history of approaches to human understanding in the Western tradition, Gadamer defends an ontological claim: interpretation is our way of being in the world; it is not a cognitive task that we might choose to take up under certain circumstances to investigate a fact in the world that exists independent of our inquiry. He concludes: "Interpretation is not an occasional, post facto supplement to understanding; rather, understanding is always interpretation, and hence interpretation is the explicit form of understanding" (Gadamer 1989, 105). Gadamer uses the metaphor of "play" to explore the ontology of human understanding. When engaged in play there is an interaction that is defined by neither player. An individual neither induces nor creates play; rather, it occurs "not only without goal or purpose, but also without effort. It happens, as it were, by itself" (Gadamer 1989, 105). The playfulness of hermeneutical activity generates meaning that only later appears to be independent of this hermeneutical activity.[10]

Gadamer argues that the dialectic of question and answer is the implicit playful structure of meaningful human experience (Gadamer 1989, 361–62). Textual interpretation is a dialogic encounter in which the reader and the text are at play. A reader comes to the text with his own horizon—or "forestructure of meaning"—which is an "opinion and a possibility that one brings into play and puts at risk" before the horizon of meaning that is the text (Gadamer 1989, 388). On the other hand, the text stands as a provocation that cannot be wholly subordinated by the reader's perspective. Reading is a fusion of these indeterminate horizons and "is what takes place in conversation, in which something is expressed that is not only mine or my author's, but common" (Gadamer 1989, 388). It bears emphasis that this is not a methodological claim about how we might best interpret a text. Gadamer is making an ontological claim: there is no meaning of the text that exists independent of the interpreter's hermeneutical activity.

Gadamer uses the provocative term "prejudices" to characterize the reader's forestructure of meaning. Because the reader is situated she can never encounter a text free of her personal history of experiences and expectations. Through a playful encounter in the structure of a dialogue, the reader's horizon and the horizon of the text meet.

> The interpreter is, therefore, first aware of a distance between the text and his own horizon which leads, in the process of understanding, to a new, comprehensive horizon transcending the initial question and prejudices. The experience he makes in the course that leads to a new understanding is a hermeneutic one. . . . (Gadamer 1989, 112–13)

Meaning is a product of the fusion of horizons, and so no text can have an essential and unvarying meaning because it is appropriated continually by historically situated readers. Any effort to lodge a text in a supposedly closed and objective past culture is a falsification of the text, which has the potential for meaning only because it invites a prejudiced reader into a dialogic encounter.

Apprehending a text as a static and closed meaning from the past would require an interpreter from nowhere. Gadamer captures this point by arguing that the text is really the ongoing "history of its effects" with previous interpreters.[11] Thus,

> . . . if we are trying to understand a historical phenomenon [such as a text] from the historical distance that is characteristic of our hermeneutical situation, we are always subject to the effects of effective-history. It determines in advance both what seems to us worth enquiring about and what will appear as an object of investigation. . . . (Gadamer 1989, 300–301)

The text provokes the reader to explore its meaning for the reader's situation because of its historical arc. In legal terms, those texts that have been deemed authoritative for the decision maker speak to her about a case, whereas other legal documents do not. Hermeneutical activity is the application of a traditionary text in the present and is not a process of neutral retrieval of a fixed meaning lodged in the past. Gadamer emphasizes that the "recovery of the fundamental hermeneutic problem" is to overcome the objectifying tendencies of the modern scientific method (Gadamer 1989, 307–41).[12] "Application does not mean first understanding a given universal in itself and then afterward applying it to a concrete case. [Application] is the very understanding of the universal—the text— itself" (Gadamer 1989, 341).

At this juncture, Gadamer turns to Aristotle's ethics as a model of the philosophical inquiry into understanding (Gadamer 1989, 312–24). Aristotle rejected Plato's doctrine of ideas in favor of a model of ethical knowledge that consists of bringing general tenets to bear in the circumstances of a concrete case. In this regard, he distinguishes the intellectual virtue of *phronesis* (exhibiting practical wisdom fitting for the occasion) from both *episteme* (having knowledge of matters that can be certain) and *techne* (demonstrating a skill).

> To summarize, if we relate Aristotle's description of the ethical phenomenon, and especially the virtue of moral knowledge to our own investigation, we find that his analysis in fact offers a kind of *model of the problem of hermeneutics*. We too determined that application is neither a subsequent nor merely an occasional part of the phenomenon of understanding, but co-determines it as a whole from the beginning. Here[, as with Aristotle's ethics,] application did not consist in relating some pregiven universal to the particular situation. The interpreter dealing with a traditionary text tries to apply

it to himself. But this does not mean that the text is given for him as something universal, that he first understands it per se, and then afterward uses it for particular applications. Rather, the interpreter seeks no more than to understand this universal, the text—i.e., to understand what it says, what constitutes the text's meaning and significance. In order to understand that, he must not try to disregard himself and his particular hermeneutic situation. He must relate the text to this situation if he wants to understand at all. (Gadamer 1989, 324)

Understanding occurs only in application, which is a fusion of the horizon of the effective-history of the text and the questions posed by the reader.[13]

We need not wonder how this ontological argument relates to law, because Gadamer argues that legal practice exemplifies his philosophical thesis (Gadamer 1989, 324–41). Although hermeneutical philosophy was warped by methodological scientism during the past two centuries, legal practice remained dogmatic in its efforts to address practical problems requiring prompt resolution. He argues that legal hermeneutics is not a special case of hermeneutical activity, but rather is a practice that is capable of restoring the philosophical unity of hermeneutical activity by reestablishing the ontological significance of application (Gadamer 1989, 328).

> The work of interpretation is *to concretize* the law in each specific case—i.e., it is a work of *application*. The creative supplementing of the law that is involved is a task reserved to the judge, but he is subject to the law in the same way as is every other member of the community. It is part of the idea of a rule of law that the judge's judgment does not proceed from an arbitrary and unpredictable decision, but from the just weighing up of the whole. Anyone who has immersed himself in the particular situation is capable of undertaking this just weighing-up. This is why in a state governed by law, there is legal certainty.... [and yet] the idea of a perfect legal dogmatics, which would make every judgment a mere act of subsumption, is untenable. (Gadamer 1989, 329–30)

We can, then, distinguish what is truly common to all forms of hermeneutics: the meaning to be understood is concretized and fully realized only in interpretation, but the interpretive activity considers itself wholly bound by the meaning of the text. Neither jurist nor theologian regards the work of application as making free with the text. (Gadamer 1989, 332)

The practice of judges vividly reveals the nature of human understanding.[14]

2.1.2 JUDGES AND LEGAL HISTORIANS. We can assess the import of
philosophical hermeneutics for the fixation thesis by reviewing Gadamer's comparison of the activities of a judge and a legal historian. Gadamer acknowledges that the task of a judge deciding a case and the
task of a legal historian seeking to explicate the meaning of a law might
seem to be radically distinct (Gadamer 1989, 325). In fact, this was the
prevailing view in the nineteenth century, when theorists assumed that
the original meaning of a text could be recovered through historical
research. Under this model, a judge was bound to refer to the original
meaning of a legal text but would not be bound by that meaning as she
dispensed justice. The dogmatic application of a legal text to a particular case was something altogether different from the philological inquiry
into the original meaning of the law as uncovered through historical research. Gadamer acknowledges that "the jurist is always concerned with
the law itself"—assumed to be a historical fact—but he also stresses that
the judge must "determine [the law's] normative content in regard to the
given case to which it is to be applied" (Gadamer 1989, 326). Under this
conception, the judge would consider the historically defined meaning of
the law, but that meaning would not determine the results in a particular case.

At this juncture, Gadamer would appear to be endorsing the fixation
thesis by distinguishing the judge's dogmatic role from the historian's retrieval of meaning. But this distinction is one of orientation and methodology that does not undermine the unity of hermeneutics as an expression of the ontology of understanding. Gadamer rejects the claim that a
historian can recover original meaning, and he criticizes the belief that a
judge might first understand the original meaning of a text and only later
apply it to a dispute. In short, Gadamer reasserts the unity of hermeneutics by finding that the historian too can understand only through
application.[15]

> But how can [the historian] know [the original meaning]? Can he know it
> without being aware of the change in circumstances that separates his own
> present time from that past time? Must he not then do exactly the same thing
> as the judge does—i.e., distinguish between the original meaning of the text
> of the law and the legal meaning which he as someone who lives in the pres-

ent automatically assumes? The hermeneutical situation of both the historian and the jurist seems to me to be the same in that, when faced with any text, we have an immediate expectation of meaning. There can be no such thing as a direct access to the historical object that would objectively reveal its historical value. The historian has to undertake the same reflection as the jurist. Thus the actual content of what is understood in each of the two ways is the same. The above description of the historian's approach, then, is inadequate. Historical knowledge can be gained only by seeing the past in its continuity with the present—which is exactly what the jurist does in his practical, normative work. . . .

[One might argue that a] legal historian who turns to the legal cultures of the past, and certainly any other historian who is seeking to understand a past that no longer has any direct continuity with the present, would not recognize himself in the case we have been considering—namely a law still in force. He would say that legal hermeneutics has a special dogmatic task that is quite foreign to the context of historical hermeneutics.

In fact the situation seems to me just the opposite. Legal hermeneutics serves to remind us what the real procedure of the human sciences is. Here we have a model for the relationship between past and present that we are seeking. The judge who adapts the transmitted law to the needs of the present is undoubtedly seeking to perform a practical task, but his interpretation of the law is by no means merely for that reason an arbitrary revision. . . .

On the other hand, the historian who has no juridical task before him but is trying to discover the legal meaning of this law—like anything else that is handed down in history—cannot disregard the fact that he is concerned with a legal creation that needs to be understood in a legal way. . . . Is this not true of every text—i.e., that it must be understood in terms of what it says? Does this not mean that it always needs to be restated? And does not this restatement always take place through its being related to the present? . . . The truth is that historical understanding always implies that the tradition reaching us speaks into the present and must be understood in this mediation—indeed, *as* this mediation. *In reality then, legal hermeneutics is no special case but is, on the contrary, capable of restoring the hermeneutical problem to its full breadth and so reestablishing the former unity of hermeneutics, in which jurist and theologian meet the philologist.* (Gadamer 1989, 327–28)

There are no objective facts about the past that exist in the present, independent of our motivated inquiries. Rather, history is our mode of being; as finite beings we can never rise out of our historical situation.

Paul Ricoeur provides a customarily careful and detailed explora-
tion of the nature of the historian's craft in a manner that develops Gadamer's thesis. History aspires to objectivity, but it is not objective in the
manner of the natural sciences because its object is human experience
and the historian's subjectivity is inescapably involved in the craft of recounting history (Ricoeur 1965, 21–40).[16] In particular, Ricoeur argues
that philosophy is historical in the sense that every philosopher engages
with the history of the emergence of reason, but he insists that the history of philosophy is a product of the questions posed by philosophers
and is never a retrieval of something wholly lodged in the past.

> And since he too has a limited subjectivity and approaches that meaning of
> history with a preconception of what is to be looked for (but whoever looks
> for nothing finds nothing), the philosopher rediscovers in history the mean-
> ing he had suspected was there. Shall we say it is a vicious circle? Not at all,
> for this meaning remains presentiment until history intervenes in order to
> raise this presentiment of meaning to a definitely articulated and true under-
> standing. (Ricoeur 1965, 35)

All historical understanding is a play of objectivity and subjectivity. History is "an extensive development of meaning and . . . an irradiation of
meanings from a multiplicity of organizing centers. No man who is im-
mersed in history, however, can arrange the total meaning of those radi-
ated meanings" (Ricoeur 1965, 39). We must distinguish the sequence of
physical acts in the natural world from history, which is a product of ongoing human understanding.

Joseph Margolis offers an elegant account of history in these terms,
although he criticizes Gadamer for not being radical enough (Margolis
1993). Margolis emphasizes that our historicity is thoroughgoing, and so
our "theory of history may have to acknowledge that the theory of history—and history itself—have histories" (Margolis 1993, 2). The key distinction, he emphasizes, is between history and a sequence of physical
events:

> history (*and* the historical past) need not be "finished" or "closed"—in the
> sense in which *the physical past is closed* (or is past or has passed or is gone
> or is no more). It's a matter entirely different from that of the reversibility of
> states of the world. *History need not be the mere passage—or the mere chron-
> icle of the passage—of physical time* . . . . Let us close this much of the ar-

gument with a single suggestion. Grant that the historical past *entails* the physical past, but is not reducible to it. Imagine that the historical past is conceptually more *complex* than the physical past but indissolubly *incarnated* in it, logically *emergent* with respect to it. (Margolis 1993, 158–59, 161)

Gadamer, Ricoeur, and Margolis describe history as the experience of historicity, rather than as a closed horizon that can be investigated as an empirical fact. The historian is enmeshed in an ongoing hermeneutical project that is distinct from a sequence of physical events.

Gadamer's hermeneutical account of the historical nature of understanding accords with the work of professional historians. The key insight of the "hermeneutical circle" is recognition of the reciprocal influence of text and context to arrive at understanding. A text cannot be broken into empirical atoms of fixed meaning that can then be pieced together. Similarly, historians do not pretend that they piece together bits of data to create a coherent understanding of a selected period in history (Gienaap 2015; LaCapra 1983). This is not a methodological choice that we might debate; rather, it is the recognition that the ontology of understanding is itself a historical process.

This ontological account of the historicity of understanding, as exemplified in legal practice, is not a relativist or skeptical philosophy. The impossibility of "fixed meaning" should not be worrisome. We can achieve knowledge of the law, and of history, but this knowledge is not to be measured according to the standards of mathematics. The rhetorical knowledge that girds law is a social activity under conditions of probability rather than a cognitive achievement regarding certainties (Mootz 2006). Gadamer celebrates the development of tradition in a way that should make perfect sense to lawyers and judges: we operate within a historically defined and rhetorically secured arena in all aspects of our life, and the experience of knowledge and progress is no less real even if we acknowledge the absence of a perspective from outside this history.

2.1.3 THE FIXATION THESIS IS ONTOLOGICALLY IMPLAUSIBLE. We now return to Solum's detailed elaboration of the fixation thesis to explain why it is false in light of contemporary hermeneutical philosophy. Solum barely acknowledges the roots of the "interpretation-construction" distinction in Francis Leiber's efforts to bring nineteenth-century German hermeneutics to bear on American legal thought.[17] Rather than an innovative conceptual insight forged by modern theorists, the "interpretation-construction" distinction arose within the framework of the romantic (intentionalist) hermeneutics of a previous century and hearkened back to the origins of legal argumentation in ancient Greece and Rome. In the context of contemporary hermeneutics, this old distinction has become untenable on its own terms; it was precisely this failure that led Gadamer to describe the inevitability of "application" as the fundamental hermeneutical problem. Adopting such a retrograde approach to meaning gives rise to contradictions in Solum's approach. Given linguistic drift and the importance of context to meaning, how does Solum propose that a contemporary interpreter can shed herself of all prejudices and regain the communicative content of a document that supposedly remains untainted by the history of its effects? Solum regularly acknowledges that he is not arguing for any particular communicative content of the Constitution because it would require a massive research effort (Solum 2015, at 29, 71, 74). But this recognition of severe epistemic challenges points toward the ontological impossibility of conceptually separating the "meaning" of a text and its significance for the reader who seeks the meaning.

Consider Solum's claim that meaning is contextually fixed in the historical period in which the text was generated. At the beginning of his article he makes an intuitive appeal with a deceptively framed question about how we would approach a historical artifact from the thirteenth century.

> And it would be very odd indeed for someone to suggest that we could better understand the letter if we were to disregard the thirteenth-century context in which it was written and instead imagine that the letter had been written today under different circumstances. Ignoring the time and place at which the letter was written would seem like a strategy for misunderstanding. (Solum 2015, 2)

The critical, but unstated, assumptions at work in this example are that the objective of the contemporary interpreter is to understand what the letter would have meant in its original context and that the historical context is either wholly determinative of meaning or it is completely disregarded by the reader. In short, Solum assumes the posture of a historian approaching the document, in which case his point is trivial and yet still false. Historians certainly explore the original understanding of texts as part of their work, but this obvious point is problematic in at least three respects (see Symposium 2015).

First, Solum assumes that there is a historical fact to be recovered. This simply is not the case. Originalists do not recover an original public meaning in the same way that we might investigate on which date Lee surrendered to Grant. The "communicative content" of a text is not an empirical fact resulting from actual persons understanding the texts in question at the time of the enactment. There is no physical event in the past that we seek to recover. Most new originalists concede that the "communicative content" of a text must be retrieved through a *hypothetical construction* of how reasonable persons at the time of enactment *would have understood* the text (Feldman 2014, 285–86).[18] There is no "public meaning" that exists independent of an effort by the legal theorist to reconstruct the communicative content that the text in question would hold for a "reasonable person" at the time of enactment. The reasonable person is a venerable fiction of legal doctrine, but it is a fiction nonetheless. Step Feldman notes that "historical research uncovers contingencies and contexts" (Feldman 2014, 288) rather than certainties, and this makes the hypothetical reconstruction of a "reasonable person" highly problematic (Feldman 2014, 302).[19] He explains that a "rather large obstacle . . . blocks reasonable-person originalism. . . . Namely, historical thinking leads to complexity rather than to univocal and determinate factual nuggets" (Feldman 2014, 298; see Gienaap 2015). Put simply, "the construct of a reasonable person brings normative dimensions with it. . . . Short of an authorial consensus possibility that allows us to rely on actual role players rather than hypothetical ones, it is the choices interpreters make for whatever role player they choose to deploy that will typically determine the meaning to be assigned" (Bennett 2011, 107–8). By hiding the construction at work, and smoothing the complexities, the practitioners of originalism have wide ambit to "find" their prejudices as linguistic facts.

> When closely examined . . . reasonable-person originalism devolves into an easily manipulated method that invites constitutional interpreters (such as Supreme Court justices) to project their political preferences into the reasonable-person construct. In the words of the legal historian Saul Cornell, reasonable-person originalism turns 'constitutional interpretation into an act of historical ventriloquism.' . . . Instead of being grounded in history . . .

> reasonable-person originalism runs aground and wrecks on the complexities
> of historicism. Like other forms of originalism, reasonable-person original-
> ism fails to lead us to a fixed and objective constitutional meaning. (Feldman
> 2014, 303–4 [quoting (Cornell 2011, 301)])

Solum provides no argument that constructing the linguistic usages
in the past in terms of a reasonable person is of a different character
than any other effort to determine historical meaning (Feldman 2014,
303n105).

Second, Solum's simple example assumes that historians operate in
an objective realm without prejudices guiding their inquiry. For what
purpose is a historian attending to the letter, and how does this purpose
shape the historical inquiry? The historian, no less than any other interpreter, is engaged in hermeneutical activity in which understanding occurs only in application. Simply by seeking to understand this historical
document rather than millions of other available documents, the historian is guided by prejudices that lead her to apply the text to the historian's concerns. A historian would never "ignore" the context of a document, of course, but it is implausible to claim that historians seek to, or
can plausibly claim to, recover the original communicative content without the influence of present concerns. Any such claim would represent
a profound misunderstanding of the work of historians.[20] This is not to
deny the existence of historical facts, but rather to deny that there can be
an unfiltered access to facts that exist independent of the inquiry being
undertaken. Historical truths are not freestanding facts in the world, but
rather arise from our contemporary, motivated questioning of the past.

Third, Solum argues that it is intuitive that we would approach the
letter as a historian might, but this ignores the fact that the letter may be
read for many purposes. Solum concedes that "meaning" can have many
dimensions—applicative, purposive, and communicative (Solum 2015,
19)—but he recognizes that the fixation thesis is plausible only by limiting meaning to communicative meaning, and so he narrows the scope of
inquiry accordingly. Rather than hypothesizing a generic letter from the
thirteenth century, consider how we would read a letter written by the
leader of the Persian invaders who reconquered Jerusalem in 1245, successfully killing or expelling the Christian and Jewish inhabitants. The
letter is of interest because the leadership of ISIL is promoting the letter
as an example of resolve that their contemporary fighters must display.
Would CIA analysts approach the letter as Solum describes? It is not

sensible to claim that the text has become completely untethered from its communicative content in this case, but it is also absurd to believe that the analysts would attempt to act merely as completely disinterested historians. Solum might argue that ISIL has in effect "reauthored" the letter in a contemporary context, or that ISIL leadership woefully misunderstands the communicative content of the letter, and so on. But it is this kind of situation that readers of old texts regularly face, particularly in the legal setting. Historians do not look at ancient texts randomly and without a purpose; they always are motivated by a question that is partly shaped by the historical resonance of the text to present concerns. Gadamer's concept the effective-history of a traditionary text addresses this dynamic. Solum offers no reason why legal actors should approach authoritative texts as if they were historians of the "communicative meaning" rather than as they currently do and in the manner celebrated by Gadamer for being in accord with our hermeneutical nature.

Solum brackets all of these fundamental problems by claiming to undertake a very modest project with regard to the fixation thesis. When Solum acknowledges core issues, he tends to leave the arguments "for another day" (Solum 2015, 29). Critics recoil from the idea that communicative meaning should have legal effect, but Solum insists that this question is distinct from the inquiry into the nature of communicative meaning. Similarly, critics question whether communicative meaning of the constitution can be sufficiently determinate, but this is a matter of how to elaborate the communicative meaning rather than a question of its existence. But of course, these moves simply evade addressing the fundamental hermeneutical reality. Solum does not *defend* the claim that meaning exists independent of an interpreter. He simply *assumes* that it exists! The problems of indeterminacy—vagueness, ambiguity, and lack of historical evidence—are posited as second order problems, but in the real world the epistemic limitations will swallow new originalism, undermining Solum's guiding presuppositions and providing evidence that he has set himself an impossible, rather than merely difficult, task.[21]

2.2 Of Straw Men and Contemporary Readers

We may now ask how Solum avoids addressing the contemporary hermeneutical critique of the fixation thesis. He does so by assuming that his readers will accept the concept of fixed communicative meaning as a conceptual matter, and then he characterizes his critics as those who

seek to follow the meaning of the text for contemporary readers rather
than the communicative meaning fixed at the time of enactment. He al-
leges that his critics make a choice motivated by normative concerns
rather than as a challenge to the plausibility of the fixation thesis. In fact,
Solum's critique of the approach taken by adherents of "contemporary
reader's meaning" involves misdirection from the important ontological
questions.

Solum's articulation of the contemporary reader's meaning approach is revealing. He suggests that proponents of contemporary reader's meaning principally believe that the legal text has a unified meaning for contemporary readers that is more salient than the meaning that
was fixed at the time of enactment. Oddly, Solum feels the need to make
an assumption that he contends may not be empirically warranted. "Of
course, different readers may understand a text differently, *but let us assume* that at any particular point in time, the community of contemporary readers of a text will have a shared understanding of the meaning
of the constitutional text" (Solum 2015, 62; emphasis added). This is—to
say the very least—an extremely curious beginning. Solum asserts again
and again that it is simply intuitive that the words of the text have a fixed
meaning among the community of interpreters at the time of enactment.
But when we fast-forward to contemporary readers there is suddenly a
need to "assume" that a community would share a uniform meaning. If
Solum's argument is premised on a fixed meaning at the time of enactment, then it would seem to follow that at any subsequent time there is a
similarly fixed meaning by considering the semantic meaning that those
words would hold for a community of interpreters at that given point in
time. The "problem" of linguistic drift is precisely this dynamic in action: the words might remain the same, but they are understood by a
subsequent community of interpreters differently. At the same time, linguistic drift is posited as a danger that would lead contemporary readers astray, such as by applying a constitutional provision relating to "domestic violence" to criminal conduct by persons who abuse their spouse
(Solum 2015, 63). This leads Solum to conclude that there really is no vi-
able choice: we either read the text sensibly in the manner in which it was
originally understood, or we invite all sorts of mischief as a result of linguistic drift (Solum 2015, 64).

This is a false choice. First, it assumes that meaning has no tempo-
ral depth. Solum appears to be suggesting that either we embrace the
original understanding or we fast-forward and posit a contemporary un-

derstanding of the semantic meaning without any concept of an ongoing practice between the time of enactment and the present. Contemporary readers, he suggests, would take up the constitutional text and try to sort out the meaning of "domestic violence" armed with nothing but a contemporary sense of this two-word term. Gadamer's philosophical hermeneutics emphasizes that such an account of a distinct and immutable contemporary meaning is no less false than the claim that there is a fixed original understanding. Is it coherent to hypothesize that the Constitution appears suddenly to a contemporary reader, like a recently discovered letter from the thirteenth century, such that the contemporary reader will have difficulty understanding the text without a historiographical inquiry? This, of course, is never the case. The constitutional text has an unbroken history of interpretation and legal effects that frame our inquiries when we consult the text with a contemporary question. No practicing lawyer would assume that contemporary lawyers seeking to understand the impact of the "domestic violence" clause of the constitution will be misled by certain contemporary uses of that phrase in other contexts. Solum's hypothetical ignores the effective-history of the constitutional text, the prejudices brought to bear in arguing for the meaning of that text for a contemporary dispute, and the radical—ontological—indeterminacy of meaning.

Solum's mistake becomes clear when he concludes by asserting that rejecting the constraint made possible by the fixation thesis is to invite hermeneutical nihilism.

> Why not say that the meaning of the equal protection clause is that Congress is constitutionally required to enact legislation to create a Scandinavian-style social welfare state? Why not say that the constitutional text that seems to require that the president be thirty-five years of age actually requires that he be a mature member of the Republican Party? Presumably, the answer to these questions is that those interpretations of the text would be unreasonable. But why? What makes them unreasonable? The answer, of course, is that those interpretations cannot be tied to the conventional semantic meanings of the words at the time and in the context in which the Constitution was adopted. (Solum 2015, 70)

Such hyperbole is disappointing. The answer to the question posed, "of course," is that the meaning of the constitutional text is bound by many factors, including the historical trajectory of interpretations over time

that stand against efforts to convert the meaning of the text into a radically indeterminate matter of the interpreter's will. There is no responsible argument for the interpretations that Solum proposes, but this is
not because meaning can be fixed at any particular point in time. Instead, stability comes from ongoing practices that persist through time
and establish a rhetorical range for reasonable applications of the text.
The deep and troubling problem with new originalism is revealed in this
strange paragraph, which suggests that when new originalists discover
that their project is impossible they will succumb to hermeneutical vertigo and accede to the tired canard that "anything goes." Meantime, outside the ivory tower, judges will continue doing what they have always
done: engaging in the meaningful practices of common law, statutory,
and constitutional interpretation.

2.3 Legal Practice is Intransigent in the Face of the Fixation Thesis

Undertaking the historical factual inquiry prescribed by Solum would
constitute such a radical deviation from our legal tradition that we should
reject it even if it were a plausible strategy. One needn't be a Burkean to
suggest that we should not upend foundational legal practices built up in
England and then in the United States over hundreds of years unless a
very high standard of proof is met. Conceptual clarity and rigor are all
well and good in the academy, but one must not lightly reject current
practices that provide social stability.

It bears emphasis that Solum does not refer to an actual legal system
that has embraced the centrality of the fixation thesis as an important element of practice. His argument is unabashedly scholarly and conceptual. In contrast, Gadamer argues that the pragmatic evolution of legal
practice (even in the very different context of Germany's civil code tradition) reveals the ontological character of understanding as always involving application. Using theoretical reflection to explore practices that
work might lead us to find that these practices exemplify deeper philosophical truths; it would appear far more doubtful that exploring supposed philosophical truths might guide us to develop more effective
practices that are radically different from current practices. The burden
of disruption, I argue, rests with the new originalists.

2.3.1 WHY PRACTICAL EFFECTS MATTER TO THEORISTS. Describing the
problems that putting new originalism into effect would cause is not a

crude plea in favor of the unreflective status quo against the superior insights of theoretical critiques. Practical difficulties are of no moment if the theoretical insights of new originalism are true. However, Gadamer emphasizes the deep connection between theory and practice, and we should be wary of any philosopher who seeks to theorize without attention to practice. One of the most problematic aspects of new originalism is the tendency of its adherents to begin with a stark theoretical program and then to judge current legal practices by this standard. This misunderstands theory to be an objective stance outside of practice, rather than a comportment to practice that loosens the immediacy of practical engagement. Gadamer's philosophical hermeneutics is a theoretical engagement with hermeneutical activity, but it does not seek to direct that activity by providing a method. This parallels Aristotle's *Nicomachean Ethics*, which is a theoretical reflection on practical engagement that is descriptive rather than directive (Mootz 2003, 706–9). Gadamer writes that the theoretic stance of his philosophical hermeneutics

> only makes us aware reflectively of what is performatively at play in the practical experience of understanding. And so it appears to me that the answer given by Aristotle to the question about the possibility of a moral philosophy holds true as well for our interest in hermeneutics. His answer was that ethics is only a theoretical enterprise and that anything said by way of a theoretic description of the forms of right living can be at best of little help when it comes to the concrete application to human experience of life. And yet the universal desire to know does not break off at the point where concrete practical discernment is the decisive issue. The connection between the universal desire to know and concrete practical discernment is a reciprocal one. So it appears to me, heightened theoretic awareness about the experience of understanding and the practice of understanding, like philosophical hermeneutics and one's own self-understanding, are inseparable. (Gadamer 1981, 112)

Ivory tower theorizing is inapt regarding legal hermeneutics, and so close attention to the hermeneutical activity of lawyers and judges is a critical element of theorizing about the potential confusions or deficiencies of that practice.

By arguing that legal practice lends support to Gadamer's ontology of human understanding I should not be misconstrued as arguing that the severe epistemic difficulties of implementing new originalism mandate Gadamer's ontological conclusions. The argument against the fixation thesis is ontological. The severe epistemic difficulties simply confirm that the degree to which contemporary practices accord with the ontological character of understanding is instructive. Just as Gadamer discussed the practice of law as an "exemplary" instance of human understanding, this chapter illustrates the ontological claims of philosophical hermeneutics by describing the intransigence of legal practice in the face of the new originalist agenda. The epistemic difficulties of implementing new originalism are an unsurprising confirmation of the ontology of human understanding.

Finally, it is entirely conceivable that some new originalists might remain agnostic about the ontological critique of the fixation thesis. Regardless of the nature of human understanding, they might argue, our legal system would benefit if judges acted "as if" they could retrieve fixed meaning from the past. Putting the ontological question to the side, these critics would celebrate the political and social benefits of requiring judges to articulate a "hypothetical original understanding," knowing full well that it is a fiction. By highlighting the severe practical problems that would follow from this approach, this section provides pragmatic grounds for rejecting new originalism to the extent that it is offered solely as a political strategy and not as a serious philosophical position.

2.3.2 THE IMPLAUSIBILITY OF IMPLEMENTING NEW ORIGINALISM. It should be clear that embracing the fixation thesis, which Solum claims is intuitive, would amount to a profound upheaval in current practices.[22] American legal practice would have to change fundamentally and dramatically if we accepted the truth of the fixation thesis. Although not determinative of cases in itself, communicative meaning would certainly be extremely important for adjudication. At a minimum, this would suggest that judges should be trained in the modern techniques of historical investigation (broadly construed as including historical, philological, linguistic, sociological, and psychological elements) rather than being trained in doctrinal legal analysis and then engaging in amateurish efforts to recover a hypothesized fixed historical meaning. To push the point, the Supreme Court might be counseled to engage a team of legal historians (as broadly construed) to analyze briefs and to provide an analysis of textual meaning to which they could refer in a case. Members of the team would not have to exercise judgment if textual meaning is an empirical fact that can be investigated and known. The court's expert researchers might not reach a definitive conclusion about particular provisions (due to either lack of evidence or contradictory evidence), but this finding in itself would be important for the determination of cases.

Introducing professional experts of communicative meaning into the judicial process might not seem too radical a departure, but the implications extend much further. What possible reason could exist to wait for individual cases before determining the meaning of constitutional clauses? A research team could begin work immediately to determine the singular and immutable meaning of various constitutional terms, providing all potential parties with a clear understanding of the fixed textual meaning in advance of disputes. This highly efficient and proactive exercise might not run afoul of the "case or controversy" requirement because it would not predetermine any particular disputes. Judges would always have to construct the textual meaning as applied to the case at hand, but an advantage would be gained by framing the dispute with predetermined explanations of the fixed textual meaning of the clause in question. Of course, perhaps the first assignment would have to be an investigation of the fixed meaning of article 3, section 2, clause 1 of the Constitution.

From this, it would also follow that lower courts should certify questions about the meaning of constitutional provisions so that they might go about their work of construction more efficiently. It would be impractical to expect every district court to undertake massive historical research into constitutional provisions, and it would seem illogical for courts to reach decisions in the absence of the meaning of the controlling provisions. Practically speaking, of course, courts might have to proceed with their dockets in the ordinary course until such time as the certified questions could be answered. In this case, courts would be in the curious position of constructing the result in a case with reference to the "preliminary" meaning of constitutional provisions.

All of this suggests that the Supreme Court would face a huge workload problem. Solum repeatedly emphasizes the tremendous amount of research required to discern the communicative content of an aged legal text. At the constitutional level this is perhaps acceptable, given the relative brevity of the text. But how would the court possibly deal with the massive amount of statutory and regulatory text that controls modern life? Solum concedes that the meaning of a private contract or of a judicial opinion might be determined differently due to the divergent contexts,[23] but it is difficult to understand why the communicative content of a constitutional provision would be determined in a different manner than the communicative content of a statutory or regulatory provision. Many statutes are ancient and encrusted with interpretations (perhaps, in Solum's mind, misunderstandings) of the textual meanings, and so the challenge would be quite significant.

Finally, we might encourage the Supreme Court to determine the communicative content of statutes and regulations as soon after they are enacted as possible. Given the effects of linguistic drift, it would be imperative to capture the communicative content quickly and then record it for posterity. There would be interesting dynamics at work, of course, with Congress undoubtedly responding with amendments when it was dissatisfied with the judicial articulation of the communicative content of its statutes. In the end, however, we might hope to be guided nearly from the beginning by a clear understanding of the textual meaning. It does not take much reflection to recognize that the text of the law itself would then be displaced by the historical findings about the communicative meaning, and these findings themselves would have to be understood by parties far into the future.

I should think that the implausibility, if not absurdity, of these suggested practices is apparent. The existence of fixed textual meaning is a comforting fantasy, but trying to get to the fixed meaning turns out to be a bit of a nightmare. The legal historian is subject to the ontological conditions of understanding no less than the judge, even if their practices are different. All understanding is application. Solum never addresses why we should believe that an empirical determination of meaning might be achieved in a manner that can be communicated without that communication itself being subject to interpretation as time passes. Would a definitive articulation of the communicative content of the Second Amendment in *Heller*—a wildly generous supposition, to be sure (Mootz 2010)[24]—be subject to an equally difficult task of retrieval 200 years from now? In which case, isn't it clear that the "fixed" meaning is always subject to retrieval through application?

More important, how would we articulate the precise task for our legal historians? "Determine the communicative content of the Second Amendment, which is an empirical fact to be discovered" would appear to be the charge, but how exactly would the inquiry begin? Without a motivation of some kind on the part of the researchers, there would be little traction for the inquiry. Can we really determine what the Second Amendment meant to the people of the time without posing a question of application, such as what the Second Amendment means regarding the private ownership of firearms? How can the researchers determine the full scope of the textual meaning without considering numerous such questions of application? And then we are back to the wisdom of our constitutional ban on advisory opinions. These fundamental difficulties are not inconvenient epistemic limits that ivory tower scholars might place to the side; rather, they are strong indicators of an ontological error in articulating the practice in question.

3. A Brief Reply to Professor Solum

Professor Solum has generously responded to my chapter in this volume in the course of restating his argument for the fixation thesis. I wish to provide a very brief reply to his response in the interest of sharpening the issues. First, Solum argues that Gadamer reinscribes the interpretation-construction distinction by distinguishing the work of the historian from the work of a judge. I argued at length for the opposite reading of Gadamer, who commonly is read to argue that all understanding involves application, which is to say that there is no interpretive recovery without a constructive element. We can leave our debate about Gadamer's philosophy to the readers, but even if Solum's atypical reading is a correct exegesis of Gadamer, I would continue to adhere to my ontological reading of Gadamer, even if it extends beyond Gadamer's own argument.

Solum contends that I err by arguing against the existence of original meaning by claiming that it is extremely difficult to recover and is always subject to revision as our biased investigations become more precise. This is a valid point, but it misses the mark. I make clear that my challenge is ontological and that the insuperable difficulties for implementing originalism merely lend force to an ontological argument that stands on its own. More important, the insuperable difficulties serve as a caution against embracing new originalism "as if" it were ontologically plausible solely as a practical effort to constrain judges.

The unavoidable point of difference between me and Solum is my central claim that the fixation thesis is ontologically implausible. This important point can be sharpened by posing two questions: Is my hermeneutical ontology plausible, and what effect would adopting this ontological perspective have on constitutional theory and practice?

Solum contends that Gadamer's hermeneutical ontology appears to be a skeptical denial of reality, but I argue against the existence of "objective facts about the past that exist in the present" only after distinguishing a sequence of physical events from our understanding of those events as facts. Human understanding of the world is hermeneutical, but this is not to say that the world is generated subjectively. Gadamer's "fusion of horizons" between what appears to be lodged in the past and present experience is expressly meant to undercut subjectivism. Solum makes a commonsense appeal that the original understanding of article 1, section 3 of the Constitution must certainly have been that precisely "two" senators represent each state, seeking to overcome my ontological challenge by providing one example. This seemingly undeniable "original understanding" would appear to be an "objective fact" in these sense required of the fixation thesis.

Solum's example draws its force from the persistence of mathematical understanding through time. When dealing with primary qualities of the world, such as number or shape, we have persistent shared experiences that engender a vigorous philosophical debate about whether these qualities are mind-independent. It would stand to reason that we would have a very strong sense that people at the time of the nation's founding would have understood "two" precisely as we understand this number, simply because of the unbroken experience of this number from that time to the present. But this confident judgment is no less the product of a fusion of horizons than a judgment about how the founding generation would understand equality among citizens.

In contrast, Solum makes clear that he rejects the "reasonable person" construction of the original understanding, claiming instead that the original understanding is an empirical fact no different than any other physical event in the historical sequence. But it is precisely at this point that Solum's ontological commitments become suspect. Does he claim that "meanings" exist as facts in the world, independent of hermeneutical activity? Such a position seems utterly fantastic. We might approach the problem by imagining that every single person at a given point in time in the past might have actually read and understood a particular document and attempt to reconstruct that understanding. Of course, this strategy confronts the unimaginable complexity of the "reasonable person" construction of meaning. Even if we grant that historical records provide (debatable and wholly incomplete) glimpses of how certain persons understood words and phrases, the project of constructing a supposed fixed and uniform meaning understood by all persons at the time would be a fictitious construction of a meaning. There simply is no plausible means to assert a unitary "meaning" shared by ordinary persons at a particular point in time without adopting a reconstruction of the reasonable person.

I conclude my reply to Solum by elaborating the impact on constitutional theory and practice that follows from embracing the ontology of philosophical hermeneutics. Gadamer's philosophical hermeneutics leads us to embrace the ethical dimensions of interpretive activity and to take responsibility for maintaining a resolute openness to meaning. Our best defense against subjective manipulation of meaning, or the false humility of deferring to a fixed meaning, is to acknowledge our nature as hermeneutical beings and to cultivate the rhetorical and exegetical practices that have developed in exemplary fashion in the legal realm. It is time to get over our originalist fixation and confront our humanity.

4. Conclusion

The fixation thesis propounded by the new originalists is false. The practice of understanding in all its various manifestations is intransigently hermeneutical, despite the conceptually complex efforts of theorists to insulate highly selective legal practices (constitutional litigation at the Supreme Court level) from the destabilizing risk of hermeneutical activity. Gadamer explores how legal practice is particularly immune to the lure of theoretical certainty, given the exigencies of the practice and the critical function it plays in society. To put the matter bluntly, the legal order is too important for social survival to be led astray by palliative theorizing. The hermeneutics of legal practice reveals a great deal about our nature as hermeneutical beings because the legal system cannot afford the luxury of a conceptual fixation.

By neglecting the ontology of human understanding, legal theorists permit the new originalist program to get off the ground with an intuitive appeal to a "fixed" meaning. Later efforts to argue on behalf of a "living constitution" will wilt in the face of the constraint principle: Who can successfully argue against the comforting fantasy of judges who discern objective meaning without having to make judgments? Gadamer's ontological account of hermeneutical activity and meaning derails the new originalist program at the outset, refusing to grant the seemingly minor concession of the fixation thesis. The debate is not over, of course, because a Gadamerian cannot compel the new originalist to accept her principles by force of logic or empirical proof, any more than the new originalists can compel the Gadamerian. But the debate is now where it should be: on the rhetorical field of persuasive arguments about our nature as communicative beings, a nature that is reflected vividly in our most important practices.

Notes

1. I would like to thank Saul Cornell and Robert Bennett for very helpful discussions about an earlier draft and Ian McGlone (McGeorge class of 2017) for his excellent editing. I am particularly grateful to my colleague Brian Slocum for involving me in this very interesting project.

2. Professor Solum's draft article was slightly revised and published in *Notre Dame Law Review* 91, no. 1 (2015): 1–78. In his contribution to this volume, Solum retraces most of the steps of his argument about the fixation thesis before considering my critique. Because some of his phrasing changes I have kept all citations to the February 3, 2015, draft of the article that is forthcoming in the *Notre Dame Law Review*.

3. "Communicative content is simply the meaning of the text: you need more than meaning to get legal effect. . . . [F]or the Fixation Thesis to have any logical implications for legal practice, it must be combined with some other premise (like the Constraint Principle)" (Solum 2015, 32; see generally Chiang and Solum 2013; Solum 2013b).

4. Solum notes that judges may need to supply legal content if the communicative content of the text is vague, ambiguous, lacking, or internally contradictory (Solum 2013a, 509–10). However, he argues that courts should not contradict the communicative content, even if they might in some cases extend the meaning beyond the communicative content (ibid., 512–13). He assumes the normative power of the communicative content in the course of differentiating it from legal content.

5. As Step Feldman emphasizes, "The goal of originalism has always been purity [and the] key to attaining purity is history" (Feldman 2014, 284).

6. Fagles 2006, 76 (Bk II, 61–62). Apologies to Virgil.

7. I am either consistently correct or doggedly wrongheaded. This part of the article follows from my first publication (Mootz 1988). Perhaps I have a fixation?

8. It is unhelpful to ask whether color is an objective feature of physical objects *or* the subjective projection of a viewer. All perception, including the perception of color, is the product of a hermeneutical relationship between the world and the observer. Maurice Merleau-Ponty anticipated the philosophical implications of this fact in *Phenomenology of Perception*.

> [A] sensible datum which is on the point of being felt sets a kind
> of muddled problem for my body to solve. I must find the atti-
> tude which *will* provide it with the means of becoming determi-
> nate, of showing up as blue; I must find the reply to a question
> which is obscurely expressed. And yet I do so only when I am in-
> vited by it, my attitude is never sufficient to make me really see
> blue or really touch a hard surface. (Merleau-Ponty 1962, 214)

In a recent book defending a new take on color adverbialism, Chirimuuta suggests that it would be more accurate to state that we "see brownly" than to say
that we "see brown" because the perception of color "involves a complex interaction between objects and seeing animals" (Chirimuuta 2015, 6). Beginning
with the fact that "*colors are real, but just not mind-independent*" (ibid., 187),
color "adverbialism asserts not only that colors are perceiver-dependent properties but that they are properties of perceptual interactions rather than of the
perceived object or mind-brain" (ibid., 213). I should emphasize that Chirimuuta
specifically does not extend this thesis to all perception, as I am suggesting in the
text, but does gesture in this direction (ibid., 177–78, 213–14).

9. Chirimuuta describes common, and inaccurate, assumptions throughout
history about how we perceive color (Chirimuuta 2015, 19–42).

10. Drawing on Heidegger, Gadamer insists that "understanding is not a
method which the inquiring consciousness applies to an object it chooses[,] and
so turn it into objective knowledge; rather, being situated within an event of tradition, a process of handing down, is a prior condition of understanding. *Understanding proves to be an event* . . ." (Gadamer 1989, 309).

11. "Just as the individual is never simply an individual, because he is always
understanding with others, so too the closed horizon that is supposed to en-
close a culture in the past is an abstraction" (Gadamer 1989, 304; see generally
300–307).

12. Gadamer describes the concept of the "history of effect" (*Wirkungsge-
schicte*) in support of the claim to truth that texts make upon us. A traditionary
text loses its claim of truth if it is approached only in its historical context.

> The text that is understood historically is forced to abandon
> its claim to be saying something true. We think we understand
> when we see the past from a historical standpoint–i.e., transpose
> ourselves into the historical situation and try to reconstruct the
> historical horizon. In fact, however, we have given up the claim
> to find in the past any truth that is valid and intelligible for our-
> selves. (Gadamer 1989, 303)

The claim to truth arises from the history of effects that connects the text to contemporary readers, rather than remaining a supposedly fixed document lodged
wholly in the past.

13. I have repeatedly referred to Gadamer's idea of the "fusion of horizons," and so it is important to note that this concept is widely misunderstood. Gadamer does not suggest that the past and present are wholly reconciled within a new, unitary, horizon. Instead, the "fusion of horizons" is meant to serve as a critique of the idea that is central to the fixation thesis: that there is a historical meaning, and a wholly distinct contemporary horizon in which the historical meaning will be deployed. Instead, the hypothesized "original meaning" shares a historical trajectory with contemporary recovery of meaning, such that there are no fixed horizons that are immutable. *"Rather, understanding is always the fusion of these horizons supposedly existing by themselves"* (Gadamer 1989, 306). At this point we are able to see that his concept of the "fusion of horizons" is just to restate the ontological claim that all understanding occurs through application.

14. George Taylor argues that Paul Ricoeur's more extensive writings about legal hermeneutics provide a more precise account of legal practice.

> I was much taken in *The Just* with Ricoeur's extremely insightful elaboration of what the process of legal application entails. Ricoeur's precision here goes far beyond Gadamer. "The application of a rule," Ricoeur says, "is in fact a very complex operation where the interpretation of the facts and the interpretation of the norm mutually condition each other." Ricoeur argues that legal application includes both interpretation and argumentation, and he draws a parallel between these two and his earlier interplay between explanation and understanding. Argumentation is necessary, because the extension of law to a new application is not a mere intuitive leap but requires a judgment of fitness, which requires analysis—explanation. (Taylor 2010, 95–96)

Taylor is correct in this assessment, but in this same vein I have argued that the (admittedly implicit) centrality of the rhetorical tradition to Gadamer's philosophy works as a supplement that exceeds Ricoeur's insights (Mootz 2011).

15. I provide an uncharacteristically long quotation from *Truth and Method* on this point for several reasons. First, it is the pivotal move in the book and is central to my refutation of the fixation thesis. Second, it highlights Gadamer's Platonic (conversational) method of inquiry, even as it reinforces Gadamer's rejection of Plato's doctrines. These quoted paragraphs could be stipulated using mathematical symbols or concise and carefully constructed sentences, but Gadamer is appealing to his reader in a different manner than modern philosophers are wont to do. In an interview late in his life, Gadamer answered a question about the charge by philosophers that his lectures were vague and not precise.

> GADAMER: . . . [T]he people who write that do not realize how flattered I feel. It is not so terribly easy to speak in such a way

> that many ideas are awakened in a person without his being
> hammered on the head.
> QUESTION: Do you mean that to express one's self clearly and
> distinctly is not necessarily the right way?
> GADAMER: It may be a cultivated thing to eat with a knife and
> fork, but that is not the right approach in philosophy. (Gada-
> mer 1992, 7)

Gadamer, much like Nietzsche, is an incisive theorist in the rhetorical tradition
who writes and speaks to persuade his audience about matters that are not subject to compelling proof. In his introduction to a series of speeches given by Gadamer about social issues, translator Chris Dawson writes:

> If we are looking for specific claims supported by watertight ar-
> guments, then, we shall find Gadamer irritating and shallow. But
> if we are looking for ways of approaching really deep questions
> about the world and our place in it, or if we are looking for some
> kind of orientation in modern society and are frustrated by the
> lack of any external viewpoint from which to examine it, we shall
> find Gadamer's historical rhetoric thrilling and invigorating.
>
> We must not be deceived by Gadamer's chatty style, which . . .
> conceals a wealth of subtle thinking and artistry. Gadamer deals
> with real and serious problems, and goes only so far with them
> as he is sure he is justified in doing. (Dawson 1998, xxxvii)

We should recall that my intentions in this article are similar. We can establish
no "proof" that the fixation thesis is false, but we can explore the question with
attention to lived experience and the nuances of interpretation. My efforts are
wholly rhetorical; my argument is that they cannot (productively) be otherwise.

16. Ricoeur's discussion of the historian's subjectivity shaping the object of
study, and of history constituting the historian's subjectivity, is similar to Gadamer's notion of the fusion of horizons (Ricoeur 1965, 21–40).

17. Solum provides a history of originalist thought over the past three decades that assumes that distinguishing interpretation and construction is a new
and important development (Solum 2015, 5 n.21). "Originalists themselves only
began to embrace the interpretation-construction distinction in the late 1990s—
and that process is still underway: without a distinction between communicative
content and legal content, claims about fixation could not be formulated clearly"
(ibid., 30 n.79). At one point he acknowledges Lieber's work but seeks to distinguish it as an "imperfect" theoretical effort (ibid., 10 n.39). In fact, Lieber advanced the intentionalist approach of romantic hermeneutics, but he leavened
any potential results with the equitable activity of construction. One might say
that Lieber didn't imperfectly appreciate the fixation thesis as much as he rejected it (Mootz 1994).

It bears emphasis that Solum exhibits the historicity of understanding, which is to say that his legal philosophy has an effective-history. There is no fixed jurisprudential question handed down from the past to which we return without intervening history having an effect on our inquiry (see, e.g., Symposium 2015).

18. Feldman discusses a number of theorists as examples, but he notes that Solum does not expressly adopt this qualification in any detail. However, it would appear necessary for Solum to admit the inevitability of some form of reconstruction of ordinary usages in a manner that bears the hallmarks of what Feldman terms "reasonable-person originalism" (Feldman 2014, 302 n.102). See my "A Brief Reply to Professor Solum" at the end of this chapter.

19. The comical use by judges of dictionary definitions from the period of enactment highlights the wholly constructive character of their undertaking. Judges refer to dictionaries from the past to claim that the hypothetical "ordinary" or "reasonable" person of the time understood the word in question in a definitive manner, as part of the present effort to construct a hypothetical account of the understanding of the reasonable person. This use of dictionaries by courts is highly suspect both theoretically and in practice (Brudney and Baum 2013). This follows from the fact that dictionaries are used by originalists to construct a hypothetical historical fact, rather than to uncover a fixed truth.

20. Consider the superb book by Barbara Tuchman, in which she looked to the past from the turbulent twentieth century to understand how civilization managed to survive the devastation of the Black Death and extreme social dislocations (Tuchman 1978). She argues that if "our last decade or two of collapsing assumptions has been a period of unusual discomfort, it is reassuring to know that the human species has lived through worse before" (ibid., xiii). Tuchman goes to great lengths to ensure the integrity of her award-winning historical analysis, but she well recognizes Gadamer's theme, as elaborated by Ricoeur, regarding the impossibility of wholly objective history. "One must also remember that the Middle Ages change color depending on who is looking at them. Historians' prejudices and points of view—and thus their selection of material—have changed considerably over a period of 600 years" (ibid., xvii).

Some scholars hew to the hope that the limitations on historians are not insuperable, as if a scientific approach that avoids logical fallacies could permit Tuchman to reveal the history of the Middle Ages without her subject "changing color" (see, e.g., Fischer 1970). Hence the scathing response to her book by some medievalist specialists, undoubtedly disconcerted that she did not have a PhD and eschewed a faux-scientific approach to recovering the "true" Middle Ages, immune from present interests and perspectives (see, e.g., Bacharach 1979).

21. Solum expressly avoids these questions. "If it were the case that the actual text of the Constitution was radically indeterminate, then, depending on how you look at things, we might say that the Fixation Thesis was irrelevant. For the

purposes of this article, we shall simply put that objection to the side" (Solum 2015, 41).

22. Solum acknowledges the reality of legal practice as a hermeneutical activity involving prejudiced readers of texts with an effective history, but he does so in the way most theory-driven critics address reality: with regret. "Misunderstandings or deliberate distortions introduced by the Supreme Court could affect the way contemporary speakers and authors use constitutional language. . . . Courts, scholars, and citizens can and do use fragments of the constitutional text to convey communicative content that differs from the original meaning" (Solum 2015, 38–39). To this observation, we can only revert to Gadamer's lesson that this situation will always obtain because it is the nature of hermeneutical activity.

23. In a recent article Solum distinguishes the activities of interpreting oral contracts, constitutional clauses, and judicial opinions (Solum 2013a, 492–506).

24. In District of Columbia v. Heller, 554 U.S. 570 (2008), Justice Scalia authored the majority opinion on behalf of five justices, claiming first to uncover the original understanding of the Second Amendment as protecting individual gun ownership (ibid. at 576–628), and only after this fifty-page exegesis did he "turn finally to the law at issue here" (ibid. at 628). Saul Cornell has definitively repudiated the fantasies girding Justice Scalia's opinion in *Heller* (see, e.g., Ruben and Cornell 2015; Cornell 2009; Cornell 2008; Cornell 2006). Robert Bennett points out that Solum lauds the avowed methodology of *Heller* but offers no real indication of how we can possibly understand the original meaning of this provision among competent speakers at the time of enactment. Once again, Solum *assumes* the semantic linguistic fact of the matter, and can provide no real analysis.

> The *Heller* case provides an example of choices (often shaped by normative considerations) that will often be required in interpretation. Solum rightfully depicts Justice Scalia's majority opinion in *Heller* as sounding in original-meaning originalism. But Scalia's approach focuses attention alone on the meaning of the words *the right to keep and bear arms*, with no particular concern for the rest of the Second Amendment language. Solum may well disapprove of that stance, for he insists that linguistic context can help wrestle down meaning, and he tells us that "[t]houghtful critics of Justice Scalia's opinion believe that the Second Amendment was intended to apply *only* to weapons used in connection with service in a state militia." In any event, when the introductory language of the amendment is brought into the interpretational picture, the possibility emerges that some quite ordinary readers of the amendment as

a whole would think the right announced was to be constrained by the announced introductory purpose. This latter interpretation, however, is hardly an objectively verifiable fact of the interpretative matter. To the contrary, the Second Amendment provides yet another example of serious ambiguity, the resolution of which would inevitably turn on normative considerations. These include the policy question of whether in this day and age a generalized right to bear arms is a good idea. Solum might claim that the ambiguity could be resolved by struggling hard enough with the words of the Second Amendment in context, but until he has done the struggling and produced that objectively verifiable ambiguity-resolving meaning that others would clearly rush to embrace, the claim rings pretty hollow. There is simply no reason to think that either language in context or patterns of language usage are up to the task that Solum insists on assigning to them. (Bennett 2011, 176–77)

To put emphasis on the point here, this is not just a claim of methodological difficulty. Rather, it is indication of an ontological confusion on Solum's part.

References

Bacharach, Bernard S. 1979. "Review." *American Historical Review* 84:724–25.

Bennett, Robert W. 2011. "Originalism and the Living American Constitution." In Lawrence B. Solum and Robert W. Bennett, *Constitutional Originalism: A Debate*. Ithaca: Cornell University Press.

Brudney, James J., and Lawrence Baum. 2013. "Oasis or Mirage: The Supreme Court's Thirst for Dictionaries in the Rehnquist and Roberts Eras." *Social Science Research Network*. Posted January 2. http://ssrn.com/abstract=2195644.

Chiang, Tun-Jen, and Lawrence B. Solum. 2013. "The Interpretation-Construction Distinction in Patent Law." *Yale Law Journal* 123:531–614.

Chirimuuta, M. 2015. *Outside Color: Perceptual Science and the Puzzle of Color in Philosophy*. Cambridge: MIT Press.

Cioffi, Frank. 1998. *Freud and the Question of Pseudoscience*. Chicago: Open Court.

Cornell, Saul. 2006. *A Well Regulated Militia: The Founding Fathers and the Origins of Gun Control in America*. Oxford: Oxford University Press.

———. 2008. "Originalism on Trial: The Use and Abuse of History in *District of Columbia v. Heller*." *Ohio State Law Journal* 69:625–40.

———. 2009. "*Heller*, New Originalism, and Law Office History: 'Meet the New Boss, Same as the Old Boss.'" *UCLA Law Journal* 56:1095–125.

———. 2011. "The People's Constitution vs. The Lawyer's Constitution: Popular Constitutionalism and the Original Debate over Originalism." *Yale Journal of Law and the Humanities* 23:295–337.

———. 2015. "Originalism as Thin Description: An Interdisciplinary Critique." *Fordham Law Review Res Gestae* 84:1–10. http://fordhamlawreview.org/assets/res-gestae/volume/84/Cornell.pdf.

Dawson, Chris. 1998. Translator's introduction to *Praise of Theory: Speeches and Essays*, by Hans-Georg Gadamer, xv-xxxviii. New Haven: Yale University Press.

Fagles, Robert. 2006. *Virgil: The Aeneid.* New York: Viking Press.

Feldman, Stephen M. 2014. "Constitutional Interpretation and History: New Originalism or Eclecticism." *Brigham Young University Journal of Public Law* 28:284–350.

Fischer, David Hackett. 1970. *Historians' Fallacies: Toward a Logic of Historical Thought.* New York: Harper & Row.

Gadamer, Hans-Georg. 1981. "Hermeneutics as Practical Philosophy." In *Reason in the Age of Science*, translated by Frederick G. Lawrence, 88–112. Cambridge: MIT Press.

———. 1989. *Truth and Method.* Translated by Joel Weinsheimer and Donald G. Marshall. 2nd rev. ed. New York: Continuum.

———. 1992. "The German University and German Politics." (Interview.) In *Hans-Georg Gadamer on Education, Poetry, and History: Applied Hermeneutics*, edited by Dieter Misgeld and Graeme Nicholson, translated by Lawrence Schmidt and Monica Reuss, 3–14. Albany: State University of New York Press.

Gienaap, Jonathan. 2015. "Historicism and Holism: Failures of Originalist Translation." *Fordham Law Review* 84:935–56.

LaCapra, Dominick. 1983. "Rethinking Intellectual History and Reading Texts." In *Rethinking Intellectual History: Texts, Contexts, Language*, 23–71. Ithaca: Cornell University Press.

Margolis, Joseph. 1993. *The Flux of History and the Flux of Science.* Oakland: University of California Press.

Merleau-Ponty, Maurice. 1962. *The Phenomenology of Perception.* Translated by Colin Smith. London: Routledge and Kegan Paul.

Mootz III, Francis J. 1988. "The Ontological Basis of Legal Hermeneutics: A Proposed Model of Inquiry Based on the Work of Gadamer, Habermas, and Ricouer." *Boston University Law Review* 68:525–617.

———. 1994. "The New Legal Hermeneutics." *Vanderbilt Law Review* 47:115–43.

———. 2003. "A Future Foretold: Neo-Aristotelian Praise of Postmodern Legal Theory." *Brooklyn Law Review* 68:683–719.

———. 2006. *Rhetorical Knowledge in Legal Practice and Critical Legal Theory.* Tuscaloosa: University of Alabama Press.

———. 2010. "Ugly American Hermeneutics." *Nevada Law Journal* 10:587–606.

———. 2011. "Gadamer's Rhetorical Conception of Hermeneutics as a Key to Developing a Critical Hermeneutics." In *Gadamer and Ricoeur: Critical Horizons for Contemporary Hermeneutics*, edited by Francis J. Mootz III and George H. Taylor, 83–103. New York: Continuum.

Ricoeur, Paul. 1965. "Objectivity and Subjectivity." In *History and Truth*, translated by Charles A. Kelbley, 21–40. Evanston, IL: Northwestern University Press.

Ruben, Eric M. and Saul Cornell. 2015. "Firearm Regionalism and Public Carry: Placing Southern Antebellum Case Law in Context." *Yale L.J. Forum* 125:121. Posted September 25. http://www.yalelawjournal.org/forum/firearm-regionalism-and-public-carry.

Solum, Lawrence B. 2013a. "Communicative Content and Legal Content." *Notre Dame Law Review* 89:479–519.

———. 2013b. "Originalism and Constitutional Construction." *Fordham Law Review* 82:453–537.

———. 2015. "The Fixation Thesis: The Role of Historical Fact in Original Meaning." February 3. http://ssrn.com/abstract=2559701. A slightly revised version was published in *Notre Dame Law Review* 91:1–78.

Symposium. 2015. "Jurisprudence and (Its) History." *Virginia Law Review* 101:849–1202.

Taylor, George H. 2010. "Ricoeur and Law: The Distinctiveness of Legal Hermeneutics." In *Ricoeur Across the Disciplines*, edited by Scott Davidson, 84–101. New York: Bloomsbury Academic.

Tuchman, Barbara W. 1978. *A Distant Mirror: The Calamitous 14th Century.* New York: Knopf.

CHAPTER EIGHT

Legal Speech and the Elements of Adjudication

Nicholas Allott and Benjamin Shaer

1. Introduction

In this study, we pursue two ideas about legal speech.[1] One is that this speech can be fruitfully studied if we approach it not as a sui generis phenomenon but as a variety of verbal interaction, with more uniting it than distinguishing it from other varieties, including ordinary face-to-face communication and literary texts. The other, which takes the first as its point of departure, is that we can gain a better understanding of legal speech by recognizing its complexity in speech act terms and distinguishing speech act content from more strictly legal content.

In much of our previous work, our interest in the speech act content of legal speech has been oriented toward the legal meaning that a legislature intends to convey through the enactment of a given statute, seen as a complex utterance that creates new social facts. Here, we focus on what judges do with legal speech in handing down judgments. While we have looked at the legislature as a "speaker," any study of what judges do needs to look at their role as both "hearers" (of statutes and previous cases) and "speakers" (of judgments). Of course, the terms "speaker," "hearer," legal "speech," and "utterance" are all an awkward fit for the legal context, given that statutes and judgments are typically presented in writing, and the use of these terms inevitably draws attention to the difference between this form of communication and the ordinary language interactions that these terms are more commonly used to describe.

We will address this by sketching a general picture of verbal communication and then showing how legal speech represents a particular elaboration of this.

Doing so will allow us to set the stage for our discussion of adjudication and for the following central claim. This is that adjudication is best described in speech act terms as a "verdictive" (Austin 1962; Bach and Harnish 1979), also known as a "representative declaration" (Searle 1976, 15). Such speech acts are reports of findings that make them the case officially. Classic examples include a line-call in tennis and a cricket umpire giving a batsman out. On Austin's (1962, 153) description, a verdictive is a "judicial act," which "consist[s] in the delivering of a finding, official or unofficial, upon evidence or reasons as to value or fact, so far as these are distinguishable." As such, "[v]erdictives have obvious connexions with truth and falsity, soundness and unsoundness and fairness and unfairness." Searle and Bach and Harnish improve on Austin here in making clear the contrast and relation between such acts and what Bach and Harnish call "effectives" and Searle "(nonrepresentative) declarations," which are speech acts that make such and such the case without also reporting a finding, such as naming a ship or saying "I do" in the wedding ceremony. Searle makes both the relationship and contrast explicit in his discussion of the difference between representative and nonrepresentative declarations (Searle 1976, 15–16). Bach and Harnish class effectives and verdictives together as "institutional" speech acts.[2]

For us, two aspects of this work are especially noteworthy. One is its highlighting of verdictives as speech acts that function within a set of institutional rules and conventions (Bach and Harnish 1979; see also Sperber and Wilson 1986, 244–45). The other is the complex nature of this type of act, which involves at least assembling evidence or reasons and issuing a decision on the basis of them—all of which, of course, depends on a court coming to a reasonable understanding of the content of the laws and other legal texts that drive its ultimate decision. Characterizing judges' adjudications in speech act terms as "verdictives" properly places decision-making rather than uncovering meanings at the heart of "judging" activity; but it also makes the point that the adjudication is not simply a free choice but a finding about how things stand.

That much is fairly uncontroversial. However, we suggest that this characterization of what judges do implies a contrast with the traditional picture of judging as essentially "interpreting what others have decided"

(Endicott 2012, 110). We also take issue with the claim of Endicott and others that much of what is commonly placed under the rubric of "legal interpretation" is not, in fact, a matter of interpretation at all. For Endicott, interpretation is "a creative reasoning process of finding grounds for answering a question as to the meaning of some object" (Endicott 2012, 109), where this answer ascribes to this object not "what everyone [already] knows if they are familiar with the object, but [. . .] a meaning that someone else might dispute" (Endicott 2012, 110). Crucially for him, it does not involve various processes some might see as basic to any kind of interpretation. These include "[u]nderstanding the law," which for Endicott only sometimes "requires a creative intellectual process of finding reasons for an answer to a question (which might have been answered differently) as to the meaning of the object" (Endicott 2012, 121). When this is not required, the law is understood "without needing to interpret" (ibid.). Endicott has also argued that what judges do when they precisify the meanings of certain terms in statutes is not interpretation, since it is not an investigative activity but a creative one.

Now, we agree with Endicott that whatever "legal interpretation" is, only part of it is plausibly identified as "utterance interpretation," where this is a process of attempting to determine the utterance content of legislative speech. We likewise agree that the process of reaching a verdict that resolves a legal dispute may involve a great deal of "creative" activity, and thus that legal reasoning may include any or all of the five ingredients that Endicott enumerates. Where we depart from him, though, is in our claims that (1) understanding the law and (2) precisifying vague terms that have been left deliberately unspecific by the legislature are interpretive activities—the former necessarily, the second only in some instances, as we explain below. This makes it more natural to see these aspects of reasoning as parts of the complex interpretative process in which judges are engaged, rather than seeing them as outside of this process.

On the other hand, while the judicial activity in question is indeed traditionally (and no doubt strategically) called "legal interpretation," at heart it is not an effort to interpret legislative speech. Instead, it is—as Endicott himself argues—an effort to resolve a dispute related to certain instances of legislative speech through an act of decision-making. Arguably, then, judges' primary role in legal communication is not as the hearer of the legislature's speech, called upon to understand what this speech means. Rather, it is as decision makers, called upon to do something: namely, to decide, on the basis of this speech, which party wins the dispute. In other words, adjudication responds to a request for action—in this case, making a decision that resolves a dispute.

Yet, it is equally clear that in responding to a request for a decision by parties to a dispute, the judge must (at least in cases not involving purely common law disputes) track the relevant intention or intentions expressed by the legislature in enacting the legislation that figures in the dispute. Accordingly, utterance interpretation in a strict sense is a necessary part of the process of judicially deciding the dispute. Moreover, although the legal content of the legislative speech on which judges ground their decision may contain indeterminacies, these are not obviously different in kind from the semantic indeterminacies that hearers must sometimes resolve in ordinary utterance interpretation. The information that the hearer can appeal to may come from a range of sources; regardless of its source, however, it is no less part of the interpretative process if the hearer appeals to it in working out a speaker's meaning. This holds likewise for legal speech, as we will explain.

Another way to see our departure from Endicott on point (1) involves his understanding of "interpretation" itself, which is based on an effort to capture "legal interpretation" in terms of Wittgenstein's (1953) distinction between noninterpretative "rule-following" and true interpretation (Endicott 1994, 2012). We believe that this understanding misconstrues the process of arriving at the meaning in putatively "noninterpretative" cases as well as in some "interpretative" ones. In particular, it fails to recognize the degree to which meaning-seeking activities involve significant inference. As such, it pulls legal interpretation as a phenomenon away from what are plausibly seen as other (albeit highly differentiated) varieties of the same phenomenon.

The heart of the problem here, as we see it, is that Endicott's claims about legal reasoning and interpretation (and those of some other legal scholars such as Andrei Marmor) are not grounded in a realistic picture of the process of working out meanings . Here we agree instead with another strand of legal scholarship, including the work of Dworkin. Relevant here is Dworkin's remark that "[w]hen we are trying to decide what someone meant to say [. . .] we weave assumptions about what the speaker believes and wants, and about what it would be rational for him to believe and want, into decisions about what he meant to say," and his claim that the same process is involved, albeit with its "difficulties [. . .] greatly increased," in interpreting "the utterances [. . .] of an institution like a legislature" rather than a "real person" (Dworkin 1997, 117). Dworkin's views here are very much in line with much recent philosophy of language and with contemporary linguistic pragmatics—in the latter of which it has become a commonplace that the hearer's task of inferring what the speaker meant is basic to verbal communication.

In what follows, we will be sketching this consensus view of modern linguistic pragmatics as it has grown out of work by the philosopher Paul Grice, showing how it provides a firmer foundation for the analysis of adjudication—in particular, by highlighting the commonalities between legal and other speech. Among the happy consequences of such a foundation, we will suggest, is a clearer understanding not only of adjudication and other aspects of legal speech but also of the strong parallels between them and other forms of communication. This permits an understanding of adjudication as a phenomenon far less alien than legal scholarship sometimes makes it out to be. In this respect, then, our discussion of adjudication serves a demystifying (and perhaps deflationary) purpose, helping to remove some of the obscurity surrounding the legal domain and placing legal speech squarely within the larger domain of verbal interaction.

Rejecting Endicott's claim about what counts as "interpretation" is not so much about substituting one meaning of the term "interpretation" for another. Rather, it is about seeing the working out of the content of an utterance or text, whether a legal or literary text or ordinary speech, as never simply about "grasping" rules and instead always about inferring speaker meanings. This is so even though the process may often be spontaneous and intuitive rather than voluntary and reflective. Pragmatic inference is often not occurrently conscious, although it is typically reconstructible after the fact.[3] We take this form of meaning determination as basic to all forms of verbal interaction—that is, driven by inference to the best explanation and exploiting whatever information is relevant to this task. It is this picture of verbal communication, then, that we take to describe the communicative aspects of adjudication and of legal speech more generally, the particularities of which emerge as a reflection of particular (institutional) assumptions, choices, and constraints, just as other varieties of verbal interaction, such as literary interpretation, reflect different ones.

Turning to the disagreement with Endicott about precisification, it is worth emphasizing that we are sympathetic to a key point he is making here: namely, that the term "legal interpretation" can obscure the distinctions between various things that judges do. In particular, we agree with Endicott that there are examples of such precisifications that are not instances of interpretation in the sense of recovering the meaning of the text or inferring what the legislature intended to convey. However, we think that there is a further distinction to be drawn in such cases. In some, the court does something that the legislature intended when it interprets a term more precisely than the legislature specified; in others, it acts against this legislative metaintention about how the statute should be read and used. Accordingly, the former are instances of proper interpretation, whereas the latter are something else.

In what follows we will be pursuing the idea that adjudication represents a complex event—that is, a constellation of activities that together form the act of judging—by laying out what we see as its components.

2. Legal Speech as a Variety of Verbal Communication

As already noted, we take as our point of departure for this investigation a picture of verbal interaction traceable to Grice (1957, [1967] 1989). This picture is captured in his claim that utterance content is constitutively determined by certain speaker intentions and—Grice's great innovation—that interpretation is a matter of the hearer inferring those speaker intentions (Sperber and Wilson 1986, 25). As such, interpretation of an oral or written text is a type of inference to the best explanation, where the production of the text is what is to be explained and the explanation is in general a matter of what it was that the speaker intended to communicate. In other words, in order to understand an utterance, the hearer infers what the speaker has intended to convey, using the linguistic material uttered as a clue; if the hearer can infer these intentions, then communication succeeds.

2.1. Inference in Verbal Communication

Now, for some readers, the claim that utterance content must be *inferred* might be an implausible one. Yet there is a simple, and compelling, argument for it: this is that hearers do not have direct access to speakers' minds and so must work with available clues to what the speaker means, in the form of the audible and visible traces of the speaker's behavior. The insight is that no simple decoding story can adequately explain verbal communication—there is in general no simple connection between movements and sounds (or marks on paper or a screen), on the one hand, and the content of an utterance, on the other.

Some might object that in verbal communication, we simply say what we mean rather than providing clues to our meaning. In other words, finding out what the speaker means is indeed a matter of decoding rather than inferring this meaning. This, as we have described elsewhere (Allott and Shaer submitted), appears to be the position of Andrei Marmor (2008), who claims that, except in very rare cases, the content the legislature prescribes is precisely the content determined by the syntax and semantics of the expressions uttered. It also seems to be what Endicott (2012) is suggesting (in a rather different philosophical idiom) in claiming that "rule-following" processes such as responding appropriately to "a red traffic light" when "approach[ing it] in your vehicle" are "noninterpretative," given that these do not involve "the interpreter's task of finding reasons for ascribing one meaning to it rather than another" (Endicott 2012). He likewise seems to be suggesting this in quoting the "attractive" view of Marmor (2005, 117) that the term "interpretation" is best reserved for cases in which "there is nothing more to explain or understand about [the] meaning" of the particular formulation of a rule and "a new formulation of the rule" is required, "which would remove the doubt."

The cogency of this objection to the inferential view of determining meanings is undermined by a number of considerations. One is Bach's (2006, 24) observation that even in cases where the speaker means precisely what she has said, the hearer must infer that that is so. The speaker might have been speaking ironically or metaphorically, rehearsing a line from a play, or the like. Another is that it is not obviously even possible for a speaker to mean precisely what is encoded by the sentence that she utters, given that the linguistic meanings of words and sentences may not be plausible candidates for speaker meanings or components of these meanings. It is well known that this applies to the interpretation of indexical expressions like *it*, where decoding of the sentence at most determines that there is some singular inanimate entity being referred to, thus still requiring the hearer to infer what that entity is. But there is an emerging consensus in lexical semantics (Levin 1993; Levin and Hovav 2005; Chomsky 2000; Leben 2015; see also Laurence and Margolis 1999, 54) and in pragmatics and the philosophy of language (Carston 2002, 359–60; Carston 2012; Recanati 2004, chap. 9; Pietroski 2010; Allott and

Textor submitted; Collins 2011) that even standard "content" words such as *red*, *car*, and *pour* have "gappy," "partial," or "schematic" encoded meanings that fall short of determining properties or extensions. According to this view, parsing a sentence and combining the meanings of its words according to the rules of syntax and semantics will never or almost never yield a proposition, that is, something with truth conditions.

Even if we assume that compositional sentence meaning (abstracting away from indexicals) is truth-apt (i.e., capable of being true or false), there is still another reason to see pragmatic inference as ubiquitous in arriving at "what is said" by a speaker in uttering a sentence. This is that the contribution made by the basic context-invariant meanings of the words uttered typically falls short of what the speaker intends to communicate (Sperber and Wilson 1986; Bach 1994). We argue elsewhere that this is so even for legislatures enacting statues (Allot and Shaer submitted). Here we will have more to say about the roles of both inference and relevant evidence in guiding inferences when we discuss Endicott's claims about "noninterpretative" aspects of legal reasoning in section 3.

2.2. *Legal and Other Forms of Communication*

The picture of verbal interaction just sketched forms the basis of the claim that we wish to defend about legal speech in general and adjudication in particular. This is that these can be characterized in essentially the same way, modulo the properties of legal speech that derive from institutional constraints on it. As we have argued elsewhere (Allott and Shaer submitted), legal speech, like ordinary communication and literary interpretation (among other varieties of verbal interaction), displays the properties of the picture just sketched, "draw[ing] on the same basic cognitive and communicative abilities" and thus plausibly captured in essentially the same terms. As we have seen, these include "the notion of inferential communication itself, the distinction between explicit and implicit communication, [. . .] expressions of attitude, and so on" (Wilson 2011, 70).

Also important to this general picture of verbal interaction is the role of information that is "relevant" to the process of inferring speaker meaning in the sense that it can be related to available background information "to yield conclusions that matter" to the hearer (Wilson and Sperber 2004, 608). As defined by Sperber and Wilson, the notion of "relevance" involves a trade-off between cognitive effects and processing effort, so that an input to cognitive processing will be worth attending to because "it is *more* relevant than any alternative input available to us at that time" (Wilson and Sperber 2004, 608). In this technical sense, then, "relevance" applies to a cognitive trade-off. However, we suggest that this notion can usefully be—indeed needs to be—extended to other trade-offs between effects and the expenditure of resources involved in legal and other forms of "offline" interpretation, as we briefly describe in what follows.

Given this picture of verbal interaction, we can attribute many of the key differences between legal and other forms of communication to the specific ways in which these different forms of communication elaborate this picture in drawing on the principles that structure the institutional domains to which these forms respectively belong.[4] In the case of legal communication, these principles—rich enough to constitute a "culture of law," as Kahn (1999) describes it—commonly engage broader institutional goals to shape and constrain legal communication in various ways. Such principles include "the near-total ban on testimony about legislators' private understandings" (Nelson 2005, 359), which—though decidedly alien to most face-to-face communication, where the hearer's ability to immediately confirm or disconfirm what the speaker has meant can be taken for granted—speaks to such concerns as "the need for citizens and their lawyers to have fair notice of the law's requirements and for voters to be able to understand what their elected representatives are up to" (ibid.). Such principles also include interpretation-guiding ones such as stare decisis, substantive canons of construction such as the rule of lenity ("penal laws are to be construed strictly"), and textual canons such as *ejusdem generis* (prescribing that the meaning of general terms be restricted to the same class as the specific terms that precede them in a list).

Another special (although not unique) feature of legal communication is the possibility of a significant displacement in both space and time between the creation of a text and its interpretation. This gives rise to another special feature: namely, the potentially wide and temporally as well as spatially dispersed nature of the intended audience of legal speech. This feature, in turn, leads to a calculation of "relevant" information very different from that associated with ordinary utterance comprehension, whose "almost instantaneous" nature means that normally "in practice the only evidence and hypotheses considered are those that are immediately accessible" (Sperber and Wilson 1986, 66).

In legal communication, by contrast, both the time available to assemble evidence and the range of potential evidence are considerable, meaning that the trade-off is between professional or institutional as well as cognitive effort and effect. As we have already noted, this trade-off is a very complex one, which involves identifying evidence that is not only relevant but also consistent with legal principles that serve to avoid the consideration by decision makers of evidence that may have a prejudicial effect on their decisions, even if relevant.

Of course, legal communication is also distinguished from other varieties of communication by the particular institutional speech acts that it gives rise to. These acts can be seen as complex, consisting of a number of subevents. In other words, it is possible to see legal communication from a bird's eye view as well as from increasingly closer views. From the furthest remove, legal speech might seem to consist simply in an authoritative speaker, the legislature, conveying a message, a statute, to an authoritative hearer, the court. But this is not accurate. At the least, we need to replace this picture with one that contains at least two types of speech act: one of enacting a statute, in which the legislature is the main actor; and another of rendering a verdict related to this statute, in which the court is the main actor.

A more interesting insufficiency of a conception of adjudication simply in terms of the author and receiver of a legal text is signalled by the frequent observation in the legal literature (made recently by, for example, Tushnet (2014, 58) and Marmor (2011)), that the relationship between legislatures and courts is "dialogic"; this underscores the roles of both courts and legislatures as actors and their anticipation of each other's actions. As we have put it elsewhere (Allott and Shaer, submitted):

> What the legislature intends to communicate is constrained by how it expects its utterance to be interpreted, and at least some members of the legislature (or the drafters working on their behalf) will know about noscitur a sociis, reading down, and the like, and in fact rely on them. That is, they are aware that courts will interpret what they say in a manner that extends beyond strictly linguistic meaning, so that the text that they create reflects their anticipation of that fact.

Legal communication can also be decomposed into an array of further subevents on both speaker's and hearer's sides of the interaction. For example, the enactment of legislation in certain jurisdictions involves development and drafting of a bill, debates and committee examination in the legislature, votes, publication in an official gazette, and then formal enactment, including official assent by the head of state. Moreover, the actual "communication" of the contents of the statute takes the form of its final publication and dissemination to the public and arguably does not "crystallize" until some member of the public is subject to it and some court authoritatively establishes its interpretation.

In previous work (Allott and Shaer forthcoming), we have described the speech act of "enactment," associated with the legislature. As already noted, our focus here is on the "verdictive" speech act, associated with the courts. We pursue an analysis of the later speech act in the next section.

3. The Speech Act of Adjudicating

To proceed with our discussion, it might be helpful to first see how the activity of adjudication is generally understood. The standard legal definition, as found, for example, in *Black's Law Dictionary*, is "[t]he legal process of resolving a dispute; the process of judicially deciding a case." What this definition naturally highlights is the decision-making at the heart of adjudication. This understanding of adjudication is reflected in Austin's (1962) speech-act description of it, quoted earlier, as a "verdictive," which likewise highlights the act of decision-making involved in making a finding based on "evidence or reasons." This understanding can also be found in a second prominent definition of "verdictive," that of Bach and Harnish (1979, 111), which emphasizes verdictives' institutional nature:

> *Verdictives* are judgments that by convention have official, binding import in the context of the institution in which they occur. Thus, to call a runner out, to find a defendant guilty, or to assess a piece of property is not just to make a judgment; given the position and attendant authority of an umpire, a judge, or a tax assessor, it is also to make it the case, if only so far as the relevant institution is concerned, that what is judged to be so is so in fact.

Moreover, although Bach and Harnish do not say so explicitly, adjudication seems to be a clear case of a verdictive that "create[s] institutional rights and obligations" and, like other conventional illocutionary acts,

also both "further[s] . . . some institutional practice, process, or procedure" and "affect[s] the institutional status of persons or things."

What both of the above definitions of "verdictive" also very clearly
signal is the complexity of this speech act. As it happens, the nature of
this complexity has received considerable attention in the legal and philosophical literature (e.g., Endicott 1994, 2012; Solum 2010, 2013; Sorensen 2001), which has highlighted its "creative" or "inventive" aspects
as well as its more narrowly "interpretative" ones.

3.1. "Interpretative" and "Noninterpretative" Aspects of Adjudication?

One very compelling analysis of adjudication, as described earlier, is
that of Endicott (1994, 2012). Noting the traditional description of what
judges do, which is mostly "interpreting what others have decided (the
parties, the legislature, framers of a constitution, states that signed a
treaty, previous courts . . .)," Endicott points out that judging may involve far more than essentially following rules laid down by others—although in cases where judges "depart from what others have decided,
they have a natural inclination to see what they are doing as interpreting what those others have done" (Endicott 2012, 110). We agree with all
of this.

More controversially, though, Endicott claims that many components
of legal reasoning "need not involve interpretation." The components in
question are the following ones (Endicott 2012, 111):

1. Resolving indeterminacies as to the content of the law
2. Working out the requirements of abstract legal provisions
3. Deciding what is just
4. Equitable interference with legal duties or powers or rights
5. Understanding the law

Let us focus first on the last of these components. In order to understand
what Endicott is getting at here, it is necessary to see that his analysis
of legal interpretation is based on Wittgenstein's (1953, §201) view of interpretation as contrasting with (mere) "rule-following," as captured in
the following: "There is a way of grasping a rule which is not an interpretation, but which is exhibited in what we call 'obeying the rule' and
'going against it' in actual cases." Endicott appeals to this distinction in
his attempt to distinguish legal "rule-following" from legal "interpreta-

tion," as in the traffic light example mentioned earlier and in the following passage:

> Deciding what is to be done according to law sometimes takes interpretation. But no need for interpretation arises if no question arises as to the meaning of an object. If you approach a red traffic light in your vehicle, you need to know what it means, but the legal rule does not give you the interpreter's task of finding reasons for ascribing one meaning to it rather than another. (2012, 109)

Endicott himself concedes that Wittgenstein's distinction is controversial (Endicott 2012, 120), and it seems fair to ask how convinced we should be by it—and in particular by Endicott's claim that there may be no need for interpretation in deciding what is to be done according to law.

Recall our earlier discussion about the role of inference in utterance interpretation. If we apply our conclusions to Endicott's claims about "noninterpretative" phenomena, including the aspects of legal reasoning just enumerated, we can see that these claims clash with more realistic accounts of how we work out meanings in a range of cases.

Consider first Endicott's traffic light example, as just given. On reflection, this description of traffic light "rule-following" is not very convincing, since responding appropriately to a signal or utterance quite certainly requires both inference and decision-making. After all, even understanding what is meant by a particular red light involves appropriately inferring that it is directed, for example, only at drivers in control of road vehicles and not, say, at pedestrians, to whom a different signal may apply, or at tram drivers on an adjacent track; and that it is used here with its conventional meaning and force, is not used in accordance with some different code, is not merely decorative or part of a film set, and so on. This is so even if such alternatives are not actively considered.

Moreover, the red light is part of a system of signs, appropriate responses to which clearly involve a great deal of decision-making—including whether a driver should proceed left on a green light when there is oncoming traffic or should slow down or speed up when seeing the traffic light turn yellow. Admittedly, many of the inferences and even decisions involved here become routinized for experienced drivers, who usually make them with little conscious thought or consideration of alternatives. Yet, if not only interpreting but also *responding* to traffic lights involved no such processes, it would arguably be difficult to explain why two drivers at the same light might respond differently to it—accelerating at a yellow light, say, rather than slowing down—and cause an accident in one case but not the other.

Similar comments apply to Endicott's claim about understanding the law. In his (1994) study, he asserts that "[u]nderstanding is an ability, and interpretation is an activity" (461). In Endicott (2012, 121), he elaborates on this claim as follows:

> you might, if you wish . . . say[] that all understanding requires interpretation. Yet sometimes, gaining an understanding requires a creative intellectual process of finding reasons for an answer to a question (which might have been answered differently) as to the meaning of the object. Some understanding does not require that process. . . . A good grasp of the context and the language may mean that there is no question as to how a person is to be understood.

If these remarks are meant to imply that the understanding of a text can be achieved without a process of inferring meaning, then we disagree. Of course, there is a distinction to be drawn between activity aimed at understanding an utterance and activity aimed at providing reasons for an interpretation. These are examples in the domain of utterance interpretation of what Mercier and Sperber have recently dubbed "intuitive" and "reflective" inference, respectively (Mercier and Sperber 2009). Modern pragmatics shows that "grasping" meanings of utterances involves not only the decoding of conventional signs but also inference—albeit often intuitive rather than reflective. And as far as we can see, it makes no sense to deny that intuitive inference is an activity.

We also doubt the wisdom of assuming that any particular process of reading of law involved in judging falls purely on the intuitive side, given the "offline" nature of this reading process, which grants time for judges to ponder alternative readings—as, of course, there is very good reason to do, since the stakes are so high. There is an interesting parallel here with literary interpretation. Carston (2010) argues that interpretation of novel and extended metaphors involves occurrently conscious inference, and we suspect that something similar is true of much judicial interpretation of statutes and case law.

In these respects, then, we disagree with Endicott's claim that interpretation need not be involved in understanding the law. As we have said, though, we are inclined to agree with him that judges also make creative decisions about the content of the law, beyond what the legislature has strictly intended to convey, on the basis of principles of justice and equity. In other words, part of what is commonly called "legal interpretation" need not be a matter of working out the meaning of the text.

However, we think that it is worth looking closely at actual cases to see what respective roles interpretative and purely creative judicial activities play in them. Given that coming to understand speaker meaning is a matter of inference to the best explanation and that, we suggest, a key aspect of such an explanation in the judicial context is the attribution of intentions to enact just laws, not to infringe against equity, and so on, then appealing to considerations of equity and justice may often not be independent of the interpretative process after all but instead part of it.

To take an item from Endicott's list, "equitable interference with legal duties or powers or rights," Endicott says the following about "an ambulance enter[ing] [a] park to rescue a person who has been injured," notwithstanding "a town bylaw [that] prohibits vehicles in the park" (2012, 118):

> The driver's behavior may show no disrespect for the rule of law. Is that because the bylaw is best interpreted as meaning something like "vehicles are prohibited in the park except in an emergency"? Or is it because of noninterpretative considerations?
>
> The [latter] considerations . . . are that driving the ambulance into the park in an emergency is morally justified . . . by a concern for the injured person, and is compatible with due respect for the local authority's jurisdiction to regulate the use of the park, even though the authority has banned vehicles. (2012, 118–19)

Elsewhere, we have analysed a possibly analogous example from the Canadian case *Montreal (City) v. 2952–1355 Québec Inc.* This involved article 9(1) of Montreal's noise bylaw, which provided that "the following noises, where they can be heard from the outside, are specifically prohibited: (1) noise produced by sound equipment, whether it is inside a building or installed or used outside." The majority judgment in this case interpreted "noise" in clause (1) as meaning "noise that interferes with the peaceful enjoyment of the environment" (Sullivan 2008, 166), in accordance with the technique of "reading down," according to which a provision is read as if "words of restriction or qualification" have been added (Sullivan 2008, 165). We took this technique to be the institutionalized

legal version of either one or another process familiar in the pragmatics literature: "free enrichment," whereby a constituent for the effect of
the noise is added to the proposition expressed; or "lexical narrowing,"
whereby the property indicated by an expression—in this case "noise"—
is "narrowed down" to a more specific property, in this case the one described by the court. Significantly, the inferential process of moving from
a less to a more specific property may, in ordinary and legal communication alike, be motivated by any number of data that come to the hearer's
attention and are deemed relevant to the determination of the speaker's meaning. That these data may come from different sources does not
make them any less a part of an interpretative process.

We think that it is an open (and interesting) question whether a judge
in the hypothetical vehicle case would infer in a similar way that the bylaw is best understood as meaning something like "vehicles are prohibited in the park except in an emergency." In a real case of this type, we
suspect that the police or a public prosecutor would choose simply not
to prosecute, on grounds of equity and the general policy of serving the
public interest. If the case were actually to reach a court, a judge might
solve the problem by attributing to the legislature the enriched meaning
that we suggest. And we do not think that it is clear that the judge would
be wrong in doing so, given that this decision would be based on the reasonable assumption that the legislature intends the laws it enacts to be
equitable. Similar remarks apply to another putatively noninterpretative
aspect of legal reasoning, that of "[d]eciding what is just."

Endicott also discusses two more obviously compelling instances of
"noninterpretative" reasoning processes: namely, "[r]esolving indeterminacies as to the content of the law" and "[w]orking out the requirements of abstract legal provisions" (2012, 111). What makes these more
plausible candidates for the "noninterpretative" claim is simply that a
case can be made that there truly is no content to determine here and
thus no interpretation to be performed: what is left for the judge, then, is
to create content rather than to probe existing content.

Endicott offers as an example of resolving indeterminacies in legal
content the European Court of Human Rights case *Bankovic v. Belgium* (52207/99) (2001), in which the court had to decide whether the
article 1 right to life had been contravened by actions taken by the Bel-
gian military in bombing Belgrade. The judges treated this as a question of the interpretation of the word *jurisdiction* in the sentence "The
High Contracting Parties shall secure to everyone within their jurisdic-

tion the rights and freedoms defined in Section I of this Convention." Endicott argues, however, that interpretation ends with the understanding that "the framers [of the ECHR] had not determined the jurisdiction at all" (2012, 113). The content of the relevant part of the convention, in the sense of what the framers meant by what they uttered, was just that there was an obligation to secure the rights within the jurisdiction.

We find convincing Endicott's characterization of the legal content of this instance of *jurisdiction* and of the court's activity in determining the meaning of this term as an activity that creates rather than investigates legal content. However, we are less convinced by the conclusion that he draws from this. Endicott remarks about these cases that it is a "mistake," though an "easy and attractive" one, to think of them "as a matter of interpretation," given "just how extravagantly the law may leave matters for decision by the parties to a transaction, or by an institution that must resolve a dispute" (Endicott 2012, 109–10). A tacit premise of this argument, and the locus of our disagreement with him, is that interpretation is exhausted when the existing content of the law has been discovered. We think that a better criterion for what is properly called judicial "interpretation" is activity that aims to discover and respect the intention of the legislature. And while this may seem to be no more than a verbal dispute, we think that our way of describing the situation has two virtues: it naturally allows for a distinction between two importantly different modes of creative judicial behavior, and it may provide an answer to a general worry raised by Sorensen (2001) about judicial adjudications.

Here is the connection to Sorensen's point. If the process of resolving legal indeterminacies involves no interpretative considerations, then we face the following problem. At least in "absolute borderline" cases, in which legal indeterminacies cannot be resolved even in principle by the provision of additional information, this resolution would seem to be open to Sorensen's (2001) worry about judges' decisions. This is that given a judge's duty "to be decisive" but also to uphold the law, the judge "cannot say 'The defendant is guilty but I have no belief one way or the other about his guilt' [but instead] quietly resigns himself to an insincere verdict" (388). Endicott regards resolving such indeterminacies as a "noninterpretative" process, but Sorensen's worry suggests that we should not reach that conclusion unless we have no reasonable alternative.

Of course, one might try to address Sorensen's worry by pointing to Bach and Harnish's (1979, 111) nonveridical characterization of verdictives, according to which all they do is make it the case that such-and-such rather than constituting true or false assertions. According to this view, judges cannot be insincere in rendering a verdict, since they are simply creating new social facts. This, however, is unlikely to satisfy those sympathetic to Sorensen's point. Sorensen (2001, 402) himself acknowledges the possibility of responding to the claim of judicial insincerity in speech act terms by highlighting the "performative" nature of adjudication, remarking that "when a judge declares the defendant guilty, the defendant is thereby guilty. Saying so makes it so." But this would not address his worry, which is not over whether the verdict as a speech act does or does not have truth conditions vacuously satisfied by the making of the act but over how the judge can *justify* the verdict. This point is crucial, since verdicts, while they certainly "make it the case that such-and-such," must nevertheless be grounded in (good) reasons for doing so (unlike effectives, as noted earlier).

A more promising avenue for addressing Sorensen's worry is the one taken by Asgeirsson (2013). Asgeirsson's argument is that "[w]hen legislatures deliberately use vague language" they are creating for courts the task not of "find[ing] out whether absolute borderline *F*s really are *F*s" but of "engag[ing] with the *normative question* whether *x* ought—relative to the purposes of the law—to count as an *F*." Moreover, Asgeirsson takes this "judicial response to this legislative 'request'" to be, under at least certain circumstances, a valuable one. From our perspective, what is worth emphasizing here is that what judges do with absolute borderline cases on this characterization, though clearly involving considerable creativity, can still be readily understood as part of interpretative activity and not outside of it. We see it as very plausible that judges are guided in these "hard" cases by the aim of respecting the intention of the legislature that enacted the relevant provision. The legislature's meaning intention does not determine a jurisdiction in section 1 of the ECHR, but legislatures may—and, we suggest, typically do—have intentions other than their intentions to mean. The legislature may be presumed to have intended to leave it to the court to decide the extent of the jurisdiction using its best (normative) judgment. Thus, we think that it is possible to reconcile our claim that resolving legal indeterminacy in such cases is an interpretative activity with Endicott's observation of the "extravagant" degree to which "the law may leave matters" to be decided by judges and others.

In considering this matter, it may also be useful to think about the distinction between legal speech act content and the content of the law. We have argued elsewhere (Allott and Shaer submitted), expanding on Raz (2001) and others,[5] that these do come apart in at least some instances. One familiar way in which they can come apart is that in which the speech act content of the statute falls short of determining its legal content, as it arguably does in American First Amendment doctrine, where the text of this amendment refers only to Congress's lawmaking powers but the doctrine also "applies to judicially created defamation law" (Solum 2013, 480). Another is that in which a statute's legal content falls short of determining the content of the law, as it did in *Riggs v. Palmer* (1889), an American case in which the court decided that a murderer could not inherit from his victim, even though the relevant "local wills legislation was silent on the issue" (Holland and Webb 2003, 101). Arguably, this case is best understood as signalling that the content of the law was not fully determined by the meaning of the statute, since that would clash with the important principle of common law that a wrongdoer should not benefit from his own wrong.

The legal indeterminacies that Endicott points to might also be instances of a mismatch between utterance content and the content of the law, although their resolution is somewhat different from those just discussed. In both of the latter types of mismatch, the activity of the court can be seen as largely investigative. For example, in *Riggs v. Palmer* the content of the law, while fully determined neither by the speech act content of the relevant statute nor by the statute's legal content, was arguably determined by (supervened on) its combination with principles of common law. In Endicott's example of more purely creative activity by the court, the content of the law before the judgment does not seem to determine the content of the law after the judgment. The court, in setting out a jurisdiction, created new legal content, resolving the indeterminacy in the content of the law to at least the extent needed to give a verdict in the case.

We see this as an appropriate response by the court to the (literal) request from the parties to the case to resolve the problem at issue and to the figurative "standing request" from the legislature to resolve indeterminacies that it has intentionally created, to the extent necessary to determine each case, in a manner consistent with justice, equity, the common law, and so on. This accords with Endicott's claim that "the framers [of the ECHR] had not determined the jurisdiction at all"; however, it also offers a way to understand the task of resolving such an indeterminacy as part of an inferential process of determining what a court has been (as it were) "asked to do" in making a decision involving vague or general legal terms. From this perspective, the task of the judge when faced with such a legal indeterminacy is much like the task of the employee asked by the boss to choose the best candidate, as in an example discussed by Sorensen. To be sure, the encoded meaning of the phrase "the best candidate" does not determine a particular candidate. However, the employee cannot fulfill the task at hand without going beyond the phrase's linguistic meaning and, with the aid of whatever information is relevant, making a decision about who that "best candidate" is. Nevertheless, we are *not* claiming that the legislature, in enacting a provision of the nature of section 1 of the ECHR, makes a speech act of requesting a judge (or anyone else) to determine the jurisdiction. Rather, the court, in taking on the task of determining the jurisdiction, was respecting a metaintention of the legislature about how the speech act and legal content that it has enacted are to be treated.

We briefly consider two objections to our account of such cases. One is that it is a rather unsatisfactory answer to Sorensen's worry. While, according to our account, a court can sincerely find a defendant guilty in an "absolute borderline" case when its finding rests on a vague term whose extension is at issue, that is only because the court has fixed the extension of this term de novo (at least to the extent of determining a verdict in the case in hand). A defendant might rightly claim that he could not have known that he was guilty before the verdict was handed down. A more philosophically inclined defendant might further claim that, as a metaphysical matter, his guilt must have been indeterminate until the verdict—including (and crucially, one might argue) at the time of the conduct in question.

One response to this objection might be to point out that it is well established that judicial decisions have retrospective effect, in that a "court setting [a] new precedent" is not merely creating new law "from [the] moment" it hands down its decision but is instead "stating the law as it always has been" (Holland and Webb 2003, 137).[6] In this sense, then, the content of the law at any given time supervenes on the content not only of extant statutes and case law, but also of future case law. Admittedly, though, this supervenience claim might well be seen only as a useful fiction and is one to which we would not wish to commit ourselves in full metaphysical seriousness. Even assuming that the response is plausible, the defendant's epistemological objection would surely still have force.

Returning to the *Bankovic* example, we can see that it was impossible to know prior to the decision what extension the court would give to the occurrence of *jurisdiction* in section 1 of the ECHR. But that, we submit, is just the way that the law works in such cases. While not especially satisfactory, the alternatives to this kind of judicial creativity—such as specifying at enactment all extensions of vague terms in statutes, or not legislating in areas that require the use of vague terms—are infeasible, undesirable, or both.

A second objection to our account of judges' resolution of legislative indeterminacy is that the metaintentions of the legislature that we postulate are mysterious entities whose existence calls for considerable suspension of disbelief. What might likewise elicit skepticism is the use of the term "interpretation" in cases of the type that Endicott sets out, which might seem nothing more than a conventional fig leaf. We submit that a distinction between cases such as *Bankovic*, where a court acts properly in fixing an extension, and ones in which it acts improperly in doing so is at the least intuitively plausible. The much-discussed American case of *Smith v. United States* (1993) (see, e.g., Scalia 1997, 23–24, 116) is for many commentators an example of such improper adjudication. In that case, the majority decided that the phrase *use or carry a firearm* in the relevant statute had an extension that included a barter in which a gun was exchanged for drugs. Many commentators have agreed with Justice Scalia's dissenting opinion that the meaning of the phrase was in fact "to use a firearm as a weapon"—even if many (including us) might see this meaning as the relevant one simply because this is almost certainly what the legislature meant by the phrase and not because it was this phrase's "ordinary meaning." We would add that the majority was also wrong to think that the legislature had intended to leave the meaning open to judicial determination of this sort, at least on this dimension.[7] What is more, we think that a felicitous way to describe this intuitive difference between *Smith* and *Bankovic* is as a difference in the metaintentions of the legislature and the extent to which the court has complied with them.

3.2. So, What Is Adjudication After All?

In the previous section, we cast a skeptical eye on Endicott's claim that much of what is commonly placed under the rubric of "legal interpretation" is not in fact "interpretative" at all. What we argued for, instead, was a broader conception of the interpretative process involved in judicial decision-making. We argued that understanding the speech act content of the legislature is necessarily an interpretive activity, although not one that is necessarily reflective or occurrently conscious, and that this is consistent with a cognitively plausible account of verbal interaction more generally. On the other hand, we agreed with Endicott that some judicial rulings involve creative (rather than investigative) activity in determining whether some behavior falls within the extension of a vague term. But here, too, we argued that this activity should be regarded as genuinely interpretative, in the sense that the aim of the activity is to respect a legislature's intentions about the way that its laws will be interpreted and used (and thus intentions that must be discovered, or at least "intuited").

A point worth emphasizing, however, is that notwithstanding our skepticism about some of Endicott's claims, we think he has shed much-needed light on the complexity of adjudication and on the implausibility of the traditional picture of judging as essentially limited to interpreting the content of others' speech. The question that inevitably remains, though, is how this complexity is best characterized.

If we return to the definitions of "verdictive" given earlier, we can see these as pointing directly to some plausible candidates for description as the components of adjudication. Austin's (1962, 153) description is especially helpful here, since it lays out many of these components. We suggest that they include at least the following (which in practice may not reflect separate processes): (1) identifying the question or questions facing the court; (2) working out the utterance content of relevant statutes, court documents, and other legal texts; (3) assembling relevant evidence and reasons and making the relevance of each explicit; (4) reaching a decision about the question or questions in (1); and (5) making it the case that a new legal situation holds. One benefit of recognizing this complexity in adjudication is that it offers some insight into why, even though a verdictive does not (or not only) constitute an assertion but creates a new situation (as already noted), a court cannot justify a verdict simply "by citing the performative nature of [the judge's] declarations" (Sorensen 2001, 403). This is because it is component (3) of the adjudicative process that serves to justify the decision. This component normally culminates with the communication of the relevant evidence and reasons by "representative" speech acts—typically, assertions. It is often inappropriate for judges to simply write, say, "I would uphold this appeal"—that is, just producing the verdictive itself—without also stating their reasons for doing so.[8] The clearest example of this point is when a judge concurs with the lead opinion given by a colleague, since she could simply produce the verdictive but will usually say something about her reasons, even if it is just that she agrees with the lead opinion.

4. Conclusion

In this study, we have sought to show that legal speech is best seen not as a radically distinct verbal phenomenon but rather as one variety of verbal interaction, albeit with various distinctive properties that follow from the institutional nature and goals of the legal domain. We first sketched a general picture of verbal communication as essentially inferential, drawing on recent work in linguistic pragmatics that takes its inspiration from the work of Paul Grice. We then focussed on the complex activity of adjudication. This we analyzed in speech act terms as a "verdictive," explaining how this act encompasses a number of subactivities. In doing so, we paid particular attention to Endicott's (2012) claims about the "interpretative" and "noninterpretative" aspects of judging. Significantly, we rejected some specific claims of his regarding the "noninterpretative" nature of certain components of adjudication. We argued (1) that the general picture of verbal communication that we had sketched earlier implies that understanding the speech act content of the law is an interpretative, inferential activity; and (2) that a court creatively determining extensions of vague terms is also performing interpretation, if it is attempting to respect certain intentions of the legislature in doing so. However, we affirmed Endicott's insight that adjudication is a far richer activity than it is painted by the traditional views with which he took issue, according to which the judge's task is largely to follow the decisions of others. We agreed, instead, that judging may also involve far more "creative" activity.

Notes

1. We have defended these claims elsewhere (e.g. Allott 2013; Allott and Shaer, forthcoming; Allott and Shaer, submitted).

2. For more on the speech acts in legal speech, particularly the role of effectives, see Allott and Shaer (forthcoming).

3. On the availability of pragmatic inference, see Recanati (2004, chap. 3); Garcia-Carpintero (2001). On tacit but reconstructible inference more generally, see Grice (2001); Boghossian (2014, 2).

4. This discussion is based on Allott (2013).

5. Raz writes that "[t]he law is systemic, and each of its rules derives its meaning not only from the utterance that created it but from other parts of the law" (2001, 418).

6. This notion of judicial decisions as "retrospective" is well established in law, as its appearance in Holland and Webb (2003), a standard English text on legal rules, makes clear. Holland and Webb (2003, 137) go on to observe that "[t]his retrospective effect of precedents" was plainly signalled in the 1998 House of Lords case Kleinwort Benson Ltd v Lincoln City Council (1998). They also point to the significant consequences that may arise "when a higher court alters the law by overruling a line of established precedents." For example, "commercial contracts concluded on the old law are in danger of being open to a different interpretation from that intended when they were formed; so too property deals, licences, employment contracts and so on."

7. However, we do think the legislature had intentionally left the meaning of the vague terms *use (as a weapon)* and *firearm* open to judicial precisification. A court could properly consider (given a case that turns on it) whether, for example, paint guns or laboratory lasers are firearms for the purposes of the act and whether firing a gun as a signal counts as using it as a weapon.

8. In Canada, the duty of a judge trying a criminal case without a jury to give reasons for conviction or acquittal was established in law in the Supreme Court case R. v. Sheppard (2002). For discussion, see, e.g., Stewart (2009).

References

Allott, Nicholas Elwyn, and Benjamin Shaer. Forthcoming. "The Illocutionary Force of Laws."

——. Submitted. "In Defence of Inferential-Intentionalism about Legal Interpretation." In *The Pragmatic Turn in Law: Inference and Interpretation*, edited by Janet Giltrow and Dieter Stein. Berlin: De Gruyter Mouton.

Allott, Nicholas, and Textor, Mark. Submitted. "Lexical Modulation without Concepts." *Dialectica*.

Austin, John. L. 1962. *How to Do Things With Words*. Oxford: Clarendon Press.

Asgeirsson, Hrafn. 2013. "Vagueness and Power-Delegation in Law: A Reply to Sorensen." In *Current Legal Issues 15: Law and Language*, edited by Mark Freeman and Fiona Smith, 344–355. Oxford: Oxford University Press. http://papers.ssrn.com/abstract=2039900.

Bach, Kent. 1994. *Thought and Reference.* Oxford: Oxford University Press.

———. 2006. "The Top 10 Misconceptions about Implicature." In *Drawing the Boundaries of Meaning: Neo-Gricean Studies in Pragmatics and Semantics in Honor of Laurence R. Horn,* edited by Betty J. Birner and Gregory L. Ward, 21–30. Amsterdam: John Benjamins.

Bach, Kent, and Robert M. Harnish. 1979. *Linguistic Communication and Speech Acts.* Cambridge: MIT Press.

Boghossian, Paul. 2014. "What Is Inference?" *Philosophical Studies* 169:1–18.

Carston, Robyn. 2002. *Thoughts and Utterances: The Pragmatics of Explicit Communication.* Oxford: Blackwell.

———. 2010. "XIII-Metaphor: Ad Hoc Concepts, Literal Meaning and Mental Images." *Proceedings of the Aristotelian Society* 110 (3): 295–321.

———. 2012. "Word Meaning and Concept Expressed." *Linguistic Review* 29:607–23.

Chomsky, Noam. 2000. *New Horizons in the Study of Language and Mind.* Cambridge: Cambridge University Press.

Collins, John. 2011. *The Unity of Linguistic Meaning.* Oxford: Oxford University Press.

Dworkin, Ronald. 1997. "Comment." In *A Matter of Interpretation,* by Antonin Scalia, 115–28. Princeton: Princeton University Press.

Endicott, Timothy. 1994. "Putting Interpretation in Its Place." *Law and Philosophy* 13:451–79.

———. 2012. "Legal Interpretation." In *Routledge Companion to Philosophy of Law,* edited by Andrei Marmor, 109–122. Abingdon, UK: Routledge.

Garcia-Carpintero, Manuel. 2001. "Gricean Rational Reconstructions and the Semantics-Pragmatics Distinction." *Synthèse* 128:93–131.

Grice, H. Paul. 1957. "Meaning." *Philosophical Review* 66:377–88.

———. [1967] 1989. "Logic and Conversation: William James Lectures." In *Studies in the Way of Words,* 1–143. Cambridge: Harvard University Press.

———. 2001. *Aspects of Reason.* Oxford: Clarendon Press.

Holland, James A., and Julian S. Webb. 2003. *Learning Legal Rules: A Students' Guide to Legal Method and Reasoning.* 5th ed. Oxford: Oxford University Press.

Kahn, Paul W. 1999. *The Cultural Study of Law: Reconstructing Legal Scholarship.* Chicago: University of Chicago Press.

Laurence, Stephen, and Eric Margolis. 1999. "Concepts and Cognitive Science." In *Concepts: Core Readings,* edited by Eric Margolis and Stephen Laurence, 3–82. Cambridge: MIT Press.

Leben, Derek. 2015. "Neoclassical Concepts." *Mind & Language* 30:44–69.

Levin, Beth. 1993. *English Verb Classes and Alternations: A Preliminary Investigation.* Chicago: University of Chicago Press.

Levin, Beth, and Malka R. Hovav. 2005. *Argument Realization*. Cambridge: Cambridge University Press.

Marmor, Andrei. 2005. *Interpretation and Legal Theory*. 2nd ed. Oxford: Hart.

———. 2008. "The Pragmatics of Legal Language." *Ratio Juris* 21:423–52.

———. 2011. "Can the Law Imply More Than It Says? On Some Pragmatic Aspects of Strategic Speech." In *Philosophical Foundations of Language in the Law*, edited by Andrei Marmor and Scott Soames, 83–104. Oxford: Oxford University Press.

Mercier, Hugo, and Dan Sperber. 2009. "Intuitive and Reflective Inferences." In *In Two Minds: Dual Processes and Beyond*, edited by Jonathan S. B. T. Evans and Keith Frankish, 149–170. Oxford: Oxford University Press.

Nelson, Caleb. 2005. "What Is Textualism?" *Virginia Law Review* 91:347–418.

Pietroski, Paul M. 2010. "Concepts, Meanings, and Truth: First Nature, Second Nature, and Hard Work." *Mind & Language* 25:247–78.

Raz, Joseph. 2001. "Sorensen: Vagueness Has No Function in Law." *Legal Theory* 7:417–19.

Recanati, François. 2004. *Literal Meaning*. Cambridge: Cambridge University Press.

Scalia, Antonin. 1997. *A Matter of Interpretation: Federal Courts and the Law*. Princeton: Princeton University Press.

Searle, John R. 1976. "A Classification of Illocutionary Acts." *Language in Society* 5 (1): 1–23.

Shaer, Benjamin. 2013. "Toward a Cognitive Science of Legal Interpretation." In *Current Legal Issues 15: Law and Language*, edited by Mark Freeman and Fiona Smith, 259–91. Oxford: Oxford University Press.

Solum, Laurence. 2010. "The Interpretation-Construction Distinction." *Constitutional Commentary* 27:95–118.

———. 2013. "Communicative Content and Legal Content." *Notre Dame Law Review* 89:479–519.

Sorensen, Roy. 2001. "Vagueness Has No Function in Law." *Legal Theory* 7: 387–417.

Sperber, Dan, and Deirdre Wilson. 1986. *Relevance: Communication and Cognition*. 1st ed. Oxford: Blackwell.

Stewart, Hamish. 2009. "The Trial Judge's Duty to Give Reasons for Judgment in Criminal Cases." *Canadian Criminal Law Review* 14:19–35.

Sullivan, Ruth. 2008. *Sullivan on the Construction of Statutes*. 5th ed. Markham, ON: LexisNexis.

Tushnet, Mark. 2014. *Advanced Introduction to Comparative Constitutional Law*. Cheltenham, UK: Edward Elgar.

Wilson, Deirdre. 2011. "Relevance and the Interpretation of Literary Works." *UCL Working Papers in Linguistics* 23:69–80.

Wilson, Deirdre, and Dan Sperber. 2004. "Relevance Theory." In *The Handbook of Pragmatics*, edited by Laurence R. Horn and Gregory L. Ward, 607–32. Malden, MA: Blackwell.
Wittgenstein, Ludwig. 1953. *Philosophical Investigations*. Oxford: Blackwell.

Cases cited

Bankovic v. *Belgium* 52207/99, (2001) 11 B.H.R.C 435, [2001] Eur. Ct. H.R 890.
Kleinwort Benson Ltd. v. *Lincoln City Council*, [1998] 4 All E.R. 513.
Montreal (City) v *2952–1355 Québec Inc.*, [2005] 3 S.C.R. 141, 2005 SCC 62.
R. v. *Sheppard*, [2002] 1 S.C.R 869, 2002 SCC 26, 162 (Can.).
Riggs v. *Palmer*, 115 N.Y. 506 (1889).
Smith v. *United States*, 508 U.S. 223 (1993).

CHAPTER NINE

Deferentialism, Living Originalism, and the Constitution

Scott Soames

In this chapter, I will compare two recent versions of originalism—my own, which I call "deferentialism" (Soames 2013), and Jack Balkin's (2011) living originalism. After beginning with a brief summary of the leading theoretical ideas of the former, I will contrast those ideas with the conceptual apparatus provided by the latter. The final two sections of the chapter will illustrate the significance of conceptual differences between the two approaches to several constitutional test cases.

1. Leading Ideas of Deferentialism

Deferentialism articulates correctness criteria for the interpretation of legal texts by legally authorized judicial actors. The theory rests on three claims.

(1) The legal content of a statute or a provision of a written constitution *cannot* be identified with either the semantic content of the text or the legal or political rationale for its passage; it *can* be identified with what was said, asserted, or stipulated by lawmakers or ratifiers in passing or approving it.[1]

(2) In applying the law to the facts of a case, the legal duty of a judge is to reach the verdict determined by the stipulated content, unless (a) that content is vague and, as a result, it doesn't determine a definite verdict; or (b) the content, the surrounding law, and the facts of the case determine inconsistent verdicts; or (c) the contents and facts are inconsistent with the rationale of the

law, which is the chief publicly stated purpose that proponents of the law advanced to justify it.

(3) In cases of type (2a-c), the judicial authority must *make new law* by articulating a minimum change in existing law that maximizes the fulfillment of the
original rationale for the law.

Principle (1) identifies the content of a legal provision with what a reasonable person who understood the linguistic meanings of the words in
the text, the publicly available facts, the history of the lawmaking context, and the background of existing law into which the law in question
is expected to fit would take to have been asserted or stipulated by the
lawmaker in adopting the text. Sometimes the lawmaker is a legislative
body, sometimes it is an administrative rule-making body, sometimes it
is the chief executive issuing an executive order, and sometimes it is another judge, or court majority, whose written opinion modified a previous version of the law. What gives the assertive or stipulative speech acts
of these institutional actors the force of law is their position in the constitutionally based legal system that the populace as a whole acknowledges as authoritative. It not necessary that the populace itself possess
detailed and extensive knowledge of the contents of all the various laws
that are relevant to them, but it is necessary that the governed have access to that knowledge through the services of members of the legal pro-
fession to whom the asserted or stipulative contents of the laws are more
directly communicated.

Principle (2) covers cases in which vagueness or inconsistency leave
judicial authorities no choice but to modify existing legal content in
some way. Since courts are designed to mediate between the immense
and unforeseeable variety of possible behaviors, on the one hand, and
the legally codified general principles designed to regulate them, on the
other, judges are frequently required to precisify legal provisions in order to reach determinate decisions in cases in which the antecedent contents of those provisions neither determinately apply, nor determinately
fail to apply, to the special facts of the case. Inconsistency is also a constant concern. Since the body of laws in modern society is enormously
large and complex, the task of maintaining consistency is never-ending.
Typically the inconsistency is not generated by two laws that flatly contradict each other—so that no possible pattern of covered behavior
could conform to both—but rather by the combination of two of more
laws with some possible, but unanticipated, behavior. Since the range of

such behavior—which, if it occurred, would generate inconsistency—is without foreseeable bounds, no legislative process, no matter how careful, precludes the need for judicial resolutions of inconsistencies. The same can be said for inconsistencies between a law's content and its rationale that are generated by unanticipated circumstances following its implementation.

The point of principle (3) is to limit the scope of the authority of judges to legislate by requiring such judicial legislation to be maximally deferential to the original lawmakers. Judges are required to reach a decision by resolving vagueness and inconsistency in ways that balance two potentially competing values—minimizing changes in antecedent legal content and maximizing the rationale of the original lawmakers for adopting that content. In order for this principle to do its job, the rationale of a law must be understood to consist not of the aggregate of causally efficacious factors that motivated individual legislators to pass it, but rather of the chief reasons, publicly offered, to justify its adoption.

The Affordable Healthcare Act of 2010 is a case in point.[2] Among the motivators of individual members of Congress were political payoffs in the form of special benefits for their states or districts, political contributions from groups favoring and companies profiting from the act, and the desire to advance the fortunes of their party and the agenda of their president, plus an ideological commitment to expanding government control over the economy and introducing a more socialistic system of medicine. But none of these were part of the rationale of the legislation in the sense relevant to deferentialist jurisprudence. Instead, its rationale was (1) to expand health insurance among the previously uninsured without jeopardizing existing plans that the already insured were satisfied with; (2) to reduce the total amount the nation spends on health care without sacrificing quality; (3) to reduce the annual cost of health insurance and health care for most citizens, especially the poor, who would be subsidized; (4) to equalize access to health care while preserving free choice among health care providers; and (5) to make both health insurance and health care more reliably available by loosening their close connection with employment.[3]

When the rationale for a law is understood in this way, it is typically both public and knowable. Since recognizing that rationale need not involve endorsing it oneself, judges who are called upon to use it to modify the content of the law in resolving hard cases need not be put in the position of substituting their own normative and political judgments for those of the original legislators. This is crucial if the judiciary is to be genuinely deferential. There are, however, certain unpleasant realities about the nature of the rationale for a piece of legislation that must be clearly recognized for what they are, if judges are to appeal to legislative rationale in deferentialist adjudication.

One of these is that the publicly stated arguments advanced for a proposed law can be deceptive, sometimes deliberately so. The public values to be served by a piece of pending legislation are routinely exaggerated. Worse, sometimes supporters know perfectly well that the public values that must be invoked in order to pass the legislation will be subverted, in whole or in part, rather than served by its passage.[4] In short, the rationale for a law can be manipulated. Instead of closing their eyes to this, deferentialist judges should be alert for opportunities to use evidence of such manipulation to enhance the integrity of the democratic process. A law the rationale for which is contradicted by its content together with the facts arising from its implementation is for that very reason at risk of substantial judicial modification, or even invalidation.[5] In a judicial regime known to be deferentialist, legislators will realize this and will have an incentive *not* to pass laws the contents of which subvert the rationales offered for them. So, far from being a problem for deferentialism, this is a normative argument for it.

The kind of case just discussed must be sharply distinguished from a different sort of conflict between content and rationale. Sometimes supporters of legislation the rationale for which has been honestly presented are able to secure passage only by creating a loophole that wins the votes of certain interested parties at the cost of weakening or partly subverting the overarching rationale for the original version of the proposed law. Because in this case there is compromise without deception, the rationale for the resulting legal product must be understood to have been implicitly modified to accommodate the change in the content that was required for passage. A deferentialist judiciary will take this into account to ensure that the unamended version of the legislation that failed to win majority support is not later enacted by judicial rectification.[6]

Finally, there may be some cases in which a legislative majority is achieved and a bill is passed by groups of legislators the aims of which are so fragmented and difficult to aggregate that the shared common ground among them is minimal. In these cases, the overall rationale for the legislation will not be very substantial and the opportunity for subsequent judicial rectification of the content of the law will be limited. If such rectification is contemplated, the role of one of the two deferential-ist values to be maximized—the fulfillment of stated rationale—will be sharply diminished. As a result, judges will be more tightly constrained to make the minimum modification of existing content that allows a def-inite result to be reached. Since this is, arguably, a desirable outcome, neither deceptive rationales, compromised rationales, nor rationales that resist substantial aggregation create fundamental normative difficulties for deferentialism.

This is one of the factors that leads me to believe, as I have argued elsewhere, that deferentialism is normatively superior to, and descrip-tively more accurate than, its competitors (Soames 2013, 612–17). The descriptive claim is based on the separation of powers, which is rooted in American tradition, embedded in federal and state constitutions, and widely accepted today. The normative claim is that more expansive con-ceptions of the judiciary put too much legislative authority beyond the reach of democratically elected representatives and, in so doing, put the integrity and competence required for faithful judging at risk by invest-ing too much authority to change the law in those whose task is to impar-tially decide what its content is.

Deferentialism is a narrowly circumscribed theory of criteria govern-ing statutory and constitutional interpretation by American judges. Be-cause the same principles govern both, the differences between the two types of interpretation are due to differences between constitutions and statutes. Although some constitutional provisions are precise and deter-minate, others are sweeping generalizations couched in vague and ab-stract language. As a result, their application to new cases in unforeseen circumstances is often less than fully determinate, with judges called upon to modify their contents based on their similarly sweeping ratio-nales. By providing criteria for making such changes, deferentialism de-limits one important form of legitimate constitutional change outside the amendment process. But it is not a theory of all such change. The practices of key governmental actors—to initiate military action, to in-troduce vast new governmental agencies and institutions, to make recess appointments to fill vacancies that didn't occur *during* a recess, to make unilateral changes in legislation without congressional approval, and the like—can and sometimes have, when unchecked, adjusted constitutional boundaries. Such practices don't fall within the scope of deferentialism, except to the extent that courts may, and sometimes must, recognize the new constitutional content they generate.

The deferentialist conception of judicial modification of constitutional content is the natural consequence of four basic truths: (1) The Constitution contains sweeping principles the contents of which encompass both a determinate core and an indeterminate periphery; (2) to apply this content to new circumstances requires periodic adjustments of content; (3) making these adjustments is primarily the job of the Supreme Court; (4) because the court does *not* have the constitutional authority to act as an independent political body, the adjustments it makes must be aimed at preserving the core assertively stipulated contents of constitutional provisions to the maximum extent possible, while authorizing only those changes that further the fulfillment of the original rationales of constitutional provisions.[7]

2. How Living Originalism Contrasts with Deferentialism

Deferentialism's single-minded focus on the role of the judiciary contrasts with Balkin's living originalist theory, which provides no explicit criteria reserved for the judiciary in guiding its application of the Constitution to difficult cases. Instead, his general remarks are aimed at all political actors who seek to further the founding project launched by both the Declaration of Independence and the Constitution.[8] Despite this difference, the two theories both insist on what they call *fidelity to the Constitution*. Deferentialism requires fidelity to asserted contents and their original rationales. Living originalism requires fidelity to "original meanings" of constitutional passages, which, Balkin insists, neither determine nor are determined by the way the original framers expected those passages to apply in particular cases.

This terminological difference signals no practical difference between the two theories when what Balkin calls "constitutional rules"—that is, highly determinate passages—are concerned. Examples are "there are two houses of Congress," "each state has two senators," and "if no candidate receives a majority of the Electoral College, the President is determined by a vote in the House of Representatives, where each state gets a single vote; in similar circumstances the Vice President is determined by the Senate." When applied to these provisions, Balkin's *original meaning* and my *asserted content* yield equivalent results. This is significant. Balkin realizes that some "constitutional rules" may be neither normatively optimal nor even consistent with the overall democratic spirit of the Constitution—for example, rules that each state, no matter what size, is represented by two senators and that each has a single vote in the House to determine the president in case of an Electoral College tie. It's not hard to imagine arguments for changing these rules based on fairness, equality, or the need to bring our governing principles up to date. Yet, Balkin maintains, they can't be changed by judicial interpretation. Why not?

Because, he argues, the Constitution is the law, which, like other law, remains in force until repealed (Balkin 2011, 55). I agree. How, in a nation of laws not subject to explicit time limits, could it be otherwise? What about provisions Balkin calls "standards and principles"? Though subject to more indeterminacy than "rules," surely they too must have some core determinate content. Doesn't it deserve fidelity for the some reason? Although I think so, Balkin's answer is unclear. Addressing this point, he says:

> Sometimes it is difficult to produce a rule to cover a wide variety of future situations, and so a standard or principle must do. Thus, choosing a standard or principle normally means that adopters are delegating the task of application to later generations. . . . If adopters cannot use hardwired rules but do not want to delegate so much to future generations they can choose *historical* principles or *historical* standards. . . . For example, adopters can choose language like "Congress shall make no law abridging the freedom of speech *as understood at the time of the adoption of this Constitution*". . . . To be faithful to such a norm, later generations must ask how such a principle would apply according to the *understandings* of the previous time. Generally speaking . . . the U.S. Constitution does not use this type of language. And this fact is quite important to constitutional construction today. (Balkin 2011, 40; emphasis added on all except "historical")

Balkin's message is that because the Constitution doesn't use *historical* principles or standards, it delegates the determination of the legal contents of its principles and standards to later generations. To whom does it delegate?[9] Although his answer is "to all of us," surely, whatever is delegated to others, the court is the central locus of authority *to create law by applying constitutional principles*. Balkin sees the court as applying the *linguistic meanings* of constitutional texts. When the meaning hasn't changed, the court will apply what he calls their, rather than the framers', *understanding* of that meaning. It will, he says, "inevitably interpret according to contemporary 'meaning' in the sense of contemporary *applications* . . . . As a result, vague and abstract clauses will likely reflect *contemporary understandings* rather than *original understandings* . . . . [This] is consistent with the preservation of the original semantic meaning of enacted laws over time" (Balkin 2011, 43–44; emphasis added on " contemporary understandings" and "original understandings").

What are these things called *different understandings* of the same meaning? Perhaps they are *what is asserted or stipulated* by different uses of the same constitutional text. This would have two virtues. First, the asserted content of a use of a constitutional clause is what those who use it are committed to and what they intend to guide the actions of others—which is what we are after when the Constitution is used to stipulate what is permissible. Second, identifying interpretive *understandings* with asserted content fits our theoretical understanding of the relationship between meaning and assertion. It is now a commonplace in the study of language that the *linguistic meaning* of a sentence cannot, in general, be identified with what is asserted by literal uses of it.[10] Asserted content of a use of a sentence is the *joint* product of its linguistic meaning plus special circumstances of the context of use, including the shared presuppositions of the participants. This joint product is what one's linguistic performance commits one to and what knowledgeable hearers reasonably take one to be committed to. It is also what different parties jointly commit themselves to when they agree on a plan, sign a contract, or ratify a constitution. In the constitutional case, it is the law to which we must be faithful. But now there is a problem, for if the framers' *understanding* of the text is the assertively stipulated law to which we must be faithful, then Balkin is wrong in insisting that it is *not* the framers' *understanding*, but the *original linguistic meaning*, to which we must be faithful.

The problem is unavoidable as long as we recognize that what we must be faithful to is the law, that asserted content is the law because it is what the framers and ratifiers committed themselves to, and that this content can't, in general, be *the meaning of the text used to assert it*, because meaning is only one of two main factors determining content. Short of disputing this third, linguistic, point, the only way out for Balkin is to maintain that although the asserted content is what the framers and ratifiers agreed to, it is *not* the law to which we must be faithful. Rather, the linguistic meaning of the text is what must be preserved, even if the content of the agreement resulting from its original use conflicts with the content some political actors use the text to assert today. Against this, I maintain that what we care about are the *contents* of our agreements—the promises made and guarantees given—not the preservation of the semantic modalities originally used.

The chief problem with living originalism is that it lacks the analytic middle ground provided by *asserted content*, which stands between the unspecific linguistic meanings of abstract clauses and the over-specific policy expectations of political actors who use them. Realizing that expected applications are too specific to be touchstones of fidelity, Balkin equivocates. Sometimes his talk of *original meaning* tracks what is really asserted content; sometimes it tracks semantic meaning that only partially determines that content. Instances of the former give the impression that living originalism is a version of originalism.[11] Instances of the latter give the impression that it is also a version of living constitutionalism. This, I believe, is an illusion; no unequivocal theory is a version of both.

3. Application of the Two Theories to Particular Constitutional Cases

I will illustrate this by comparing deferentialism and living originalism on a few well-known constitutional issues. I begin with Balkin's suggestion that there is a lesson in the fact that the framers didn't use time-specific language like "Congress shall make no law abridging the freedom of speech *as understood at the time of the adoption of this Constitution*." The lesson, he seems to suggest, is that they intended to *delegate* to future generations the authority to protect all and only the speech and communication that *future generations think should be free*, whether or not the central freedoms presupposed by the founders and ratifiers are included in the protected category. Surely, that won't do.

Here is a portion of the First Amendment: "Congress shall make no law respecting an establishment of religion, or prohibiting the free exercise thereof; or abridging the freedom of speech, or of the press . . ." What is a law *respecting the establishment of religion*, and what is it to *abridge the freedom of speech or the press*? There is, I think, no case for identifying what was stipulated in ratifying the amendment with its linguistic meaning.[12] The First Amendment doesn't tell us that Congress shall make no law of any kind applying to a religious institution and no law restricting any form of speech. The key words are "establishment" and "abridging." Americans knew what an established state religion was because several states had tepid versions of one.[13] Hence the core asserted content of the establishment clause was that the federal government must not interfere with the established religions in any state, and that it must not set up an official national religion, or endow any sect with the trappings of one. This is what cannot be transgressed without constitutional amendment no matter what "new understandings" may arise from whatever religious revivals may lie in our future. The establishment clause doesn't dictate complete neutrality toward religion vs. nonreligion, or even among all religions (provided all are free to practice).[14] If some wish to guarantee such neutrality, they need to amend the Constitution.

As for freedom of speech and press, you can't abridge something that isn't already a reality. To abridge *War and Peace* is to truncate the original. To abridge the freedom of *speech* and of *the press* was, in 1791, to truncate the freedom to speak, write, communicate, publish, and disseminate information and opinion long recognized in England and America. It is not just that the ratifiers of the Constitution *expected* the federal government not to abridge those freedoms *for the foreseeable future*; abridging them is what they *stipulated* that the government can *never* do. Of course, speech and communication today, as well as ways of regulating them, include forms that didn't exist then. The questions for current interpretation are: (1) *Which new forms of communication belong to the category protected by the original asserted content of the First Amendment?* (2) *Which new forms of regulation fall under the category originally proscribed?* (3) *Which decisions about new forms that don't fall under categories included in the original assertive content of the First Amendment would best fulfill its original rationale—which was to protect important political, cultural, educational, commercial, moral, religious, and artistic communication?* Since there is indeterminacy here, the court has considerable authority to modify the content of First Amendment guarantees in the manner specified by deferentialism. But not anything goes.

Next consider the due process clause of the Fifth Amendment: *No person shall . . . be deprived of life, liberty or property without due process of law.* What does *without due process of law* mean? Its ordinary linguistic meaning is *without the process of law to which one is due.* But if that were the assertive content of the use of the clause, it would have added nothing to the processes of law guaranteed elsewhere in the Constitution. In fact, it added a guarantee that played an important role both in the run up to the American Revolution and in state governments after the Revolution. As Chapman and McConnell (2012) have shown, the term "due process of law" appears in 1354 British statute law, where it denotes the application of existing law by a judicial body—which was prescribed by the Magna Carta as a condition limiting the king's ability to deprive a subject of his rights. It occurs again with the same assertive content in the 1628 Petition of Right and in legal writings in Britain up through the American founding, when—following the Boston Tea Party—the so-called the "Intolerable Acts" imposed by Parliament in 1774 inflamed the colonies for, among other things, inflicting punishments *without trial*. Following the Revolution, Alexander Hamilton used the term in remarks made to New York State's General Assembly 1787 in arguing that ex post facto laws against loyalists violated "due process of law" by depriving them of property without benefit of a judicial proceeding.

This was the presupposed background that generated the core assertive content of the due process clause, which guarantees that no rights involving life, liberty, and property may be deprived without the protection of a judicial process. Among these rights are those explicitly mentioned in the Constitution, which can't be abrogated by legislation, and those traditional rights (to work, travel, raise a family, etc.) that can be regulated by legislative acts. As I have argued elsewhere, in this reading, the same deferentialist principle that invalidates the decision in *Lochner v. New York*[15] invalidates the decision in *Planned Parenthood of Southeastern Pennsylvania v. Casey*[16] (Soames 2013). In both cases, the justices of the Supreme Court impermissibly inserted their policy preferences into the assertive content of a clause restricted to safeguarding procedural rights.[17]

How and why does such judicial overreach occur? It began innocently with *Marbury v. Madison*, when the court ruled that Congress improperly granted authority *to the court itself* to issue writs beyond what is specified in the Constitution. The result of this ironic decision was that the court, in deference to its own limited authority under article 3 of the Constitution, resisted an essentially inconsequential congressional increase in its authority, thereby asserting an immensely greater authority to strike down acts of Congress nowhere explicitly asserted in the Constitution. Although this may sound suspect, it isn't. The logic of constitutional limits and guarantees requires a body, which can only be the Supreme Court, to judge when they have been violated. The same constitutional logic also requires that in adjusting the Constitution to new circumstances, the court must *not* make up new constitutional content on its own but must, to the maximum degree possible, *defer* to the Constitution. In the case of the due process clause this means that the court must not replace its original asserted content with the court's own contemporary *understanding* of *the process of law to which one is due.* Adjustments of the original content to resolve vagueness and inconsistency are justified to the extent that they fulfill its original rationale. But our system of the separation of powers grants no authority to unelected, ostensibly nonpolitical, justices to place their policy choices beyond the reach of the normal operation of representative government.

My chief worry about living originalism is that it invites such judicial overreach. It's not, I think, that Balkin is fond of judicially imposed policy. But that, I worry, is what he may be led to when *principles* and *standards* are involved. The problem is the false dichotomy drawn between semantic meaning, which is often underspecified, and what he calls "expected policy applications," which are highly specific. The problem is illustrated in his discussion of Justice Scalia.

> Justice Scalia agrees that we should interpret the Constitution according to *the original meaning of the text, not what the original draftsmen intended . . . .* But he insists that [content] . . . must be . . . applied in the same way . . . [it] would have been . . . applied when . . . [it was] adopted. As he puts it, the principle enacted in the Eighth Amendment *"is not a moral principle of 'cruelty' that philosophers can play with in the future, but rather the existing society's assessment of what is cruel. It means not . . . 'whatever may be considered cruel from one generation to the next, but what we consider cruel today [i.e. 1791]'; otherwise it would be no protection against the moral perceptions of a future, more brutal generation". . . .* Scalia's version of "original meaning" is not original meaning in my sense, but a more limited interpretive principle, "original expected application." Original expected application asks how people living at the time the text was adopted would have expected it would be applied using language in its ordinary sense (along with any legal terms of art). (Balkin 2011, 7; italics indicate Scalia's words)

Balkin criticizes Scalia for identifying *original meaning*, to which we must be faithful, with original expected applications, to which we need not be faithful. The criticism is correct to the extent that Scalia's rejection of original intention fails to distinguish what J. L. Austin (1975) called *perlocutionary intentions* (encompassing consequences one expects to follow one's speech act) from what he called *illocutionary intentions* (encompassing shared expectations one relies on to determine the content of one's speech act) (see also Soames 2011, 240–42). But Balkin's position is the mirror image of Scalia's and so is subject to a similar critique. Balkin is right to the extent that he maintains that original expected applications encompassed by the framers' perlocutionary intentions are not constitutive of constitutional content. But the critique of Scalia is incorrect to the extent that Balkin himself fails to distinguish the framers' illocutionary intentions (which encompass shared presuppositions that contribute to asserted content) from their perlocutionary intentions (which reflect mere policy expectations that don't contribute).

The significance of this distinction is illustrated by the Fourth and Eighth Amendments.

> *Fourth Amendment*: The right of the people to be secure in their persons, houses, papers, and effects against unreasonable searches and seizures shall not be violated . . .

> *Eighth Amendment*: Excessive bail shall not be required, nor excessive fines imposed, nor cruel and unusual punishments inflicted.

The key words are "unreasonable" in the Fourth Amendment and "excessive" and "cruel and unusual" in the Eighth. Because what counts as *unreasonable* varies across circumstances and times, the scope of constitutionally permitted searches and seizures may vary without changing the originally asserted content. Historical findings about those the founding generation deemed warranted may help us fix the weight *they* placed on personal privacy and security relative to other public values. This, in turn, may contribute to setting a lower bound below which the value of privacy and security can't be pushed by competing concerns. In this way, some of the founders' expected applications of the amendment may play an indirect and limited role in determining its content.

Analogous remarks apply to the Eighth Amendment prohibition of excessive bail, excessive fines, and cruel and unusual punishments. The asserted contents of the first two clauses prohibit bail and fines that are punitively out of proportion with the severity of the underlying charge or, in the case of bail, the amount needed to deter flight. The asserted content of the third clause forbids punishments that are cruel by virtue of being punitively out of proportion with the severity of the offense. The content of the amendment doesn't provide the scales by which offenses are ranked, which offenses are ranked where, or the scales and rankings of punishments. No doubt, historical research could provide information about which offenses were widely recognized in 1791 to be more serious than others and which punishments and fines for them were judged to be appropriately proportional and so not excessive, cruel, or unusual. This creates a constitutional presumption that contemporary punishments and fines for offenses that are reasonably taken to be comparable in seriousness to similar offenses at the time of the founding—murder and petty theft, perhaps—must, in order to pass constitutional muster, not be substantially *more punitive* than those for similar offenses were then. To this limited extent Scalia is right in affirming, and Balkin is wrong in denying, that prevailing historical standards at the time of the founding play some constitutive role in determining the original Eighth Amendment content to which we owe fidelity.

This is so despite the fact that the comparisons needed to arrive at defensible results in real cases are not algorithmic. Changing social circumstances can render facially similar offenses more or less serious now than before, while different punishment regimes plus increased knowledge of their deterrent effects and the long-term consequences for those subjected to them can lead to current applications that rightly differ from those expected by the founding generation. But, to the degree to which we recognize that the founders' *moral standards* concerning punishment *do* play a constitutive role in ruling out some possible punishments as *too punitive*, we must also recognize the burden they place on those today whose moral standards classify capital punishment as too extreme for any offense. The fact that many citizens share these changed standards may provide a reason *not* to impose that punishment. But it doesn't give the court grounds to find its continued use by some states to be unconstitutional.

These examples illustrate the deferentialist balance between fidelity to the Constitution and the authority of the Supreme Court to modify constitutional content when required by unanticipated circumstances. While deferentialism recognizes this authority, it places restrictive limits on it—so restrictive that some important decisions in recent decades don't pass muster (in the form they were originally rendered). This might seem to cause a conceptual problem. Since deferentialism views Supreme Court precedents on constitutional matters as generating real constitutional content, one might argue that we owe the same fealty to the new content that we once owed to the now superseded content. But how can that be? Surely, the original Constitution holds a privileged place in our jurisprudence, as the touchstone to which we must perennially return. By contrast, one might argue, it is a virtue of living originalism that it identifies the original meaning of constitutional text as that to which we always owe fealty, while demoting what it calls mere *understandings*, both original and those in Supreme Court precedents, to the status of temporary implementations that may be discarded when new circumstances prompt a change.[18] Thus, it may seem that living originalism does, whereas deferentialism does not, accord the original Constitution its proper pride of place.

Not so. A court precedent doesn't have the status of original constitutional content because its legitimacy is contingent on finding the application of that content in a case to require modifying it in accord with original rationale. When the court overturns an earlier precedent-setting decision, it must be shown either that the earlier decision failed to respect antecedent constitutional content and rationale or that new circumstances have arisen that make possible a resolution that better respects that content and rationale. Since this chain of justification stretches back to the Constitution, deferentialism properly accords it pride of place as the touchstone against which judicial decisions are evaluated. It succeeds because it correctly recognizes inherent limits on the court's authority to engage in constitutional construction.

As I have argued, I worry that living originalism doesn't consistently do so. This worry is qualified by the fact some of Balkin's most edifying discussions arrive at what are, for all intents and purposes, proper deferentialist results. I will close by recounting two cases.

4. Points of Potential Convergence

The first is his discussion of *the compact clause* of article 1, section 10 of the Constitution, which *is*, as I read it, sensitive to original asserted content and rationale. The compact clause says "[n]o State shall, without the Consent of Congress . . . enter into any Agreement or Compact with another State." Commenting on this, Balkin observes:

> The language seems to state a ban on all agreements between states with-
> out congressional consent. But such a rule . . . would be unwieldy, if not ab-
> surd; it would require Congress to pass on administrative or ministerial ar-
> rangements between states in which the federal government has no interest,
> and that pose no danger to the federal union. . . . Accordingly, the Supreme
> Court has always treated the compact clause as *stating a principle* . . . . [I]t . . .
> has held that the clause prevents combinations that increase the power of the
> states at the expense of the supremacy of the federal government. . . . Justice
> Field and later interpreters . . . *sought to understand the point of the text in
> order to understand what kind of constraint it creates. Treating the text as a
> hardwired rule was absurd*; therefore they assumed that the text was ambigu-
> ous and required construction. (Balkin 2011, 47–48; emphasis added)

Although the result is correct, the attempt to fit it into the *living originalist* framework is strained. The language of the clause is underspecified,
not ambiguous. This is common when phrases *some/any/no so-and-so*
are used, which often incorporate tacit restrictions on the subdomain of
so-and-so's quantified over. As in ordinary speech, the contribution to
assertive content made here by the use of the phrase "any agreement or
compact with another state" is determined by *the point* of its use in the
text, which is to prohibit agreements that diminish federal supremacy.
This isn't *constitutional construction*, which modifies original asserted
content in light of new facts. It is correct identification of what was asserted in a case in which asserted content is a function of more than linguistic meaning (see Soames 2009). The residual problem with Balkin's
otherwise insightful discussion of this clause is the mirror image of Scalia's otherwise insightful dissent in *Smith v. United States*, where, lacking
the analytical notion of *asserted content*, he wrongly identified it with the
ordinary linguistic meaning of the clause "uses a weapon" in a congressional statute (Soames 2013, 321–23). Here, lacking the same analytical
notion, Balkin wrongly identifies original asserted content with a *later
understanding* of *original linguistic meaning*. Fortunately, his final result
is not affected.

Balkin also gets *Brown v. Board of Education*[19] substantially right,
again for essentially deferentialist reasons. His discussion is important
both for its critique of McConnell's originalist defense of *Brown* and for
Balkin's identification of the *privileges or immunities clause* as the driver
of Fourteenth Amendment guarantees. Here is part of the Fourteenth
Amendment.

No state shall make or enforce any law which shall abridge the privileges or immunities of citizens of the United States; nor shall any state deprive any person of life liberty, or property, without due process of law; nor deny to any person within its jurisdiction the equal protection of the laws.

McConnell's (1995a, 1995b) originalist defense of *Brown* bases it on the equal protection clause, the congressional supporters of which, he argues, intended to outlaw racially segregated public schools. Balkin argues that this historical finding is not dispositive because McConnell conflates the framers' intended application of the text with its original meaning.

McConnell showed that in the years following the ratification of the Fourteenth Amendment, many . . . congressmen and senators who proposed . . . [it] argued for desegregation of schools in proposed federal legislation. . . . They supported this legislation on constitutional grounds, because they believed that segregated public schools violated the Fourteenth Amendment. . . . My point . . . is that . . . [McConnell's] research . . . is . . . unnecessary if the question is whether *Brown* is consistent with *original meaning* . . . . [He] thought that the best evidence of original meaning was evidence of original expected application. . . . [He] did not use evidence of original expected application by the *general public* and the *ratifiers* of the amendment—whom . . . [he] conceded probably strongly supported school segregation. Instead, he used evidence of original expected application by the *framers*. McConnell made his case for *original meaning* by making a case based on the *original intentions* of the framers. (Balkin 2011, 105; emphasis added; see also 226–27)

Apart from conflating *original assertive content* with *original meaning*, Balkin's critique of McConnell is correct. Assertion is not a solitary, but a social, act that involves coordinating the intentions and expectations of asserters and addressees. Because of this, the assertive contents of linguistic performances are not found solely in minds of the performers. What is asserted by a use of a text is what the performance commits the performers to, which is what knowledgeable addressees who understand the linguistic meaning of the text and are familiar with the contextual background reasonably take them to be committed to. Since it is questionable that either the general public or the ratifiers could be expected to take the Fourteenth Amendment to commit the country to banning racially segregated public schools, McConnell's finding that key congressional supporters intended it to do so does not show that its ratification established the unconstitutionality of school segregation.

Nevertheless *Brown* is deferentially justified. Balkin agrees that its chief justification lies in the equal protection clause, but much of what he says would support the claim that the privileges or immunities clause — which asserts that all citizens of the United States have rights deriving from their *national citizenship* that no state (after the Civil War) can infringe — might rightfully be viewed as a contributor. Although Balkin (2011, 192–93) calls this the *original meaning* of that clause, it is, I think, better characterized as its original asserted content. What were national rights involving public education in 1868? Since public education in America, including the territories as well as the states, was uneven, and not universally available, it is not obvious precisely what they were. Whether or not operating different and unequal schools in an area offering public schools was unconstitutional may very well have been arguable even then, even if the outcome may not be entirely clear. But whatever may be said of 1868, by 1954 changes in the general conditions of life and the role of government in the lives of citizens had removed any remaining doubt. The ubiquity and importance of systems of public education made it highly plausible that no class of citizens could be excluded from them. Since the so-called "separate but equal" systems to which African Americans were in some places confined were inherently unequal to majority systems, many descendants of those the plight of whom it was the rationale of the Fourteenth Amendment to address were unconstitutionally denied the rights of citizens. Thus, the result reached in *Brown* was deferentially correct.

So, although deferentialism and living originalism arise from different conceptions of constitutional interpretation and employ different analytic tools, they can be used to reach similar results in some important cases.[20] Nevertheless, I remain skeptical about how far this convergence can be pushed. Whereas Balkin sees and celebrates the delegation of judicial authority to alter the basic tenets of our constitutional system, I seek to minimize that delegation by restricting needed alternations to those that are maximally deferential to original asserted content and rationale. If determinate constitutional rules are sacrosanct, then, as I see it, the rationales for, and determinate parts of, the asserted contents of all constitutional provisions are similarly sacrosanct. That, in a nutshell, is deferentialism. It is also, I fear, what living originalism denies.

Notes

1. Saying, asserting, and stipulating are *speech acts*—or, in more technical philosophical terminology, *illocutionary acts*. Each involves taking a certain stance toward the representational content of the act. To say or assert that so-and-so is to commit oneself to its being true that so-and-so. To promise to do such-and-such is to commit oneself, often by asserting that one promises, to making it true that one does such and such. Stipulation is similar. For a proper authority to *stipulate* that, say, the speed limit on certain roads in California is 65 mph is for the authority to assert that the speed limit is 65 mph and for that very assertive act to be a, or the, crucial component in to making what is asserted true.

2. Patient Protection and Affordable Care Act, Pub. L. No. 111–148, 124 Stat. 119 (2010).

3. See U.S. Department of Health and Human Services, "In Focus: Health Disparities and the Affordable Care Act," http://www.healthcare.gov/news/factsheets/2010/07/ health-disparities.html (accessed Sept. 22, 2011).

4. The Affordable Care Act is a good example. Not only have (1–4) of the rationale just cited been contradicted by its implementation, but many of its supporters realized that they would be when arguing for its passage.

5. Again, the Affordable Care Act, which came close to being declared unconstitutional in *National Federation of Independent Business et al. v. Sebelius, Secretary of Health and Human Services, et al.*, 132 S. Ct. 2566 (2012), provides a case in point. After failing to secure justification, under either the commerce clause or the necessary and proper clause, for the act's individual mandate requiring citizens to buy health insurance, the majority agreed with Chief Justice Roberts that the mandate could be justified by reconstruing what had been characterized as a penalty imposed for violating it as a simple tax, justified by the tax clause, imposed on those who failed to buy insurance. Since it was politically important in passing the act that the mandate *not* be labeled by its supporters as a tax, we may conclude that *if* the mandate was not severable from the act, and *if* it was not justified by the commerce, or the necessary and proper, clauses, *then* the act's survival of depended *not* on bringing its legal content into conformity with the rationale used to secure its passage but on *increasing* the disparity between the two. Thus, Roberts's reasoning was not deferentially justifiable. Indeed, it looks even worse today than it did so when rendered on June 28, 2012, now that it has become clear that the elements of the rationale noted in the previous note have been shown to be duplicitous.

6. This answers a question raised by David Kaplan at the session on law and language at which this paper was presented on April 18, 2014, at the Pacific Division Meeting of the American Philosophical Association held in San Diego.

7. What happens when the assertive content is (relatively) clear, but the rationale is attenuated, anachronistic, or nonexistent? The Second Amendment is such a case. *A well, regulated militia, being necessary to the security of a free state, the right of the people to keep and bear arms, shall not be infringed.* Its content is given by the main clause, its rationale by the dependent clause. The content stipulates that the federal government can't impose a ban on guns and similar weapons. But it remains vague and subject to future precisification what counts as "arms" and what "infringing" on the right to bear them amounts to. The stated rationale provides guidance. Militias in 1791 were typically voluntary organizations of citizens armed to protect themselves, to keep order, to be available for military duty in emergencies when called up by the state, and even to guard against a tyrannical federal government. An argument can be made that this means that weapons reasonably serving similar functions today can be borne by citizens, subject to regulation, while other weapons, like guided missiles and atomic bombs, have no constitutional protection. Although this is reasonable, it could be countered that since there are no longer militias in the original sense, and hence no rationale for the asserted content to fulfill, that content can be disregarded as fulfilling no constitutional purpose. Since this too is not unreasonable, the issue is a gray area for deferentialism. I am inclined to think that the continued value of armed citizens capable of protecting themselves and others is a surviving remnant of the stated rationale, which, together with the priority of stated content over rationale, preserves the Second Amendment guarantee. See also Balkin (2011, 206–7), which discusses the place of the Second Amendment in the application of constitutional guarantees to the states and the changed view of its rationale in the minds of the framers and ratifiers of the Fourteenth Amendment in 1868.

8. See chapters 4 and 5 of Balkin (2011), including the references to the Declaration of Independence on pages 76 and 84. Whereas deferentialism seeks to specify the nature and limits of the *legal* authority and obligations of the judiciary in applying constitutional law, living originalism sees what Balkin calls "interpreting the Constitution" as a historical process of individual, group, and national self-definition that requires a normative attitude of "attachment" to the Constitution and "faith in the constitutional project, which is also faith in its redemption through history" (74).

9. Balkin's understanding of the open-endedness of constitutional interpretation, construed as involving the *delegation* of broad authority to future generations, is essentially connected to his picture, sketched in note 8 above, of constitutional interpretation as process of national self-definition requiring *faith* in future generations.

10. See chapter 7 of Soames 2010, which summarizes considerations advanced in the contemporary literature in support of the above thesis about the relation-

ship between meaning and assertion (even for sentences that do not contain obviously context-sensitive items like "I," "you," "today," "now," and "this"). See also Bach (1994); Neale (2007).

11. See the discussions of the compact clause, the commerce clause, and the privileges or immunities clause. The discussion of the necessary and proper clause also belongs here, though what is really going on may be a revision of asserted content to bring it in line with its rationale in the manner of the deferentialist principle (2c) above.

12. Balkin's (2011) discussion on pp. 204–5 of the "nonliteral" uses of "Congress," "speech," and "press" in the amendment doesn't, I believe, track nonliteral *meanings*. Instead, words are used with their ordinary meanings in a special context in which what is asserted goes beyond what the sentences containing them literally mean. The point is similar to cases in which metaphorical uses of words in sentences to express contents different from their literal meanings are often wrongly taken in literary criticism to be uses in which words and sentences have metaphorical *meanings*. The linguistic point is discussed in Soames (2009).

13. These varied in their exclusivity from "the Christian faith" (Delaware and Maryland) and "the Protestant faith" (New Hampshire, New Jersey, and South Carolina) to the Congregationalist Church (Connecticut and Massachusetts).

14. The matter has been muddied by the weight some interpreters give to Madison's support in Virginia's General Assembly from 1779 to 1786 of Jefferson's Bill for Establishing Religious Freedom—which enjoined a more robust separation of church and state. Madison's role in proposing and securing the adoption of the First Amendment suggest that he hoped it to be interpreted in this way. But the asserted content of the text is not determined by what a small number of its proposers and supporters intended. It is determined by what ratifiers plus reasonable and knowledgeable members of the general public understood the nation to be committed to by its adoption. The relationship between church and state established by passage of Jefferson's bill in Virginia was not typical of the other states, and the understanding of Jefferson and Madison about the proper relationship between the two was not the common one.

15. 198 U.S. 45 (1905).

16. 505 U.S. 833 (1992).

17. Since the clause is repeated in the Fourteenth Amendment, it applied to state action, which was at issue in these cases.

18. Balkin makes this point on pp. 50–58 in criticizing the view—espoused in Strauss (2010)—that our real constitution is a common law constitution of judicial and nonjudicial precedents and that we owe no special fealty to our written Constitution. In chapter 7 he balances this critique by siding with Strauss in criticizing originalists who don't recognize implicit constitutional changes that are sometimes ratified by the judiciary after being initiated by others. This criticism

of other originalists doesn't apply to deferentialism, which recognizes some constitutional change by means other than amendment or judicial decision.

19. 347 U.S. 483 (1954).

20. The same can be said about the perspectives of deferentialism and living originalism on a number of the issues involving the commerce clause and its expansive application in the last seventy-five years beyond narrow matters of trade, or even strictly economic matters (illuminatingly discussed in chapter 9 of *Living Originalism*). As before, the suggested convergence comes with the caveat that it is the *original asserted content* of the commerce clause that best plays the role of Balkin's (2011) *original meaning*. The necessary and proper clause, discussed on pp. 177–79, requires a related caveat. Although the clause empowers Congress *to do what it reasonably judges to be proper for the purpose of implementing the specifically granted powers*, more or less as Chief Justice Marshall thought, this interpretation is by no stretch of the imagination the *original meaning* of the words "The Congress shall have Power . . . to make all Laws which shall be necessary and proper for carrying into execution. . . ." It is not even obvious that the correct interpretation was *asserted* by the original use of the constitutional text, as opposed to being a revision of an unduly weak original assertion needed to achieve the clear *rationale* of the clause, which was to ensure that Congress could adopt reasonable means, consistent with other constitutional provisions, to achieve the ends it had been given the power to pursue.

References

Austin, J. L. 1975. *How to Do Things with Words*. Cambridge: Harvard University Press.

Bach, Kent. 1994, "Conversational Impliciture." *Mind and Language* 15:124–62.

Balkin, Jack M. 2011. *Living Originalism*. Cambridge: Harvard University Press.

Chapman, Nathan S., and Michael W. McConnell. 2012. "Due Process as Separation of Powers." *Yale Law Journal* 121:1672–807.

McConnell, Michael W. 1995a. "Originalism and the Desegregation Decisions." *Virginia Law Review* 81:947–1140.

———. 1995b. "The Originalist Justification for *Brown*: A Reply to Professor Klarman." *Virgina Law Review* 81:1937–55.

Neale, Stephen. 2007. "On Location." In *Situation Semantics: Essays on the Philosophy of John Perry*, edited by Michael O'Rourke and Corey Washington, 251–393. Cambridge: MIT Press.

Soames, Scott. 2009. "The Gap Between Meaning and Assertion: Why What We

Literally Say Often Differs from What Our Words Literally Mean." In *Philosophical Essays*, vol. I. Princeton: Princeton University Press.

———. 2010. *The Philosophy of Language*. Princeton: Princeton University Press.

———. 2011. "Toward a Theory of Legal Interpretation." *New York University of Law and Liberty* 6:231–59.

———. 2013. "Deferentialism: A Post-Originalist Theory of Legal Interpretation." *Fordham Law Review* 82:597–617. Reprinted in *Analytic Philosophy in America: And Other Historical and Contemporary Essays*, 320–41, Princeton: Princeton University Press, 2014.

Strauss, David. 2010. *The Living Constitution*. Oxford: Oxford University Press.

CHAPTER TEN

Deferentialism and Adjudication

Gideon Rosen[1]

1. Questions for a Theory of Adjudication

When a court is charged with reaching a verdict in a case, its first task, once the facts are clear, is to determine what the law is. In normal adjudication, the court identifies settled law and applies it to the facts to yield a verdict. When pertinent law is vague or indeterminate or conflicting, however, the court has a limited power to modify it so as to yield a determinate result.[2] In either case, the court has two distinguishable tasks: to identify settled law and then to reach a verdict, either by applying settled law or by modifying it and then applying it.

A theory of adjudication has two parts corresponding to these two judicial tasks. The first part—the theory of interpretation—is the bread and butter of traditional jurisprudence. It asks a metaphysical question—"How are the legal facts fixed or determined by acts of the legislature and other sources of law?"—and then a derivative epistemological question: "How should courts go about identifying these legal facts?" The second part is the theory of interstitial law making,[3] where the question is not so much a question of law as of political morality: "When courts are empowered to modify the law, how should they do so?"

Modern theories of adjudication mainly focus on cases in which the legal facts are grounded, to a significant degree, in explicit verbal acts whose express purpose is to make the law: statutes, constitutional provisions, administrative regulations, and the like. If there can be cases in which the law is fixed entirely by more diffuse "customs" or "practices," or by the natural law, they are not on the agenda. In these paradigm cases the basic question in the theory of interpretation is always this: What is the *legal content* or *legal effect* of an authoritative pronouncement? What difference does that pronouncement make to the legal facts?[4]

It is worth stressing that although it is common to call this a question of *interpretation*, the question, as posed, is not a linguistic question (Greenberg 2011). It is not a question about the meanings of words, or about what some person said or meant when he used some words. It is a question about the legal consequences of a speech act. We can think of the law in any given jurisdiction at any given time as determining a pair of sets (S_1, S_2), where S_1 includes the acts that are clearly legally permissible in J at t, and S_2 the acts that are clearly legally impermissible in J at t. The legal content of a provision is the difference it makes to this pair of sets: the acts it renders clearly legal or clearly illegal against the background of independently settled law. When courts seek to identify the legal content of a provision, this is what they're looking for.

If jurisprudence were a science, this part of it would consist in general principles—the *laws of legal effect*—that specify the legal content of an authoritative pronouncement as a function of its various linguistic, sociological, and normative features. This may be too much to hope for. However, it is not unreasonable to hope for an account of *which* features of a legal provision play a role in grounding its legal effects. Are the legal effects of a statute a simple function of its ordinary linguistic meaning? Do the actual intentions of legislators matter? If so, *which* intentions matter? Are the legal effects of a provision determined by the *semantic* intentions of the drafters (their intention to *mean* this or that by their words), or by their *illocutionary* intentions (their intention to *say* this or that), or by their *legal* intentions (their intention to change the law in certain ways)? Do normative facts about which legal rule would be best or most justifiable play a role in determining the legal content of an enactment or are the grounds of legal content wholly "positive"? And so forth.

Theorists sometimes write as if the answers to these questions, and the laws of legal effect more generally, are settled once and for all by the nature of law itself. But this seems to me to be quite wrong.[5] We could have a "textualist" legal regime in which the legal effect of a statute is determined (to the extent that it is determined) by its semantic meaning. But we could also have an intentionalist regime in which legal content is determined by the actual intentions of legislators—say, their intention to change the law in certain ways by means of the pronouncement—or a "hypothetical intentionalist" regime in which the legal content is determined by the intentions that it would be reasonable to impute to legislators on the basis of publicly available evidence. We could have a positivist regime in which legal content is always grounded in "descriptive" social facts, but we could also have a Dworkinian regime in which the legal effect of a pronouncement is determined by normative facts about which interpretation of the positive sources of law, including the new pronouncement, achieves the best balance between "fit" and overall justifiability (Rosen 2011). And so on.

Which regime we actually have is a matter of contingent fact. And this means that we face a good question at the metalevel: What makes it the case that we have one sort of regime rather than another? Are the laws of legal effect in any given community fixed entirely by positive social facts about how judges and other legal actors understand and apply the law? Or are they fixed in part by normative facts about which jurisprudential regime would be most justifiable? In any case, just as there is always a distinction between what this law is and what the law ought to be, there is always a distinction at the metalevel between the descriptive question, "What are the laws of legal effect in such and such a jurisdiction?," and the normative question: "What should the laws of legal effect be?"

Most developed conceptions of these laws of legal effect are *originalist* in the following bland sense: they hold that the legal effect of a given pronouncement—the difference it makes to the legal facts—is fixed when the pronouncement is made and that facts that ground this legal effect must therefore lie in the past light cone of the enactment. This is not to say that the legal content of a legal provision cannot change. The Civil Rights Act of 1964 was modified in 1972. It is rather to say that the legal content of *the Civil Rights Act of 1964*—a certain datable provision in the US Code—was fixed by facts that were in place when it was enacted.

This bland originalism can sound so bland as to be indisputable, but it is not a tautology. Our statement of the issue leaves room for views according to which the present day content of a law that was enacted at some point in the past is determined in part by intervening events that were not self-conscious acts of legislation. Suppose an ordinance prohibiting "vehicles in the park" is enacted at *t* and that it is initially indeterminate whether, say, motorized scooters are to count as "vehicles." Suppose further that over the years park officers develop a practice of issuing tickets to scooter operators—tickets that are routinely enforced by courts with no outcry from the public, despite ample publicity. It is not a contradiction or a conceptual error to say that the original ordinance now prohibits driving a Segway in the park, even if it did not when it was first enacted and even though no one set out to modify its content in the interim. Of course one might insist on calling even this view a form of "originalism" in the boring sense, on the ground that the small intervening decisions and episodes of acquiescence that ground the now-settled legal content of the ordinance collectively amount to a legislative act akin to the amendment of the Civil Rights Act in 1972. But this is artificial and unnecessary. It would be better to say that if post hoc events of this sort can modify the legal content of the original ordinance then originalism is false: the legal content of a provision is not fixed when it is made.[6] The abstract framework we've been discussing thus does not assume originalism. To the contrary, it is consistent with, and allows a clear statement of, the only sane version of the view that the law is a living thing.[7]

2. Deferentialism

Scott Soames's *deferentialism* is a theory of adjudication that seeks to answer most of the questions we have identified (Soames 2013; chapter 9, this volume). Its key tenets are as follows:

(1) The legal content of a statute or provision of a written constitution cannot be identified with either the semantic content of the text or the legal or political rationale for its passage; it *can* be identified with what was said, asserted, or stipulated by lawmakers or ratifiers in passing or approving it.

(2) In applying the law to the facts of a case, the legal duty of a judge is to reach the verdict determined by the stipulated content, unless (a) that content is vague and, as a result, doesn't determine a definite verdict, or (b) the content, surrounding law, and the facts of the case determine inconsistent verdicts, or (c) the contents and facts are inconsistent with the rationale for the law, which is the chief publicly stated purpose that proponents of the law advanced to justify it.

(3) In cases of type (2a-c), the judicial authority must *make new law* by articulating a minimum change to existing law that maximizes fulfillment of the original rationale for the law. (chapter 9, this volume)

Deferentialism is meant, first and foremost, as an account of the law as it actually is in the United States. Clause (1) specifies the actual "law of legal effect," as I have called it, privileging a notion central to speech act theory: what is *said, asserted, or stipulated* by means of an utterance. The remaining clauses specify the actual legal duties of judges in applying existing law (2) and making new law (3). But it is also meant as an account of how these aspects of the law ought to be, given a commitment to basic rule of law principles and the best version of the idea of separation of powers. In what follows, I focus mainly on Soames's descriptive claims. I have no doubt that deferentialist legal regimes are possible and that such a regime would be attractive in many ways. The questions I want to press mainly concern the question: Does deferentialism give a correct account of the laws of legal effect and the norms governing judicial lawmaking in the United States in the twenty-first century?

3. The Deferentialist Theory of Interstitial Lawmaking

The view's first distinctive claim—and its main philosophical innovation —is the suggestion that the legal content of an authoritative pronouncement is determined not by the linguistic meanings of the words and not by the actual purposes of the legislators, but by "what was said, asserted or stipulated" by lawmakers when they adopted the provision (chapter 9, this volume). The view thus sees the central question in the theory of interpretation as a problem not in semantics or psychology or normative political philosophy but in pragmatics, the theory of speech acts. I want to focus mainly on this aspect of the view. But I'll say a few words first about the theory of interstitial lawmaking that Soames builds on top of it.

The stipulated content of an enactment fixes the baseline for adjudication. This is the law to which judges owe fidelity. When it yields a verdict given the facts, the "legal duty" of a judge is to give that verdict—except when the stipulated content is "inconsistent with the rationale for the law," (2c) above, an exception to be considered shortly (chapter 9, this volume). When the stipulated content fails to yield a verdict, courts are obliged to modify the law minimally so as to "maximize fulfillment of the original rationale for the law" (ibid.). By "rationale" Soames means the official, publicly stated purpose of the provision as gleaned from the language of the provision itself ("A well-regulated militia being necessary . . ."), the legislative record, and other public materials that might be available to interpreters. This rationale is to be distinguished from the real motives and secret aspirations of lawmakers, which may be totally cynical or mercenary and which have no bearing on the law on Soames's account. It is a (possibly fictional) purpose that we impute to lawmakers on the basis of what they say and that points to some (putative) good to be achieved by means of the law. Soames notes that in many cases the rationale for a piece of legislation will be "thin." Lawmakers will have said many contradictory things about the purpose of the law, or not enough to render guidance. But where there is an identifiable rationale, deferentialism says that it should guide the court's modification of legal content.

The normative point of this requirement is familiar. It violates our constitutional conception of the separation of powers to allow unelected judges in their legislative role to substitute their values and purposes for those of the people and their elected representatives. So when the law must be sharpened, courts are obliged to implement the purposes that guided the original legislation (or, better, the public story about those purposes). The result is that at least in principle, judicial lawmaking should be a technical matter in which the judge's own values do not intrude, the question being, "Which minimal modification of existing law that resolves this case would do the best job of promoting the official purpose for which the law was enacted—a purpose that I, qua judge, need not share?"

For the most part deferentialism accords with the "standard view" of adjudication mentioned at the outset, according to which judges are obliged to apply settled law when it yields a verdict. There is an exception, however, in clause 2(c), which empowers judges to modify settled law when the verdict it requires is "inconsistent with the rationale for the law."[8] Soames gives an example of how this clause is meant to operate. Discussing Chief Justice Roberts's holding in *National Federation of Independent Businesses et al. v. Sebelius*,[9] that the individual mandate of the Affordable Care Act is constitutional as an exercise of Congress's taxing power, Soames writes:

> Since it was politically important in passing the act that the mandate *not* be labeled by its supporters as a tax, we may conclude that *if* the mandate was not severable from the act, and *if* it was not justified by the commerce or the necessary and proper clauses, *then* the act's survival depended, not on bring-

ing its legal content into conformity with the rationale used to secure its passage, but on increasing the disparity between the two. Thus Roberts' reasoning was not deferentially justifiable. (chapter 9, this volume)

The argument is compressed, but I take it to be this. The official rationale for the Affordable Care Act was not just to solve various problems
with the health insurance system in the United States but to do so *without imposing new taxes on individuals who choose not to buy insurance.*
If Roberts is right about the legal content of the act, however, the act imposes just such a tax. So even if the act, so interpreted, is constitutional
under the tax clause, it should be *modified* by the courts so as to involve
no such tax, but rather a mandate that individuals buy insurance or pay
a penalty. This must be done in order to bring the content of the act into
conformity with its stated rationale. So modified, however, the act is *unconstitutional*, at least by Roberts's lights, since Congress has no power
to impose such a mandate on his view. According to Soames, then, a
properly deferentialist adjudication of the issue would not give effect to
the actual legal content of the provision (which *would* pass constitutional
muster) but would rather modify that content and then reject the law as
unconstitutional.

This strikes me as tortured and, more importantly, as contrary to the
spirit of deferentialism. It is first of all inconsistent with a settled principle of constitutional interpretation according to which statutes are to be
construed to avoid clashes with the Constitution where fairly possible.[10]
More importantly, the underlying principle—that courts should modify
the legal content of a duly enacted statute when it clashes with extralegal dicta—is an invitation to exactly the sort of judicial meddling that
deferentialism mostly seeks to block. Suppose Congress enacts the "Put
Real Americans Back to Work Act" whose official rationale is to promote employment by reducing taxes on business but which in fact contains incentives for companies to automate production in ways that will
exacerbate unemployment. (Suppose the provision was inserted into the
bill without debate in response to input from the robot lobby.) When a
company buys a fleet of robots and claims the tax break, which is then
denied for whatever reason by the IRS, the only correct result on appeal is that given the clear language of the statute, the company is entitled to its tax break. Soames's clause 2(c) would license courts to say instead: "Since this part of the law is inconsistent with its official rationale,

we hereby modify the law as written by Congress so as to erase the tax break for automation. . . ." Whatever the merits of this sort of judicial revision, it doesn't sound like *deferentialist* adjudication to me.[11]

If we delete this clause as a friendly amendment, as I think we should, deferentialism emerges as a coherent theory of adjudication of a recognizably right-of-center sort (given prevailing political conditions). The view is doubly deferential: Courts must defer to the legislature when the law made by the legislature yields a verdict and to the legislature's official purposes when sharpening the law in hard cases. The normative rationale for this double deference is familiar:

> More expansive conceptions of the judiciary put too much legislative authority beyond the reach of democratically elected representatives and, in so doing, put the integrity and competence required for faithful judging at risk by investing too much authority to change the law in those whose task is to impartially decide what its content is. (chapter 9, this volume)

As noted above (note 1), a more pristine implementation of this idea is possible. Instead of authorizing courts to make law in hard cases, one might refer the case back to the legislature, or require "no verdict" on grounds of lenity, or allow courts to decide the case on equitable grounds in ways that do not change the law. So we might wonder whether the normative argument favors deferentialism over these purist alternatives. As a descriptive matter, however, Soames is surely right that courts in the United States have the power to sharpen law in hard cases. So if the question is "How should they use this power given that they have it?," deferentialism provides an answer.

4. The Pragmatic Turn: The Deferentialist Account of Legal Content

This preliminary discussion has focused on the deferentialist theory of interstitial lawmaking. But as noted above, the most distinctive philosophical claim in Soames's approach concerns the theory of interpretation. Soames's pragmatic turn is an intervention in a long-standing debate among originalists about which features of a legal enactment fix its legal content. Some writers regard "original textual meaning" as decisive, others point to the intentions or expectations of the drafters and ratifiers, and so on. Soames thinks that existing theories are missing a key concept, one that has been developed with real clarity only relatively recently by philosophers of language: the concept of *assertoric* or *stipulated content*.

The starting point is the uncontroversial observation that the content of an assertoric utterance—what the speaker *says* when he makes an assertion by uttering a sentence—cannot in general be identified with the linguistic meaning of the sentence uttered. If you ask me about the weather and I say, "It's raining," my assertion is the sort of thing that can be true or false, whereas the meaning of my sentence is not. Suppose I utter my sentence in New York, where it's raining, while you utter the same sentence in Los Angeles, where it isn't. Then *what I said* is true, whereas *what you said* is false, even though the sentences we uttered have the same linguistic meaning. If *semantics* aims to represent the linguistic meanings of linguistic expressions considered as repeatable types, then one of the central aims of *pragmatics* is to identify the rules or principles that determine the content of a concrete utterance— what is said, if the utterance is an assertion—as a function of the linguistic meanings of the sentence uttered and various features of the context in which the sentence is uttered. In this simple case, the meaning of "It's raining" might be given as a gappy "propositional matrix": *it is raining in* —— *at* ___, and the basic pragmatic rule might say that an assertoric utterance of a sentence of this sort, in a context with a designated place p and time t, expresses the fully specified, truth-evaluable proposition *it is raining in p at t*.

In this very simple case we have a formal rule that goes a long way toward determining the content of the utterance as a function of the meaning of the sentence uttered and overt features of the context of utterance.[12] In general, however, there is no simple rule for doing this. Suppose I open the refrigerator door and say, "There's no beer." What did I just say? Did I say that there is no beer anywhere in the universe? That's possible. If we've been having a philosophical conversation about the ontology of substances like water and gold—things allegedly designated by so-called "mass nouns"—then my remark may have been an assertion to the effect that *beer simply does not exist*. But of course it's more likely that what I said is that *there is no beer in the refrigerator*. Again, the linguistic meaning of the sentence "There's no beer" is the same in both cases, so we can't identify *what I said* with this thin meaning. The linguistic meaning is something like a function that takes us from a context of utterance in which a certain domain D is somehow salient, to the proposition that *there is no beer in D*. But in this case there's no mechanical rule for determining which domain is relevant, though any competent speaker will have no trouble in the vast run of cases.

The deferentialist theory of legal content identifies the legal content of an authoritative pronouncement with what the drafters and/or ratifiers *said or stipulated* when they enacted it. This can sound more like a tautology than like a substantive theory of legal content. It invites us to convert the question, "What is the legal effect of such and such a pronouncement?" into the question, "What did the legislature stipulate— i.e., prohibit or permit—when they enacted it?"[13] And it can be hard to hear a difference between the second question and the first. Other theories of interpretation seek to ground the legal content of a provision in manifestly prelegal facts: the linguistic meanings of words, the intentions of legislators, and so on. But on the face of it the deferentialist account simply *redescribes* the legal content of a provision as *what the legislature permitted or prohibited by enacting it*; and by itself this doesn't look like an account of *that in virtue of which* the provision has the legal content it has.

But of course the proposal is not tautological. One way to see this is to note that it entails originalism as we defined it earlier, the thesis that the legal content of a provision is settled when it is enacted (until it is deliberately revised). If we know anything about the pragmatic notion of *asserted or stipulated content*, we know that the assertoric content of an utterance is fixed at the time of utterance and can't be altered by subsequent events. So in saying that the legal content of a provision is fixed by what the drafters and ratifiers *said* when it was enacted, the deferentialist is ruling out the idea that the legal content of a provision might be a "living, evolving" thing.

The theory gains most of its substance from what Soames goes on to say about how the assertoric content of a legal provision is itself determined. One possible view in pragmatics holds that the assertoric content of a speech act—more generally, its illocutionary content, which determinate speech acts it accomplishes—is determined mainly by the actual communicative intentions of the speaker together with facts about the context. Soames's approach to the content of legal speech acts, by contrast, downplays the constitutive importance of the speaker's actual intentions in favor of a third-personal account.

In general, what a speaker uses a sentence S to assert or stipulate in a given context is, to a fair approximation, what a reasonable hearer or reader who knows the linguistic meaning of S, and is aware of all intersubjectively available features of the context of utterance, would rationally take the speaker's use of S to be intended to convey and commit the speaker to. In most standard linguistic communications, all parties know, and know they all know, the linguistic meaning of words and sentences used, plus the general purpose of the communication, and all relevant facts about what has previously been asserted and agreed upon. Because of this, what is asserted or stipulated can usually be identified with what the speaker means and what the hearers take the speaker to mean by the words used on that occasion. Applying this lesson to legal interpretation, the deferentialist looks for *what the lawmakers meant and what any reasonable person who understood the linguistic meanings of the words, the publicly available relevant facts, the recent history of the lawmaking context, and the background of existing law into which the new provision is expected to fit, would take them to have meant.* This—not the original linguistic meaning of the words they used—is the content of the law as enacted. (Soames 2013, 598)

The deferentialist theory of interpretation is thus an alternative, both to Scalia-style textualism—which privileges dictionary meaning—and to originalist views that ground legal content in what the framers/drafters in fact intended or expected their legislation to accomplish. The key constitutive facts are rather the various bits of publicly available evidence, including the linguistic meaning, on the basis of which a rational interpreter would attribute intentions to legislators. The view is thus a form of what is sometimes called "hypothetical intentionalism," [14] though it is more specific than standard versions of this approach, insisting that the relevant imputed intentions are those that bear on the assertoric or stipulative content of the legal speech act.[15]

Soames illustrates the view with the much discussed case of *Smith v. United States*,[16] in which the relevant federal statute mandates extra penalties for "any person who . . . uses or carries a firearm" in the course of drug trafficking. Smith had attempted to barter a machine gun for cocaine, so the question was whether this use of a firearm qualifies as the sort of use that triggers the extra penalties. The majority concluded that it did on the flat-footed ground that Smith has indisputably used a gun while committing his crime. Justice Scalia famously dissented on the ground that when we ask someone whether he has ever used a gun, the "ordinary meaning" of the question is, "Have you ever used a gun *as a weapon*?"[17] Soames thinks that Scalia got the right answer, though not quite for the right reason. The linguistic meaning of "use a firearm" is nonspecific. Sentences involving the phrase can be used to make a wide range of assertions. An assertoric utterance of "Smith used a gun when he bought the drugs" could be true in the case at hand. But the question is not "What do the words in the statute mean?" but rather, "What did Congress stipulate when it enacted them?," or, equivalently, "What would a reasonable interpreter familiar with the publicly available facts *take* Congress to have intended to stipulate when it enacted the statute?" And here Soames agrees with Scalia's substantive judgment: In enacting the statute, the legislature stipulated that extra penalties attach when a gun is used as a weapon.

Cases of this sort illustrate the virtues, but also some of the limitations, of the deferentialist approach to interpretation. Suppose a school imposes a dress code by posting signs that read: "On pain of expulsion, boys must wear a necktie while on school property." When Fred shows up with a necktie neatly threaded through the belt loops of his pants and is forthwith expelled, he protests by saying: "The rule *says* that boys must wear a tie, and I wore a tie, so I didn't break the rule." Somehow one suspects that Soames would be unsympathetic. Even though the linguistic meaning of the posted rule is consistent with Fred's interpretation of its legal content, any reasonable person acquainted with the linguistic and nonlinguistic facts would take the school officials to have intended to require that boys wear ties *around their necks* (in the usual way—no funny business). And yet it seems to me that by Soames's own lights, Fred has a (somewhat limited) point. Focus on the pragmatic question: Did school officials *say* that boys must wear ties around their necks? They may have intended to say this. They may have expected, reasonably enough, that their signs would communicate this intent. But did they *say* it? It's not dispositive to note that the linguistic meaning of the posted rule does not force this reading. As we've noted, what is said by means of an utterance often goes beyond the linguistic meaning of the sentence uttered. The point is rather that when a speech act is designed to establish a rule that people must comply with on pain of penalties, drafters are under considerable pressure to say exactly what they mean. Moreover a rational interpreter whose job it is to identify what was said will know this and will thus feel pressure to minimize the gap between the literal meaning of the words and what he takes the utterance to say or stipulate, and so to concede that school officials did not quite *say* that the required necktie must be worn around the neck. This provides the basis for a deferential-ist defense of the majority holding in *Smith*. To reinforce the point, think how odd it would be to *report* the content of the law at issue in that case by saying, "In the clause providing for special penalties, Congress said/ stipulated that anyone *using a handgun as a weapon* is subject to an ad-ditional five years in jail." One natural response to this report is to insist that, strictly speaking, Congress said no such thing.

These reflections suggest that there can be a gap between what a le-gal provision (literally) says and what a reasonable, informed inter-preter would take the drafters to have intended to permit or prohibit by means of it. And if these notions can come apart, the deferentialist faces a choice about which to privilege as the ground of legal content. To judge from his concrete judgments about cases, my sense is that, faced with this choice, Soames would privilege the latter. Or he might say: "In the perhaps slightly technical sense of the phrase that I have in mind, what the legislature *says or stipulates* always corresponds to what a rea-sonable interpreter would take them to have intended to permit or pro-hibit." But in that case the appeal to the theory of speech acts—to a the-oretically constrained notion of *what is said* drawn from the philosophy of language—is not really central to the view, which is best formulated explicitly in hypothetical intentionalist terms:

> The legal content of a provision is what a reasonable, informed interpreter would take the authors/ratifiers to have intended its legal content to be.

The main philosophical innovation in deferentialism does no essential work on this reconstruction, but we still have a form of originalism man-ifestly worth discussing.

Of course, when the view is formulated in this way it faces a well-known difficulty concerning the level of specificity at which the relevant hypothetical intentions are to operate.[18] Consider the holding of *Brown v. Board of Education*,[19] which Soames endorses as deferentially correct. The holding is that the Fourteenth Amendment prohibits states from es-tablishing racially segregated public schools. The *Brown* court's reason-ing relies mainly on the equal protection clause, which prohibits states from denying "equal protection of the laws" to anyone within their ju-risdictions. The court's argument is that given the social facts on the ground in the United States since the Civil War, segregated schools are "inherently unequal" and hence a violation of the constitutional guarantee of equal protection. And yet—as is now well known—the Congress that oversaw the process that culminated in the adoption of the Fourteenth Amendment operated a segregated school system in the District of Columbia and was certainly not taken at the time to have outlawed segregated schools operated by the states. Michael McConnell has shown that many *drafters* of the Fourteenth Amendment intended the equal protection guarantee to preclude any (potentially invidious) racial classification by the states (McConnell 1995). But on deferentialist grounds, the actual intentions and expectations of individual drafters are not dispositive.

> Assertive contents of linguistic performances are not found solely in the minds of the performers. What is asserted by a use of a text is what the performance commits the performers to, which is what knowledgeable addressees who understand the linguistic meaning of the text and are familiar with the contextual background reasonably take them to be committed to. Since it is questionable that either the general public nor the ratifiers expected the Fourteenth Amendment to commit the country to banning racially segregated schools, McConnell's finding that key congressional supporters intended it to do so does now show that its ratification established the unconstitutionality of school segregation. (chapter 9, this volume)

Soames goes on to defend *Brown* on deferentialist grounds as an application of the privileges or immunities clause of the Fourteenth Amendment, which precludes states from abridging the "privileges or immunities of citizens of the United States."

> [W]hatever may be said of 1868, by 1954 changes in the general conditions of life and the role of government in the lives of citizens had removed any remaining doubt. The ubiquity and importance of systems of public education had made it highly plausible that no class of citizens could be excluded from them. Since the so-called "separate but equal" systems to which African Americans were in some places confined were inherently unequal to majority systems, many descendants of those the plight of whom it was the rationale of the Fourteenth Amendment to address were unconstitutionally denied the rights of citizens. Thus the result reached in *Brown* was deferentially correct. (chapter 9, this volume)

As I understand it, the argument is this: A reasonable interpreter of the privileges or immunities clause would have taken it to prohibit state abridgment the rights of US citizens, not just as they happened to be in 1868 but as they might be at any time in the future. By 1954, the right to an (equal) public education was a right of US citizenship. Segregation in fact denies an equal public education to African Americans. So in 1954, de jure segregation was unconstitutional under the privileges or immunities clause.

One might wonder about the claim that the right to an equal public education qualifies as a right of US citizenship in the sense relevant to the provision. States are not obliged by federal law to run a system of public schools, after all. But let's set this issue aside and ask the question that deferentialism as I have interpreted it instructs us to ask about the legal content of the privileges or immunities clause of the Fourteenth Amendment. What would a reasonable, informed interpreter take the drafters/ratifiers to have intended to permit or prohibit by means of it? On the one hand such an interpreter would impute to the authors *the intention to prohibit states from abridging the privileges or immunities of US citizens, whatever they may happen to be.* On the other hand, she might impute to those same authors *the intention to permit segregation in public schools.* Now suppose that Soames is right that by 1954, at least, these intentions are not jointly satisfiable: to permit segregation is to abridge the (unenumerated) rights of citizens. It then follows that the deferentialist theory of *interpretation* yields no clear result in *Brown*. What the framers *said* or *stipulated*, when glossed as a matter of imputed hypothetical intentions, turns out be inconsistent given the facts.

Now of course this is consistent with claiming that *Brown* is deferentially correct. It is open to Soames to classify *Brown* as the sort of hard case that calls for judicial modification of the law and then to argue that the modification required by deferentialism—the minimal modification that maximizes fulfillment of the public rationale for the Fourteenth Amendment—forces the holding in *Brown* nonetheless. But this is a precarious basis on which to ratify *Brown*. We can imagine a deferentialist court reasoning rather differently: "We set aside our own moral and political judgments as irrelevant to the content of the law and notice that we can give full force to the intentions we reasonably impute to the framers of the Fourteenth Amendment by denying that access to equal public education is a right of US citizenship. These rights may include the civil rights protected in the nineteenth-century civil rights acts, and perhaps the rights enumerated in the first eight amendments; they may even include unenumerated rights that certainly would have been enumerated if there had been an issue about them, including the right to privacy, the right to marry, and so on. But public education has always been a matter for state and local government. So the minimal deferentialist modification of settled law to resolve the case is to see the Fourteenth Amendment as placing no substantive constraints on state education policy." This may not be a good argument in the end. Soames may be right about how the best deferentialist adjudication of the case would run. But one may be forgiven for thinking that this is a bit too close for comfort.

I should stress: the objection is not that the deferentialist gets the wrong answer in *Brown* and should therefore be cast into outer darkness, or even that he makes an easy case hard and thus misrepresents the jurisprudential facts. It is rather that like versions of originalism that emphasize the actual intentions or actual expectations of lawmakers, deferentialism risks giving weight to certain intentions—in this case, imputed intentions—that should have no weight at all. I think it makes no difference whether the drafters of the Fourteenth Amendment intended to permit segregated schools, or whether they are properly regarded as having so intended. What matters is their intention—real and expressed—to guarantee equal protection of the laws. Other theories of adjudication— Dworkin's, for example—do a better job of explaining why this should be (Dworkin 1988, 379–92). The Dworkinian instructs judges in hard cases to look to the real values the vague provisions of the constitution are designed to protect and to seek a result that presents the relevant legal materials, including past decisions of the court, as most justifiable as an attempt to advance those values. This is not the place to defend this approach to adjudication. So let me just record my sense that if we seek a *descriptively* adequate theory of adjudication—one that fits that actual practice or self-understanding of modern courts reasonably well—then this is a point at which deferentialism pinches.

5. Deferentialism and Substantive Due Process

Soames's most sustained discussion of the implications of deferentialism for constitutional interpretation takes up the line of cases beginning with *Lochner v. New York*[20] and running through *Meyer v. Nebraska*,[21]

Griswold v. Connecticut,[22] *Roe v. Wade,*[23] *Planned Parenthood v. Casey,*[24] and *Lawrence v. Texas.*[25] This line of cases sees the due process clause of the Fourteenth Amendment as protecting certain substantive individual rights, not enumerated elsewhere in the Constitution, against state infringement. Following Chapman and McConnell (2012), Soames argues that informed interpreters of the clause would have imputed to its authors a fairly specific intention to prohibit state executives and legislatures from discharging certain functions reserved for the judiciary. Courts can deprive individuals of "life, liberty and property," but only for the violation of a previously enacted law, and only subject to extensive procedural safeguards. According to Chapman and McConnell, contemporary interpreters of the due process clause of the Fifth Amendment took it to prohibit Congress and theexecutive from infringing these individual rights as a quasi-judicial penalty but to place no constraints on legislative action so long as it was appropriately *general* and *prospective.* The due process clause of the Fourteenth Amendment was intended to extend the same prohibitions to state governments, but again to place no substantive constraints on general and prospective legislation, or so an informed reader of the publicly available evidence would assume. So if the legal content of the due process clause is determined, as the deferentialist supposes, by the legal intentions that an interpreter of this sort would impute to the drafters and ratifiers, then every case in the substantive due process tradition was wrongly decided, at least insofar as the due process clause was essential to the argument. Soames argues further that the privileges or immunities clause cannot be enlisted to defend the court's holdings in these cases and so concludes, on deferentialist grounds, that the US Constitution does not protect a right to freedom of contract, or to marital privacy, or to "define one's own concept of existence"[26] against state infringement by general and prospective laws that amount to a reasonable exercise of the police power.

I'm not going to challenge Soames's reading of this history or his deferentialist analysis of the cases involving unenumerated rights. I would like to look instead at a line of cases beginning with *Gitlow v. New York*[27] and culminating recently in *McDonald v. Chicago*[28] that "incorporate" specific provisions of the Bill of Rights against the states. Before the Civil War it was settled law that the provisions of the Bill of Rights do not limit state action.[29] The Fourteenth Amendment was certainly designed to revise the relation between the federal Constitution and state action, but the nature of that revision was unclear from the start. In the *Slaughter-House Cases*[30] the court notoriously held that the privileges or immunities clause precludes states from infringing only a narrow range of legal rights created by the federal Constitution and deriving specifically from United States citizenship. When questions about the applicability of the Bill of Rights to the states arose in the nineteenth century, the argument was always quick and dismissive. Facing the question whether the Second Amendment right to keep and bear arms limited state action in *U. S. v. Cruikshank*,[31] the court held that since the right of bearing arms for a lawful purpose "is not in any manner dependent on [the Constitution] for its existence," the Second Amendment's declaration that it not be infringed "means no more than that it shall not be infringed by Congress."[32] In what is sometimes regarded as the first substantive decision applying a provision of the Bill of Rights against the states, the court held in *Chicago B. & Q.R. Co. v. Chicago*[33] that when state action amounts to a taking of property, compensation must be paid. It is however striking that this decision does not so much as mention the takings clause of the Fifth Amendment. Rather it interprets the due process clause of the *Fourteenth* Amendment as requiring compensation in its own right. The case is therefore dubiously read as an anticipation of the twentieth century's piecemeal incorporation of the Bill of Rights.

The first case that clearly merits this description is *Gitlow v. New York*,[34] which is standardly recognized as incorporating the First Amendment's protections of freedom of speech and of the press. But it is a curious document for this purpose. In addressing the case the court writes, "For present purposes we may and do assume that freedom of speech and of the press which are protected from abridgment by Congress by the First Amendment are among the personal rights and 'liberties' protected by the due process clause of the 14th Amendment from impairment by the States."[35] The court then goes on to argue that even given this assumption, Gitlow's conviction for disseminating revolutionary socialist literature is permissible as a reasonable limitation on this right given the state's interest in maintaining public order. The decision does not explicitly *endorse* this assumption. The incorporation of the First Amendment is assumed rather *for the sake of argument* (or so it seems), without any acknowledgment that a momentous constitutional question is at issue. Still the dissent by Holmes, joined by Brandeis, presupposes, without citation, that the "general principle of free speech . . . must be taken to be included in the Fourteenth Amendment, in view of the scope that has been given to the word 'liberty' there used."[36] All subsequent decisions then cite *Gitlow* as the case that established a substantive right to free speech protected from state infringement under the due process clause.

Fast forward to the most recent incorporation decision, *McDonald v. Chicago*,[37] which in the wake of *District of Columbia v. Heller*[38] announced that the Second Amendment right to keep and bear arms limits the states' power to regulate the private ownership of firearms. The key point for present purposes is that the court in *McDonald* takes it as settled law that the "liberty" protected by the due process clause of the Fourteenth Amendment includes every liberty protected by the first eight amendments insofar as it is "fundamental to our Nation's particular scheme of ordered liberty and system of justice."[39]

Is this line of cases deferentially justifiable? Presumably not. The argument that the protection of unenumerated rights cannot be deferentially justified under the due process clause applies equally to the incorporation of enumerated rights. If Chapman and McConnell are right about the publicly available facts, then on deferentialist grounds the legal content of the due process clause places no constraint on general, prospective legislation by the states, except insofar as it usurps the function of the judiciary. Since state laws limiting speech or private ownership of handguns do not do *that*, such laws cannot possibly be unconstitutional on due process grounds according to the deferentialist.

A more interesting question is whether incorporation can be deferentially justified under the privileges or immunities clause. It is universally acknowledged that the *Slaughterhouse Cases* were a travesty. As a deferentialist would put the point, any reasonable, informed interpreter of the privileges or immunities clause must impute to the framers and ratifiers an intention to protect a range of substantive rights from state infringement, including the various rights that Congress sought to protect by means of the Civil Rights Act of 1866. These include the right

to make and enforce contracts, to sue, be parties, and give evidence, inherit, purchase, lease, sell, hold, and convey real personal property, and to full and equal benefit of all laws and proceedings for the security of person and property . . . (14 Stat. 27–30)

But of course this list does not include the various substantive provisions of the Bill of Rights. It is now well established that the principal author of the Fourteenth Amendment, John Bingham, believed and intended that the amendment would incorporate the Bill of Rights, as did many of his contemporaries.[40] But it is equally beyond dispute that many contemporary interpreters of the Fourteenth Amendment, including the court majorities in the near contemporary *Slaughterhouse Cases* and *U. S. v. Cruikshank*, did not understand it in these terms.[41] Of course these actual intentions and imputations are not dispositive. According to the deferentialist, we are to ask what a reasonable, informed interpreter of the privileges or immunities clause would have taken the drafters and ratifiers to have intended to stipulate—permit or prohibit—by means of it. And here the only honest answer may be that such an interpreter would have imputed a range of intentions to the relevant legal actors. Soames does not say how the legal content of a provision is determined when there is diversity of this sort, but it is in the spirit of deferentialism to suppose that given such diversity, the clear legal content of the provision—the content to which courts owe fidelity—is the minimal content a reasonable interpreter would take all or most of the drafters and ratifiers to have intended to enact. When a committee drafts a rule that is susceptible of many interpretations and which was in fact understood in different ways, the only honest answer to the question "What did *they* assert or stipulate when they enacted it?" is to say: "While the individual committee members may have had many things in mind, considered collectively they only managed to assert *that* . . . ," where one simply repeats the language of the stipulation, preserving in one's report all of the vagueness that attaches to it. If this is right, then the correct deferentialist interpretation of the Fourteenth Amendment may well be that it is indeterminate whether the amendment incorporates the Bill of Rights against the states.

If we want to know whether the incorporation decisions are deferentially correct, we must therefore ask whether they are justifiable as interstitial legislation on deferentialist grounds. That means we have to ask whether the court in (say) *McDonald* was sharpening the law to fulfill the public rationale for the Fourteenth Amendment. But if the asserted *content* of the amendment is indeterminate at this crucial point, the public rationale will be equally unclear. There is a core rationale for the Fourteenth Amendment that no one disputes: the law aimed to prohibit states from applying the law unequally on the basis of race. But that simply doesn't settle whether the states can abridge the right to bear arms in a race-neutral way, and nothing in the public record surrounding the amendment yields a *shared* rationale that would settle this question one way or the other.

Needless to say, the facts may be clearer than I take them to be. But if this assessment is right then *McDonald* and many of the other incorporation decisions have the same status as the substantive due process decisions that protect unenumerated rights. They are certainly not justified on deferentialist grounds as applications or sharpenings of the due process clause of the Fourteenth Amendment, given Chapman and McConnell's account of the relevant history, and they are arguably unjustified as applications or sharpenings of the privileges or immunities clause.[42] If Americans want to protect an individual right to keep and bear arms against state action, they will have to amend the Constitution—or so deferentialism apparently entails.

6. Deferentialism and Judicial Error

Does this mean that the Second Amendment does not apply to the states—that under US law as it currently exists, New Jersey is in fact fully empowered to ban guns? If deferentialism entails this result, then whatever may be said for it as a view about how the laws of legal effect *ought* to be, it is implausible as a statement of these laws as they actually are. Whatever we may say about the law prior to 2010, as of 2010 the Second Amendment applies to the states. Any theory of US law that cannot say this is descriptively inadequate.

But as I shall now argue, the deferentialist *can* say this. The theory acknowledges that courts have lawmaking power and makes a strong claim about how that power *should* be wielded. But it says nothing about what happens when this moral/legal norm is violated. There are two sorts of case that deserve consideration:

(a) cases in which the law is in fact unsettled (so that the court's legitimate lawmaking power is triggered) but in which the court moves to sharpen the law in ways that cannot be deferentially justified;

(b) cases in which the law is in fact *settled*, though the court takes it to be unsettled and then moves to sharpen it.

To these may be added

(a) cases in which the Court does not *think of itself* as wielding lawmaking
power, but rather simply as interpreting and applying existing law, but where
in fact the court's good faith interpretation is inaccurate and would, if effective, amount to a revision in the law.

In all of these cases the court makes a mistake, at least according to the
deferentialist. The question is whether a mistake of this sort can change
the law.

Purist views on which judicial errors can never change the law have
a certain, well, purist appeal. Such views need not reject stare decisis
altogether. It is open to the deferentialist to say that just as courts are
obliged to apply settled law when it is grounded in the Constitution, duly
enacted statutes, and other deliberately legislative acts, so lower courts
are obliged to apply settled law when it is grounded in *legitimate* exercises of the lawmaking power of higher courts. But it is possible to maintain that when the courts have gotten it wrong, either by asserting power
that they did not possess, or exercising that power in violation of legal or
quasi-legal norms,[43] then whatever they and others may *take* the court to
have done, their act is not legally binding on anyone.

There is, however, something manifestly unrealistic about this sort of
purism. Such views will allow a vast gap between the law as it actually
is and the law as *everyone in the polity believes it to be*. One sometimes
hears this sort of thing from cranks who insist that since the ratification of the 1787 Constitution was illegitimate under the Articles of Con-
federation, the Constitution and everything that depends on it is null
and void. I hope we can agree that as a descriptive matter, this is simply wrong, even if the original historical claim is true. Everyone should
agree, in other words, that changes in practice and understanding that
do not quite accord with settled legal procedures can change the law, and
often do. The procedural irregularities that led to the court's astonishing
power grab in *Marbury v. Madison*[44] may have been questionable once,
but it is now a legal fact that the Supreme Court has the power of judicial
review. The question for a theory of the grounds of law is not *whether*
law can change in these ways but *when*.[45]

For what it's worth, it would be awkward for the deferentialist to deny
this. Our federal Constitution is officially one of enumerated powers, so
an interpretation of the structural parts of the constitution that gives unenumerated powers to a branch of the federal government is immediately suspect on deferentialist grounds. But deferentialism is premised

on the assumption that the Supreme Court has the unenumerated power to modify the law when it is vague or indeterminate or conflicting— a power claimed (or grabbed) in *Marbury v. Madison*.[46] Since no one should deny that the court has had this power ever since, no one should deny that judicial acts that flout deferentialist strictures can change the law.[47]

I won't attempt to say when exactly this sort of legal change occurs, but a sufficient condition is clear enough. When the court (or some other branch) announces or presupposes that some statute or constitutional provision has a certain content and proceeds to act accordingly, and when that interpretation is eventually accepted by the other branches of the government and by most citizens who bother with such things, and when the interpretation becomes entrenched, both in the sense that other parts of the law are organized around it and in the sense that people have come to rely on it, and when the law as reinterpreted is defensible as an expression of entrenched legal values, then the interpretation modifies the content of the law and so changes the law, even if it was not deferentially justifiable to begin with. Any deferentialist who thinks that the key provisions of the Bill of Rights have been incorporated against the states should accept some view of this sort.

There are, of course, two ways to formulate this thought. Proponents of the "living constitution" will say that these entrenched (mis)interpretations *change the legal content of the constitutional and statutory texts they interpret*. This need not be put as the confused claim that events in 2010 can change the *semantic meaning* or the *assertoric content* of a sentence first inscribed in 1868. It would rather be the fully intelligible claim that the *legal content* or *legal effect* of the due process clause, for example, is different now from what it was then, thanks to a tradition of interpretation and construction that satisfies the conditions laid out above. Of course the deferentialist cannot say this, since he thinks that the legal content of a provision is its assertoric content, which has to be fixed at the time of utterance. But the deferentialist can say what amounts for all practical purposes to the same thing, viz., that the 1868 due process clause has been unwittingly *amended* by the tradition of misinterpretation and entrenchment. Since a deferentialist judge seeks to interpret and apply *the law as it is*, not the *law as it was prior to amendment*, he can say that it is this amended due process clause to which he owes fidelity.

But if this is possible, there is nothing in deferentialism to rule out the

possibility that the court's substantive due process decisions announc-
ing *unenumerated* rights from *Meyer v. Nebraska* to *Lawrence v. Texas*
have similarly amended the law, so that even if some of the early decisions in this line of cases were deferentially incorrect, a suitably deferential judge may maintain that whatever may have been the case in 1868,
the Fourteenth Amendment now protects a right to privacy, for example.
The same may be said for many of the other radical, mostly liberal inno-
vations in twentieth-centurys constitutional adjudication, including the
New Deal construal of the commerce clause as a grant of massive regulatory power to the federal government.

7. Conclusion

The case for deferentialism is the case for a distinctive form of judicial
restraint. In normal adjudication, the deferentialist judge seeks to apply
the law made by the legislature, the content of which is fixed not by the
linguistic meaning of the legal text, and not by the intended downstream
consequences of the enactment, but by what the legislators *said* or *stipulated* when they laid it down. I have suggested that we should identify
this stipulated content with the content of certain intentions that an informed interpreter would impute to the authors of the law. The framers
and ratifiers of (say) the Fourteenth Amendment may have any number
of long term goals, and any number of beliefs about the consequences of
their legislative act. But according to the deferentialist, as I have interpreted the view, these real intentions and expectations are irrelevant. If
we want to know the legal content of the due process clause, we should
ask: What would an interpreter, apprised of the relevant history and context, take the framers and ratifiers to have intended the legal effect of the
provision to be?

In many cases this question will have a clear enough answer to assign determinate content to the law. On the face of it, at least, the deferentialist approach is incompatible with the Supreme Court's substantive due process jurisprudence. Not only does the due process clause
fail to protect sweeping unenumerated rights like the right to privacy,
as Soames argues; it fails to protect the enumerated rights in the Bill
of Rights against state infringement, or so I have argued. It is a harder
question whether these rights are incorporated against the states by the
privileges or immunities clause. In that case the deferentialist instructs

to ask whether an informed interpreter would take the framers and ratifiers to have intended the clause to incorporate the Bill of Rights. My
tentative view is that the deferentialist should regard this as a hard question, and perhaps as a question for which there is no determinately correct answer.

If deferentialism entails that for this reason, there is no clear fact as
to whether (say) the Second Amendment applies to the states in 2016, it
would be mistaken as a descriptive matter. Given the court's holding in
McDonald, that legal question is now settled. The deferentialist can endorse this result in two ways. He can regard the court's holding in *Mc-
Donald* and similar incorporation cases as exercises of the court's interstitial lawmaking power. In that case there will still be a real question
about whether these decisions are deferentially justifiable, since deferentialism requires courts to seek the *minimal* modification of existing
law that furthers the explicit rationale for the provision they are interpreting. Our cursory glance at the history surrounding the Fourteenth
Amendment suggests that it is at best unclear whether the incorporation cases can be justified on these grounds. The alternative is to hold
that even if the early incorporation decisions, like *Gitlow*, were deferentially incorrect, a century later it has somehow become settled law that
the due process clause incorporates the Bill of Rights against the states.
This is consistent with the letter of the deferentialist view of law, provided the deferentialist analogizes the early incorporation decisions to
(perhaps unwitting) amendments to previously settled law. If that is possible, then the law to which the deferentialist judge owes fidelity is not
the Fourteenth Amendment of 1868 but the Fourteenth Amendment as
modified by the Supreme Court over the past 150 years. A deferentialist
who takes this view can make sense of the indisputable facts of US law,
but then the view is much closer to "living constitutionalism" than its
proponents might allow.

The crucial open question is how a broadly deferentialist theory of
adjudication should understand the legal effect of deferentially *mistaken*
decisions of the past. If these decisions can change the legal content of a
statute or a constitutional provision by in effect amending it, then deferentialism counsels deference not to the *original* enactment but to the enactment as modified by the blunders of judges down through the years.
Deferentialism can still counsel restraint, inviting judges to curb their
enthusiasm for self-conscious modifications of the law guided by their
own principles. And yet it must allow that the law to which the deferen-

tialist judge owes his or her allegiance has often been made—and perhaps made well—by judges who were *not* exercising the restraint that deferentialism requires of them.

Notes

1. I am grateful to all of the participants in the conference on Inference, Intention, and Ordinary Meaning at McGeorge School of Law in 2015, where this material was first presented, and to Sherif Girgis, Alex Guerrero, Paul Gowder, and Larry Solan for very helpful comments. This paper was drafted in the spring of 2015 when I was a visitor in the School of Social Sciences at the Institute for Advanced Study in Princeton, NJ. I would like to thank the faculty and staff of the school for their supererogatory hospitality.

2. It is inevitable that settled law will sometimes be vague or indeterminate (see Dworkin 1975). But it is not inevitable that courts should have the power to modify the law to fill such gaps. In principle hard cases could be referred back to the legislature, or resolved by a rule of "lenity" that forces a verdict for the defendant when pertinent law is vague, or resolved on equitable grounds that do not create a precedent and so do not change the law.

It is nonetheless indisputable that courts have this gap-filling legislative power in the United States, and that raises a puzzle for any theorist who thinks that in our system, at any rate, the basic legal facts, including the powers of the branches of government, must be grounded in explicitly enacted law and ultimately in the Constitution. Nothing in article 3 supports the idea that courts have legislative power (or the power of judicial review, which is a separate matter). Any theorist who holds that courts have the legal power to modify the law must concede that some legal powers—hence some legal facts—are not grounded in explicit legislation.

If such a theorist is pressed to specify the facts in virtue of which courts have this power to modify the law, the answer can only be some combination of familiar ideas: courts have this power because (a) it is good that they should have it, since other ways of sharpening the law are cumbersome or otherwise normatively disfavored; and/or (b) a long-established practice of judicial lawmaking exists and somehow suffices to confer this power on the judicial branch. This will be important in section 5 when we seek to determine the limits of the judicial lawmaking power according to the deferentialist.

3. Hart's phrase (Hart 1994, 259), also called "construction" (Whittington 1999) and "rectification" (chapter 9, this volume).

4. A *legal fact*, as I use the term, is a true proposition of law, i.e., a true proposition of the form: *It is the law in jurisdiction J at time t that p.*

5. In saying this I do not dispute Solum's claim that the determinants of *semantic meaning* are settled once and for all by the nature of semantic meaning, and not by contingent considerations of politics or policy (Solum 2008). My claim is that even if the determinants of semantics meaning are fixed by the nature of meaning, the determinants of *legal effect* are not.

6. Since most self-styled originalists will concede that postenactment judicial decisions can modify the legal effect of a provision, the present framework requires the originalist to assimilate these decisions to the sort of deliberate legislative modification one sees in the amendments to the Civil Rights Act. This does not strike me as artificial. Even if a judge does not see herself as making law when she (re)states the legal content of a provision, she is fully aware of the role of stare decisis and hence of the fact that her act has consequences for the content of the law. The totally unselfconscious "modification" of the law mentioned in the text strikes me as quite different. Thanks to Sherif Girgis on this point.

7. To reiterate: The relevant antioriginalist thesis is not that the *meaning* or *asserted content* of a provision can change after it has been enacted, but rather that the *legal effect* of a provision—the difference it makes to what the law is—can change post hoc.

8. Thanks to Alex Guerrero for discussion of this point.

9. 132 S. Ct. 2566 (2012).

10. What is sometimes called the doctrine of "constitutional doubt" requires courts to construe a statute, "if fairly possible, so as to avoid not only the conclusion that it is unconstitutional, but also grave doubts upon that score." *United States v. Jin Fuey Moy* 241 U.S. 394, 419 (1916), cited in Kim (2008, 21).

11. At one point Soames remarks that the sort of conflict between content and rationale that would trigger revision under clause 2(c) must be "sharply distinguished from a different sort of conflict between content and rationale."

> Sometimes supporters of legislation the rationale for which has been honestly presented are able to secure passage only by creating a loophole that wins the votes of certain interested parties at the cost of weakening or partly subverting the overarching rationale for the original version of the proposed law. Because in this case there is compromise without deception, the rationale for the resulting legal product must be understood to have been implicitly modified to accommodate the change in content that was required for passage. (chapter 9, this volume)

So we must ask whether my imagined case involves "implicit" modification of the stated rationale. What is the test for this? My case involves neither compromise nor deception, so it's not exactly the sort of case Soames has in mind. But suppose we say that my case does involve "implicit modification of the stated rationale," so that judicial modification is not licensed by clause 2(c). Why not say the same for the Affordable Care Act? Soames's idea is that the stated rationale must be held fixed (and the content of the law adjusted if necessary) when it was part of a deceptive political maneuvering designed to secure passage of the bill. But then the inquiry courts must undertake in order to determine whether judicial modification is warranted under clause 2(c) is the sort of inquiry that courts are rightly loathe to undertake: an inquiry into the sincerity of legislators.

As a test case we might consider the various recently enacted state laws that require doctors at abortion clinics to have admitting privileges at local hospitals, ostensibly on grounds of public health, or the various voter ID laws that are officially designed to minimize voter fraud. These public rationales are presumably deceptive (though no one is fooled). The real rationales are to limit abortions and to discourage minority voting. Should a deferentialist judge applying such laws *modify their contents so as to bring them into line with their stated rationales*? That seems like an invitation to exactly the sort of judicial interference in legislation that deferentialism is concerned to avoid. Since these laws are perfectly clear on their face, a deferential court should enforce them as written (questions of constitutionality aside). It is bad enough for courts to look to legislative history when the language of the statute is clear; it is worse to look to legislative history with an eye to distinguishing genuine from sham purposes. A deferentialist, it seems to me, should want nothing to do with this.

12. Of course the "formal" rule given here is wrong. If we're in New York talking about London, and you ask about the weather, my utterance of "It's raining" might express the proposition that it's raining in London. So even the relatively simple cases are not so simple.

13. I hope it's a harmless stylistic switch to paraphrase Soames's appeal to "what the legislature *stipulated*" as "what the legislature *permitted or prohibited*." Permitting and prohibiting are stipulative speech acts, and in most of the relevant legal contexts, the only relevant stipulations will be either permissions or prohibitions. A more general treatment would acknowledge legal stipulations that don't quite fit this mold: grants of power, for example.

14. This term is not in wide currency in legal theory, but it's a standard "ism" in the theory of literary interpretation (see, e.g., Levinson 2006).

15. To be fair, Soames does not say what happens when there is a clash between what legislators in fact intended to stipulate and the stipulative intentions that a reasonable interpreter would attribute to them, so I'm guessing when I say that in his view, the real determinant of legal content is the latter rather than the former. The simplest cases to test the question will involve drafting errors that go unnoticed by legislators but which no third-party interpreter would recognize as such. Suppose the text for a complex drug law specifies aggravated penalties for people caught with (say) "$1,000 worth of cocaine," when in fact the drafters meant to write "$10,000." The natural thing to say in such a case is that while the legislature *meant to say* that special penalties attach when the deal involves

$10,000 worth of cocaine, what they *in fact said*—or *stipulated*—is that penalties attach when $1,000 worth of cocaine are involved. This is by analogy with ordinary slips of the tongue, in which a gap opens up between *what the speaker says* and *what he intends to say*. Since Soames identifies the legal content of a provision with *what the drafters said,* as opposed to *what they tried or intended to say,* I take him to privilege the interpretation of informed third parties and to assign no constitutive role to the actual intentions of the drafters.

16. 508 U.S. 223 (1993).

17. "When someone asks, 'Do you use a cane?' he is not inquiring whether you have your grandfather's silver-handled walking stick on display in the hall; he wants to know whether you *walk* with a cane. Similarly, to speak of 'using a firearm' is to speak of using it for its distinctive purpose, i.e., as a weapon." *Smith*, 508 U.S. at 242.

18. Noted by Brest (1980, 216).

19. 347 U.S. 483 (1954).

20. 198 U.S. 45 (1905).

21. 262 U.S. 390 (1923).

22. 381 U.S. 479 (1965).

23. 410 U.S. 113 (1973).

24. 505 U.S. 833 (1992).

25. 539 U.S. 558 (2003).

26. *Planned Parenthood*, 505 U.S. at 852.

27. 268 U. S. 652 (1925).

28. 561 U. S. 742 (2010).

29. Barron ex rel. Tiernan v. Mayor of Baltimore, 32 U. S. 243 (1833).

30. 83 U.S. 36 (1872)

31. 92 U.S. 542 (1875)

32. *Id*. at 553.

33. 166 U.S. 226 (1897).

34. 268 U. S. 652 (1925).

35. *Id*. at 666.

36. *Id*. at 673.

37. 561 U.S. 742 (2010).

38. 554 U.S. 570 (2008).

39. *McDonald*, 561 U.S. at 744.

40. See Aynes (1993, 79). In fact Bingham believed that the privileges and immunities clause of article 4 had already made the Bill of Rights applicable to the states, and that the main innovation of the Fourteenth Amendment was to give Congress the power to enforce the article 4 protection.

41. For example, Senator Poland of Vermont remarked in the Senate debate that "the proposed privileges and immunities clause 'secures nothing beyond what was intended by Article IV, Section 2, Clause 1,'" quoted in Fairman (1971,

1296). Other senators were simply unsure, even after extensive debate, what the legal function of the privileges or immunities clause was meant to be:

> I am decidedly in favor of the first part of the section which defines what citizenship shall be, and in favor of that part of the section which denies to a State the right to deprive any person of life, liberty or property without due process of law, but I think it quite objectionable to provide that "No State shall make any law which shall abridge the privileges or immunities of the United States," simply because I do not understand what will be the effect of that. (Reverdy Johnson, Cong. Globe. Pt. 4, 1st Sess., 39th Cong., 3041, quoted in Fairman 1971, 1297.)

42. Soames notes that when the official rationale for a provision is too vague to provide guidance, then the deferentially correct decision is the decision that effects a "minimum modification of existing content that allows a definite result to be reached" (chapter 9, this volume). I assume that outright incorporation of the relevant provisions of the Bill of Rights is not a minimal such modification, entailing as it does the sweeping invalidation of state laws that had previously been regarded as valid.

43. Soames says that the deferentialist rule for revising the law in light of its public rationale is a *legal obligation* of judges. But it's an odd sort of legal obligation; it would be odd to call Justice Kennedy a *lawbreaker* for his opinion in *Lawrence vs. Texas*.

44. 5 U.S. 137 (1803)

45. Soames acknowledges that law may change in "extralegal ways."

> [Deferentialism] is not a theory of all [legal] change. The practices of key governmental actors—to initiate military action, to introduce vast new governmental agencies and institutions, to make recess appointments to fill vacancies that didn't occur during a recess, to make unilateral changes in legislation without congressional approval, and the like—can and sometimes have, when unchecked, adjusted constitutional boundaries. (chapter 9, this volume)

But he does not discuss the ways in which nondeferentialist *adjudication* can change the law.

46. "It is emphatically the duty of the Judicial Department to say what the law is." *Marbury*, 5 US at 177.

47. This assumes—what is arguable—that a deferentialist reading of article 1, section 1 would take seriously the claim that *all* legislative power is vested in Congress and hence that even this power to make law in hard cases was not granted to the court by the Constitution.

References

Aynes, Richard. 1993. "On Misreading John Bingham and the Fourteenth Amendment." *Yale Law Journal* 103:57–104.

Brest, Paul. 1980. "The Misconceived Quest for Original Understanding." *Boston University Law Review* 60:204–38.

Chapman, Nathan S., and Michael McConnell. 2012. "Due Process as Separation of Powers." *Yale Law Journal* 121:1672–807.

Dworkin, Ronald. 1975. "Hard Cases." *Harvard Law Review* 88:1057–109.

———. 1988. *Law's Empire*. Cambridge: Harvard University Press.

Fairman, Charles. 1971. *History of the Supreme Court of the United States: Reconstruction and Reunion, 1864–88, Part One*. New York: Macmillan.

Greenberg, Mark. 2011. "Legislation as Communication? Legal Interpretation and the Study of Linguistic Communication." In *Philosophical Foundations of Language in the Law*, edited by Andrei Marmor and Scott Soames, 217–56. Oxford: Oxford University Press.

Hart, H. L. A.1994. *The Concept of Law*. 2nd ed. Oxford: Oxford University Press.

Kim, Yule. 2008. *Statutory Interpretation: General Principles and Recent Trends*. CRS Report for Congress.

Levinson, Jerrold. 2006. "Hypothetical Intentionalism: Statement, Objections, and Replies." In *Contemplating Art: Essays in Aesthetics*. Oxford: Oxford University Press.

McConnell, Michael. 1995. "Originalism and the Desegregation Decisions." *Virginia Law Review* 81:947–1140.

Rosen, Gideon. 2011. "Textualism, Intentionalism, and the Law of the Contract." In *Philosophical Foundations of Language in the Law*, edited by Andrei Marmor and Scott Soames, 130–64. Oxford: Oxford University Press.

Soames, Scott. 2013. "Deferentialism: A Post-Originalist Theory of Legal Interpretation." *Fordham Law Review* 82:597–618

Solum, Lawrence. 2008. "Semantic Originalism." Illinois Public Law Research Paper No. 07–27. http://papers.ssrn.com/sol3/papers.cfm?abstract_id =1120244.

Whittington, Keith. 1999. *Constitutional Interpretation: Textual Meaning, Original Intent, and Judicial Review*. Lawrence: University of Kansas Press.

Comments on Rosen

Scott Soames

In what follows, I make some remarks on Gideon Rosen's chapter, "Deferentialism and Adjudication," which raises issues useful for precisifying deferentialism.

1. The Role of Rationale

I begin by noting a misreading of my position on Roberts's decision upholding the Affordable Care Act. Rosen reconstructs my argument as proceeding as follows:

(1) Roberts didn't modify the content of the act as passed; he *interpreted* what it called a *penalty* for not purchasing required insurance as a *tax*.
(2) Achieving the other goals of the act without raising taxes on individuals was part of the act's rationale.
(3) Thus the content of the law as passed violated part of the law's rationale.
(4) For that reason a properly deferentialist judge should have voided it.

This isn't my argument. In my view, only (2) is correct; (1), (3), and (4) are not.

Claim (1) is incorrect because the law as passed involved not a tax but a *penalty*—which was the word used in the act—imposed on those failing to comply with the *requirement* to buy approved insurance. Since Roberts ruled that Congress lacked authority to impose such a *requirement*, he modified the stated content to render it consistent with (his reading of) the Constitution. Claim (2) is supported by proponents' insistence that the fee imposed was *not a tax* but a *penalty* for not complying with a *requirement*. Since this was done to secure passage in the face of objections, it was part of the law's rationale. Because (1) is false, (3) can't soundly be derived.

On my reading, Roberts changed the law's content by replacing a *penalty* with a *tax*. This would be deferentially acceptable if it were "a minimum change in existing law that maximizes the fulfillment of the original rationale for the law." I criticized the decision for not meeting this requirement. In the note on which Rosen relies, I reasoned as follows.

> Since it was politically important in passing the act that the mandate *not* be labeled by its supporters as a tax, we may conclude that *if* the mandate was not severable from the act, and *if* it was not justified by the *commerce*, or the *necessary and proper*, clauses, *then* the act's survival depended *not* on bringing its legal content into conformity with the rationale used to secure its passage but on *increasing* the disparity between the two. Thus, Roberts's reasoning was not deferentially justifiable.

This brief statement can be extended by considering a possible deferentialist *defense* of Roberts. The defense maintains that maximal fidelity to original content and rationale is better achieved by modifying a minor part of each than by voiding the law. This defense might have merit *if avoidance of a tax was a sincerely held part of the rationale for the law that was inessential to its passage*. But it wasn't. Due to strong opposition, the act passed by the narrowest of margins. Because the no-tax rationale was politically effective, a reasonable case can be made that, had it been abandoned, the act wouldn't have passed. This is important. When changing the content of a law to remove a conflict with other authoritative law (in this case the Constitution as Roberts interpreted it), it is generally acceptable to sacrifice a minor feature of the law's content and rationale to preserve the rest, but it is not acceptable to jettison a feature essential to its passage. Deferentialism requires deference to the exercise of legislative authority by which a bill became law—preserving, when modifications are needed, as much of the content and rationale inherent in that exercise as possible, without abandoning aspects of the law that were essential to achieve passage.

This, of course, was not spelled out in the brief discussion of Roberts's decision in my footnote. Nor was the connection made explicit between my argument there and the paragraph it was meant to elaborate.

The point of the paragraph was that lawmakers' deceptive manipulation of stated rationale for the purpose of assuring passage should not be excused in later adjudication, when sacrificing the deception becomes necessary to save the law in the process of judicial rectification. The alacrity of supporters in urging reclassification of the penalty as a tax when the constitutional issue was raised after passage suggests such deception. My criticism of the decision was meant to underline this point; if a change in the content of the law requires one to sacrifice an element deceptively introduced into to secure passage, such a change is not deferentially justified.

On my reading, the original content of the Affordable Care Act was consistent with its stated rationale. Roberts's attempt to remove what he took to be a conflict between that content and the Constitution introduced an inconsistency between an aspect of the law's original rationale and its revised content. This change might have been a defensible alternative to voiding the law, had the original content and the rationale it served not been introduced as a political expedient needed to secure passage.

For this reason, I reject Rosen's critique. However, I credit his discussion with calling attention to an overly general formulation of clause (c) in the following summary statement of my principles of judicial rectification. *"In applying the law to the facts of a case, the legal duty of a judge is to reach the verdict determined by the stipulated content, unless (a) . . . or (b) . . . or (c) the contents and facts are inconsistent with the rationale of the law, which is the chief publically stated purpose that proponents of the law advanced to justify it."* Clause (c) was intended to cover cases in which the literal application of a law's stated content to *unanticipated facts* of a particular case lead to *obviously unwanted results* that subvert or fail to advance the rationale of the law itself, or of surrounding laws, in ways that can be corrected by *fine-tuning the law's content* (see Soames 2011, 244–53). This is a proper part of deferentialism. But it's not a blank check.

To see why, imagine a hypothetical case in which the legislature foolishly triples the minimum wage to serve the stated rationale of increasing the income of certain workers without causing unacceptable job losses. Suppose further that the economic effects of the law after passage are pernicious. No matter how great the failure to achieve the law's rationale, deferentialist judges cannot rewrite it—both because the relevant economic considerations were available to the legislature at the

time of passage and because avoiding the resulting economic failure would require not a minor adjustment in the content of the law but
wholesale change or invalidation, which would exceed the authority of
judges. In this case, the literature on job losses and other economic ill effects of large mandated wage increases would rightly be seen as undercutting any claim that the chances of economic ill effects could not reasonably have been taken into account. That the possibility of such effects
was implicitly recognized is reflected in fact that the law's rationale already incorporates a clearly political judgment that only the legislature
can make—weighing the social good of increasing the economic pros-
pects of some at the expense of others. Since setting the wage rate at any
other level would merely substitute a figure already implicitly considered
and rejected by the legislators for one they accepted, no such judicial
rectification is deferentially allowed.

The recent decision in *King v. Burwell*[1] provides a similar case in
point. Proponents of the Affordable Care Act included precise language
stipulating that purchasers of mandated health insurance would be eligi-
ble for federal subsidies *only if* their policies were obtained through an
exchange established by one of the states. Backers of the legislation included this language deliberately, to create political pressure they hoped
would lead states to participate in, and eventually share the cost of, a
program they might otherwise shun. When, after passage, thirty states
declined to set up exchanges, this purpose was thwarted, threatening the
long-term financial viability of the program, unless modified by further
congressional action. Rather than open up the act to further legislative
bargaining, the executive branch, operating through the IRS, rewrote
the law to allow federal subsidies for those *not* purchasing their plans
through one of the states.

This executive change of legislative content was authorized by Justice
Roberts's decision in *King v Burwell*, primarily on the ground that the
change in content was required to fulfill the law's rationale—since otherwise the program might fail financially. But his decision can no more be
deferentially justified than could a decision ratifying unilateral action of
a president altering the dollar amount of minimum-wage legislation. In
both cases, the possibility that circumstances threatening the law's rationale—weak economic performance in one case and refusal of many
states to participate in an unpopular program in the other—were considered by legislators. Being factors that were, or could reasonably have
been, taken into account, their actual occurrence is no excuse for either

judicial or executive usurpation of congressional authority. Any deferentialist principle of rationale-based rectification of content must reflect this.

Further precisification of clause (c) of the deferentialist rectification principle is needed to incorporate the factors illustrated here. Since this isn't the place for such a reformulation, I will simply illustrate why rationale-based rectification is sometimes needed. My example is the free-exercise clause of the First Amendment, which states that *Congress shall make no law* respecting the establishment of religion *or prohibiting the free exercise thereof*. Though a useful general directive, this stated content is only a starting point. In one respect, it is not general enough, because what Congress is here prohibited from doing the president would also be prohibited from doing by executive order, except perhaps in an emergency. To the extent that this is already a settled legal matter, it is the result of previous rectifications of the content of the clause in order to fulfill its rationale. To the extent that further rectification may be needed, a decision extending the constitutional guarantee in an unanticipated case of this kind would amount to judicial fine-tuning of preexisting content of the sort I envision. In a different sort of case, the rectification may narrow the originally stated content of the clause. Since there are few limits on the range of possible activities that might be required or prohibited by the practice of some religion or other, it is easy to imagine cases in which a literal application of the stated content of the free-exercise clause would compromise the overarching rationale of our constitutional structure of democratic self-government. As before, to the extent that this is already a settled matter of our law, it is the result of previous rectification of the original stated content of the clause. To the extent that further rectification may be needed, a decision narrowing the constitutional guarantee in a novel case of the sort imagined would be an instance of judicial fine-tuning of preexisting content in the service of better fulfilling the rationale of both the free-exercise clause and the surrounding constitutional structure to which it contributes.

2. Content, Assertion, Stipulation

In identifying the original content of a piece of legislation with what the lawmakers asserted or stipulated in enacting it, I invoke a kind of illocutionary content. The concept employed, *what is said or stipulated*, is not a technical one reserved for legal language; the uses I make of it in contexts of lawmaking and adjudication are applications of the concepts employed in nonlegal contexts. In all these contexts asserted or stipulated content arises from a confluence of factors. Speakers, hearers, writers, and readers communicating in ordinary conversations, public speeches, academic seminars, planning sessions, group meetings, or through letters, text messages, newspapers, or scholarly books use language against a background of presumed shared information that shapes asserted or stipulated content. Language users in these contexts make assumptions about each other's awareness of the general purposes of the communication, the questions currently at stake, the ground already covered, the linguistic meanings of the expressions employed, and relevant background facts that participants can be expected to know without being told.

Typically these assumptions of speaker/writers and hearer/readers converge on optimal candidates for asserted/stipulated contents (among which it is not necessary to make further discriminations). Sometimes, however, participants fail to correctly identify that content because they fail to recognize what their position in the exchange would justify assuming or inferring. In such cases they miss some of what is literally asserted or stipulated because they don't live up to the normative demands of their position in the linguistic exchange. Since this content-determining idealization is a feature of ordinary assertions and stipulations, the idealization needed when using these concepts to determine *legal content* isn't a departure from the speech-act model—even though the legal idealization has some special features due to the gap between the lawmaking body and the multiple audiences to which its use of language is addressed.

It must also be noted that asserted/stipulated content can be indeterminate. It may be *determinate* that an agent asserted or stipulated at least one of several related propositions, while being *indeterminate* which ones were asserted or stipulated. Often this indeterminacy doesn't matter, but sometimes it does. When this indeterminacy occurs in a lawmaking context, and resolving or narrowing it is needed in adjudication, the indeterminacy can be treated as a kind of vagueness to be resolved in judicial rectification.

3. *Brown*, Deferentialism, and Hypothetical Intentionalism

Rosen's discussion of *Brown*[2] illustrates the importance of adhering to the speech-act model. I do regard the asserted/stipulated content of the privileges or immunities clause—which speaks of "the privileges and immunities of citizens of the United States"—as an important justifier of *Brown*. I also take its content to include "prohibiting states from abridging the privileges or immunities of US citizens, wherever they may happen to be." I see this not simply as an *intention* of the authors and ratifiers of the amendment; it is part of what they used the text to *assert/stipulate*—which, I contend, would have been grasped by a reasonable and knowledgeable audience. It was, I think, unclear what, if any, provision for public education all citizens of the United States were entitled to in 1868. But it was crystal clear that whatever those entitlements might turn out to be, they can't be denied on the basis of race. It should also have been clear that the entitlements might change over time. It follows that if access to public education was, by 1954, such an entitlement, then the stipulated content of the privileges and immunities clause plus the facts in 1954 were sufficient to justify *Brown*.

Rosen sees a problem for deferentialism in the fact that many drafters/ratifiers did not view the Fourteenth Amendment as prohibiting racial segregation in public schools and would not have endorsed it had they thought otherwise. But this cuts no ice. In 1868 there may have been an arguable case that the amendment didn't prohibit school segregation because public education was not one of the rights inherent in national citizenship. Those who favored segregation might thus have been comforted by the expectation that ratification wouldn't change things. But an expectation is all it was. Rosen protests that deferentialism risks giving weight to this expectation, which he calls *the intention to permit segregation in public schools*, when in fact it should have none. Not to worry. The amendment can't be read, nor can its ratification be understood, as involving a *stipulation* that, henceforth, segregation in public education would be constitutionally protected. Securing constitutionally protected segregation was also not part of the *rationale* for the Fourteenth Amendment. It was merely an expectation that forced desegregation wasn't in the immediate offing, coupled with a belief (by some) that it should never be. Here, I fear that Rosen's elision of my speech-act conception of legal content into a version of hypothetical intentionalism obscures needed distinctions.

4. Substantive Due Process

Regarding the *Slaughterhouse Cases*,[3] *Cruikshank*,[4] and related cases severely limiting the privileges and immunities clause (from 1873 through the turn of the twentieth century), I largely agree with Jack Balkin's (2011, see chapter 10) conclusion (though not always with his reasons) that they were wrongly decided. I haven't studied, and so won't comment on, the incorporation cases *Chicago B & Q R. Co.*,[5] *Gitlow*,[6] or *McDonald*.[7] But I agree that the questions Rosen raises are significant. If, following McConnell's and Chapman's historical analysis, I am right that many substantive due process cases over the last century plus weren't deferentially justified, then it is worth asking whether some are deferentially justifiable on other grounds. This provides further reason to clarify the original legal content and rationale of the privileges and immunities clause, which might do some of the justificatory work. I won't here prejudge the outcome of such a clarification.

5. Deferentialism and Judicial Error

I agree with much in this section of Rosen's chapter. Of course, deferentialism tells us that many cases have been wrongly decided and that those mistakes have changed the content of the law. The actions of authoritative actors, including judges and justices, change law, whether or not the changes are justified. Moreover, not all judicial changes, justified or not, are created equal. Sometimes originally unjustified changes become so entrenched and widely embedded in our system that it becomes virtually impossible, and undesirable, to wholly reverse them. This is one way that the legal contents of constitutional provisions change over time. Still, changes due to judicial error retain a degree of vulnerability. They can be challenged by showing both (a) that an earlier decision failed to respect constitutional content and rationale, while a different resolution that is now possible does a better job, and (b) that the new resolution does not seriously disrupt the existing body of law, constitutional or otherwise.

Here is how I put the issue in my original article on deferentialism.

> Because of the many anti- or non-deferentialist decisions in past decades, any
> effective renewal of deferentialism must include a strategy for dealing with
> the body of existing law created by those decisions. Since neither wholesale
> revocation nor wholesale preservation of previous non-deferentialist deci-
> sions in their current form is compatible with a lasting deferentialist judiciary,
> finding a workable middle way is the most daunting task of rectification that
> confronts deferentialism. The way to think of this task is, I suggest, to treat it
> as a sub case of *harmonization of conflicts in law*, where (at least) one of the
> laws in conflict is judge-made. When the Supreme Court finds that the facts
> of a new case create a conflict between some valid legal provision and the law
> produced by a previous decision that the Court now finds unjustified, the task
> of the Court is to remove the conflict by making the minimal changes needed
> to the conflicting laws while furthering, to the extent possible, the rationales
> for both. How this would, or should, work in particular cases is, of course,
> a large, open-ended question. But the principle of respecting both laws, de-
> spite their provenance, and aiming for limited adjustments—which may, over
> time, become cumulative—is, I think, the best general procedure. (Soames
> 2013, 617)

I may help to make this more specific. When the court finds that the
facts of a new case create a conflict between some *valid* legal provision L
and a constitutional provision L* produced by an earlier *mistaken* decision, the task is to make the least change in L* that both narrows the
previous error (by bringing the interpretation of the provision closer to
what is now seen to be correct) and removes the conflict with L. This
should be done to the extent that the consequences of the rectification
of L* for settled law are foreseeable and reasonably localized. When this
isn't so—when the mistaken L* is inextricably entrenched in a complex
body of surrounding law—the goal may have to be reduced to creating a
carve-out for L that doesn't expand the mistaken content L*. Reapplica-
tion of this rule over time may gradually narrow the impact of past erroneous judicial decisions, while avoiding unpredictably destabilizing effects on the body of existing law. In this way, rectification of previous
error may proceed, and become cumulative, without inviting disastrous
or quixotic quests.

Notes

1. 576 U.S. ___ (2015).
2. Brown v. Board of Education, 347 U.S. 483 (1954).
3. 83 U.S. 36 (1873).
4. U.S. v. Cruikshank, 92 U.S. 542 (1876).
5. Chicago B & Q R. Co. v. Chicago, 166 U.S. 226 (1897).
6. Gitlow v. New York, 268 U.S. 652 (1925).
7. McDonald v. Chicago, 561 U.S. 742 (2010).

References

Balkin, Jack M. 2011. *Living Originalism*. Cambridge: Harvard University Press.
Soames, Scott. 2011. "Toward a Theory of Legal Interpretation." *New York University of Law and Liberty* 6:231–59.
———. 2013. "Deferentialism: A Post-Originalist Theory of Legal Interpretation." *Fordham Law Review* 82:597–617. Reprinted in *Analytic Philosophy in America: And Other Historical and Contemporary Essays*, 320–41, Princeton: Princeton University Press, 2014.

Contributors

Nicholas Allott is senior lecturer in English language at the University of Oslo; he previously worked at University College London, where he completed his PhD in linguistics in 2008. He is the author of *Key Terms in Pragmatics* (Continuum, 2010) and coauthor of *Chomsky: Ideas and Ideals* (Cambridge University Press, 2016); his work focusses on pragmatics, philosophy of language, and philosophy of linguistics, including research on heuristics in utterance interpretation, lexical modulation, and the interpretation of legal language.

Kent Greenawalt, who studied political philosophy under Isaiah Berlin and H. L. A. Hart at Oxford and served as law clerk to Justice Harlan, is now in his fifty-first year of teaching at Columbia University Law School. Writing in many fields, he has been a University Professor since 1992.

Francis J. Mootz III is dean and professor of law at the University of the Pacific, McGeorge School of Law. He is widely published on the relevance of philosophical hermeneutics and rhetoric to contemporary legal theory.

Karen Petroski is professor of law at Saint Louis University. She received her PhD in literature from Columbia University and her JD from the University of California, Berkeley.

Frank S. Ravitch is the Walter H. Stowers Chair in Law & Religion and director of the Kyoto, Japan summer program at the Michigan State University College of Law. He is the author of numerous books, articles, book chapters, essays, and amicus briefs to the United States Supreme Court.

Gideon Rosen is the Stuart Professor of Philosophy at Princeton University. He is the editor (with Alex Byrne, Joshua Cohen, and Seana Shiffrin) of *The Norton Introduction to Philosophy*.

Benjamin Shaer is a government policy analyst in Ottawa and adjunct research professor in law, linguistics, and cognitive science at Carleton University. His academic training includes a PhD in linguistics from McGill University and a JD from the University of Toronto Faculty of Law, and his recent research involves the application of linguistic analysis to issues in legal interpretation.

Brian G. Slocum is professor of law at the University of the Pacific, McGeorge School of Law. Holding both a JD and a PhD in linguistics, he writes at the intersection of language and law and is the author of *Ordinary Meaning: A Theory of the Most Fundamental Principle of Legal Interpretation* (University of Chicago Press, 2015).

Scott Soames is distinguished professor and chair of the School of Philosophy at USC. The author of well-known works in philosophy of language, the history of analytic philosophy, and theories of legal interpretation, his books include *Philosophy of Language* (Princeton University Press), *Rethinking Language, Mind, and Meaning* (Princeton University Press), and *Philosophical Foundations of Language in the Law* (Oxford University Press), edited with Andrei Marmor.

Lawrence M. Solan is the Don Forchelli Professor of Law and director of the Center for the Study of Law, Language, and Cognition at Brooklyn Law School. He is the author of *The Language of Statutes: Laws and their Interpretation* and other books.

Lawrence B. Solum is the Carmack Waterhouse Professor of Law at Georgetown University. His work ranges broadly in legal theory, including constitutional theory and virtue jurisprudence.

Cases

Bankovic v. Belgium (52207/99) (2001), 206, 211

Brown v. Board of Education (1954), 233–35, 253–56, 278

Burwell v. Hobby Lobby Stores, Inc. (2014), 59

Caminetti v. United States (1917), 36–39

Chicago B. & Q.R. Co. v. Chicago (1897), 258, 279

Chisom v. Roemer (1991), 110, 115, 120–21

District of Columbia v. Heller (2008), 178, 187n24, 259

Ehime Tamagushi (1997), 99–100

Elonis v. United States (2015), 71–72, 113–14, 118, 120–21

Flores-Figueroa v. United States (2009), 19–20, 35, 79

Gitlow v. New York (1925), 257–59, 265, 279

Griswold v. Connecticut (1965), 257

Holy Trinity Church v. United States (1892), 5, 26, 42n26, 52, 75

In re Sinclair (1989), 109–10

Johnson v. United States (2000), 27

King v. Burwell (2015), 275

Lawrence v. Texas (2003), 257, 264

Lemon v. Kurtzman (1971), 97–99

Lochner v. New York (1905), 228, 256

Marbury v. Madison (1803), 228, 262–63

McDonald v. Chicago (2010), 257, 259–61, 265, 279

Meyer v. Nebraska (1923), 256, 264

Montreal (City) v. 2952–1355 Québec Inc. (2005), 205

National Federation of Independent Businesses et al. v. Sebelius (2012), 246

Planned Parenthood of Southeastern Pennsylvania v. Casey (1992), 228, 257

Riggs v. Palmer (1889), 209

Roe v. Wade (1973), 257

Slaughter-House Cases (1873), 258–60, 279

Smith v. United States (1993), 75, 211, 233, 251–53

Train v. Colorado Public Interest Research Group (1970), 23–30, 36

Tsu City Groundbreaking Ceremony (1971), 96–100

United States v. American Trucking Ass'ns (1940), 24, 30

United States v. Cruikshank (1876), 258, 260, 279

United States v. X-Citement Video, Inc. (1994), 17–20

Index

absurdity doctrine, 5–6, 51
Affordable Healthcare Act of 2010 (Affordable Care Act), 220, 236nn2–5, 246–47, 268n11, 272–75
Alito, Samuel, 60, 113, 120
ambiguity
  Berghuis v. Thompkins (2010) and, 73
  Caminetti v. United States (1917) and, 38–39
  computational system and, 76–77
  constitutional provisions and, 144, 148, 181–82n24, 233
  context and, 140–41
  contracts and, 108, 124n10, 124n11, 124–25n14
  fixation thesis and, 8
  hermeneutics and, 160, 171, 182n4
  Japanese law and, 97–100
  legal meaning and. *See* legal meaning
  lexical ambiguity. *See* ambiguity: semantic
  plain meaning rule and, 16–17, 28
  prevalence of, 4
  semantic, 7, 68–69, 77, 81–84
  speech act and, 71
  syntactic, 68–69, 78–81
  vagueness compared to, 69, 74
Anderson, Jill, 81–82
Aristotle, 162, 175
Asgeirsson, Hrafn, 208
assertoric content (assertoric utterance), 10–11, 249–52, 263
Austin, John, 10, 192, 201, 212, 230

Baaij, Cornelius, 81
Bach, Kent, 83, 192, 197, 198, 201, 207–8
Balkin, Jack
  deferentialism and. *See* deferentialism
  nonliteral meanings and, 238n12
  originalism and, 131, 218, 229–35, 237n7, 237n9
Bill of Rights, 63, 257–65, 269n40, 270n42
Bingham, John, 259, 269n40
Bobbitt, Phillip, 102n25, 133
Brandeis, Louis, 258
Brest, Paul, 131, 269n18

Campos, Paul, 3
Cardozo, Benjamin, 66, 93, 102n29
Carston, Robyn, 197, 204
categorization
  "No Vehicles in the Park" hypothetical and, 2–3, 5, 20–21
  vagueness and, 2, 7, 54, 74, 77, 210–13, 214n7
Chapman, Nathan, 228, 257, 259, 261, 279
Chomsky, Noam, 1, 68, 70, 78, 197
Civil Rights Act of 1964, 243–44
communicative content. *See* originalism; semantics
communicative intent, 32–33, 68, 84, 250
compact clause, 232–33, 238n11
concept. *See* categorization
constitutional rules, 223, 235
constraint principle. *See* originalism

construction (versus interpretation), 5,
    9–10
    constitutional interpretation and, 134–
        35, 142–44, 146–47, 157–58, 167–
        69, 177, 179–81, 185n17, 232–33,
        263, 266n3
    contextual approach, 28–36
    conventional meaning. *See* meaning
    conventional usage, 50–51. *See also* ordi-
        nary meaning
Cook, Anne, 77
critical legal studies, 88
Cunningham, Clark, 3

de dicto/de re, 81–82
deferentialism
    Balkin, Jack and, 223–26, 237n8, 238–
        39n18, 239n20, 279
    linguistic meaning and, 11, 254, 264
    "No Vehicles in the Park" hypothetical
        and, 243–44
    originalism and, 218, 223–35, 237n8,
        239n20, 250, 253–56
    pragmatics and, 10, 245, 248–52
    rule of law and, 245
    semantics and, 10, 218, 225–26, 242,
        244–49
    Soames, Scott and, 10, 244–57, 260,
        264, 267–68n11, 270n42, 270n43,
        270n45
    speech acts and, 244–45, 251, 253
    textualism and, 251
    vagueness and, 10, 218–20, 222, 244, 260,
        270n42, 277
dialogic encounter, 161, 200
dictionaries
    Chisom v. Roemer (1991) and, 121–22
    judicial reliance on, 2–3, 20–21, 115,
        128n38, 186n19
    textualism and, 251
    *White City Shopping Center, LP v. PR
        Restaurants LLC* (2006) and,
        75–76
Douglas, William O., 109
Doyle, Arthur Conan, 116
due process, 227–29, 234, 256–65, 270n41,
    279
Dworkin, Ronald, 93, 132, 194–95, 243,
    256, 266n2

Easterbrook, Frank, 108–11, 114–15,
    125n17, 125n19
effectives. *See* speech acts
ejusdem generis, 37–40, 43n47, 199
enactor intent, 55–56, 60–61
Endicott, Timothy, 74, 193–98, 202–9,
    211–13
Eskridge, William, 25, 88–89, 101n2,
    102n9, 102n20

Feldman, Stephen, 101n1, 151, 169, 170,
    182n5, 186n18
Fillmore, Charles, 3
First Amendment, 137, 209, 226–27,
    238n14, 258–59, 276
fixation thesis. *See* originalism
Flanagan, Brian, 5, 12n3, 25
Flores-Figueroa v. United States (2009),
    19–20, 35, 79
Fourteenth Amendment, 63, 137,
    233–34
Fraser, Bruce, 72
Frazier, Lyn, 77, 83
Freud, Sigmund, 156

Gadamer, Hans-Georg, 9, 89–94, 98, 101,
    101n1
    originalism and 130, 145–53, 159–87
Garner, Brian, 31, 40, 75
generative linguistics, 68–69
Green, Georgia, 18
Greenberg, Mark, 25, 242
Grice, Paul, 49, 53, 65n3, 71, 195–96, 213,
    214n3
Griffin, Stephen, 132–33

Hamilton, Alexander, 228
Harnish, Robert, 192, 201, 207
Hart, H. L. A., 2–3, 20, 25, 266n3. *See
    also* "No Vehicles in the Park"
    hypothetical
Hay, Bruce, 42n28
hermeneutics. *See* philosophical
    hermeneutics
Holmes, Oliver Wendell, 8, 105–29,
    258
Holy Trinity Church v. United States
    (1892), 5, 26, 42n26, 52, 75
Hutton, Christopher, 76

illocutionary intentions. *See* speech acts
inferential processes (inferential systems),
    23
intentionalism, 33–34, 132, 251, 278–79

Jackendoff, Ray, 68
Jackson, Bernard, 34
Jori, Mario, 34
judicial discretion, 59–60
Juhasz, Barbara, 77

Kahn, Paul, 199
Kaplan, David, 236n6
Kaplan, Jeffrey, 18
Kramer, Matthew, 111

language faculty, 1–2, 6–7, 9
    architecture of, 66–69
    computational aspects of, 68, 76–83
law and religion, 93–100
laws of legal effect, 242–43, 245, 261
legal meaning
    ambiguity and, 21, 29–30, 58, 66–67, 137
    literal meaning and, 25, 72–73
    plain meaning and, 24–28, 36–39
    pragmatics and, 51–52, 70–71, 174,
        205–6
    vagueness and, 4–6, 9, 21, 33, 58, 69, 80,
        193, 208, 241, 266n2
legal speech. *See* speech acts
legislative history
    Caminetti v. United States (1917) and,
        38–39
    legislative intent and, 29–30, 33–35, 62,
        109, 267n11
    linguistic meaning and, 28
    ordinary meaning and, 22, 31–32
    textualism and, 29, 59–60, 109, 125n19
    *Train v. Colorado Public Interest Re-
        search Group* (1976) and, 24–26,
        28–29
legislative intent
    Caminetti v. United States (1917) and, 39
    hypothetical readers and, 57, 109
    legislative history and, 29–30
    problems discerning, 30–36
legislative purpose, 31, 42n26
Leiber, Francis, 167
lexical semantics. *See* semantics

linguistic meaning. *See* meaning; ordinary
    meaning
literal meaning. *See* meaning
living constitutionalism. *See* originalism
living originalism. *See* originalism

Manning, John, 5, 29–30
Margolis, Joseph, 166–67, 197
Marmor, Andrei, 32, 35, 194, 197, 200
McConnell, Michael, 228, 233–34, 254, 257,
    259, 279
McKenna, Joseph, 38–39
meaning
    applicative sense of, 137
    communicative sense of, 137–38, 142
    conventional, 3, 27, 141, 203
    horizon of, 91, 161
    legal, 4–5, 15–16, 21–29, 40, 108, 115–18,
        122, 164–65, 191
    linguistic, 3
        as compared to interpretation cho-
            sen by court, 5, 14–31, 33–36, 40,
            42n27, 42n31, 57, 132, 200, 219, 242,
            245, 250
        constitutional interpretation and, 132,
            134–37, 142, 157, 224–27, 233–34
        deferentialism and. *See*
            deferentialism
        definition of, 16–17, 249
        determination of, 38–39, 62, 114, 197,
            210, 251–52, 277
        literal meaning and, 12n3, 41n3, 41–
            42n17, 225
        purpose and, 5
    literal
        asserted meaning and, 252–53
        contribution to legal meaning of. *See*
            legal meaning
        definition of, 12n3
        ejusdem generis and, 37–39
        nonliteral meaning and, 25–26, 28,
            238n12
        ordinary meaning and, 41n3
        objective determinants of, 14–15
    ordinary. *See* ordinary meaning
    ordinary linguistic, 227, 233, 242
    original. *See* originalism
    plain
        contextual approach compared with, 36

meaning—plain (*continued*)
    definition of, 16–19
    as source of legal meaning. *See* legal
        meaning
    *Train v. Colorado Public Inter-
        est Research Group* (1975) and,
        25–26
    pragmatic. *See* pragmatics
    purposive sense of, 137
Mercier, Hugo, 204
Miller, Geoffrey, 52
Moore, Michael, 88–89
Mootz, Jay, 8–9, 88–89, 130, 147, 149–53
Murphy, Arthur, 36

nonoriginalism. *See* originalism
"No Vehicles in the Park" hypothetical,
    205–6
    categorization and. *See* categorization
    deferentialism and. *See* deferentialism

ordinary linguistic meaning. *See* meaning;
    ordinary meaning
ordinary meaning, 124n11
    definition of, 7–8, 23, 29
    ejusdem generis and, 43n47
    generalized notions of intent and, 16, 32,
        34, 242
    legal English compared to, 119–22
    linguistic meaning and, 16, 30–31, 35–
        36, 41n3, 42n36, 53, 227, 242
    linguists and, 22, 47
    normal speakers and, 110, 114–18,
        186n18
    original expected application and, 229
    plain meaning compared to, 16, 19
    possible meaning compared to, 75–76
    Smith v. United States (1993) and, 211,
        233, 251–52
    specialized meanings compared to, 25–
        28, 238n12
    textualism and. *See* textualism
    United States v. X-Citement Video, Inc.
        (1994) and, 19
ordinary member of Congress, 110
ordinary reader, 56, 60, 187
ordinary user, 107
originalism
    communicative content and, 8, 130–31
    constraint principle and

definition of, 8, 132
Gadamer, Hans-Georg and, 147
maximalist version of, 133
minimalist version of, 133
relationship to fixation, 135–36, 142–
    44, 153–54, 159, 181, 182n3
deferentialism and. *See* deferentialism
fixation thesis and, 130
    definition of, 135–36, 157–59
    generalized version of, 138–42
    hermeneutic critique and, 145–
        53, 159, 167–71, 185n15, 185n17,
        186–87n21
    justification for, 136–44
    legal practice and, 174–76, 182n3
    living constitutionalism and, 131–32,
        145–47, 226, 265
    living originalism and, 131–32, 218,
        223–26, 229, 232, 235, 237n8,
        239n20
    nonoriginalism and, 131, 153
    original assertive content (original as-
        serted content) and, 227, 234
    original intentions and, 8, 132, 135–36,
        230, 234
    original methods and, 8, 132
    original public meaning and, 8, 132,
        135, 169
    original understanding and, 46
    contemporary understanding and,
        172–73, 225
    historians and, 168–72
    hypothetical nature of, 176, 180
    ordinary uses of language and, 46–47
    philosophy of language and, 55–56,
        62–63
    Second Amendment and, 187n24

perlocutionary intentions. *See* speech
    acts
philosophical hermeneutics
    context and, 90–95, 97–100, 102n27,
        148–49, 153, 157–58, 167–74, 177,
        183n12
    dasein and, 7, 88–92, 94, 101
    episteme and, 162
    Gadamer, Hans-Georg and, 9, 89–94,
        98, 101
    hermeneutical circle and, 167
    horizon of meaning and

connection to *dasein*, 88–89
definition of, 7
fusion of, 93, 102n28, 147, 161, 163,
    180, 183n11, 183n12, 184n13,
    185n16
history and, 167
interpretive predispositions and, 90,
    95, 97, 101, 161
texts as containing, 91–92
Japanese law and, 94–100
nihilism and, 91–92, 173
objective interpretation and, 91–92,
    149–50, 153, 161, 165–66, 170, 175,
    180–81, 183n10, 186n20, 188n24
originalism and, 130, 145–53, 159–87
preconceptions and, 7, 88–93, 97, 102n30
philosophy of language, 48
phronesis, 162
plain meaning. *See* meaning; ordinary
    meaning
Plato, 74, 162, 184n15
Poirier, Marc, 3, 18–19, 41n2
Popkin, William, 3
Posner, Richard, 33, 75–76
pragmatics
    combination with other determinates,
        69, 198
    compared to semantics, 83, 110–11
    contribution to legal meaning. *See* legal
        meaning
    deferentialism and. *See* deferentialism
    definition of, 22–23
    inference and, 70–74, 84, 195, 198, 204,
        213, 214n3
precisify, 4, 193, 219
privileges and immunities clause, 137,
    233–35, 238n11, 254–61, 264–65,
    269n40, 269–70n41, 278–79
prototypes, 76
psychology, 1–4, 9, 15, 28, 41n1, 156, 176,
    245
public meaning. *See* originalism

Rayner, Keith, 77
Raz, Joseph, 42n35, 209, 214n5
reader understanding, 55–61
Ricoeur, Paul, 166–67, 184n14, 185n16,
    186n20
Roberts, John, 236n5, 246–47, 272–75
Rosen, Gideon, 11, 272–74, 278–79

Ross, Stephen, 22–23, 28
rule against surplusage, 81
rule of law
    deferentialism and. *See* deferentialism
    Gadamer, Hans-Georg and, 146–47,
        163
    indeterminacy and, 81, 83–84
    legislative history and, 24
    ordinary meaning and, 31
    originalism and, 9, 154, 158
    speaker meaning and, 205
    vagueness and, 7
rule of lenity, 79–81, 199, 248, 266n2
rule of the last antecedent, 80–81

Sacks, Albert, 25
Scalia, Antonin, 125n17
    on *ejusdem generis*, 40
    on Holmes's normal speaker of English,
        108–11, 113, 115, 120–22
    on judicial discretion, 47
    on legislative history, 61
    on ordinary meaning, 30–31, 75
    originalism and, 55, 187–88n24, 229–31
    on purposivism, 42n26
    Smith v. United States (1993) and, 58–59,
        211, 233, 251–52
    on vagueness, 74–75
Schauer, Frederick, 66
Schiffer, Stephen, 54
Searle, John, 71, 127n35, 192
semantics
    ambiguity and. *See* ambiguity
    communicative content and, 3, 28, 134
    deferentialism and. *See* deferentialism
    definition of, 83
    generative linguistics and, 68–69
    indeterminacy and, 194, 197–98
    lexical semantics and, 28
    ordinary meaning doctrine and, 22,
        28, 31
    originalism and, 139–44, 148–52, 158,
        172–73, 187, 267n5
    living originalism and, 229, 263
    textualists and, 29, 110–11, 242
    United States v. X-Citement Video, Inc.
        (1994), 18
separation of powers, 47, 61, 64, 222, 229,
    245–46
Shapiro, David, 26

Slocum, Brian, 3, 5, 6, 41n3, 41n15, 43n47, 75
Soames, Scott
  deferentialism and. *See* deferentialism
  on meaning and assertion, 268n13, 268–69n15
Solan, Lawrence, 6–7, 9, 15, 29, 42n35, 51–52, 78, 115, 119
Solum, Larry, 187n23
  communicative content and, 82, 182n3, 182n4, 202, 209, 267n5
  fixation thesis and, 8, 156–59, 182n2, 185–86n17
  ontological implausibility of, 167–74, 187n22, 187–88n24
  implementing originalism and, 176–81, 186n18, 186–87n21
Sorensen, Roy, 74, 202, 207–8, 210, 212
speech acts
  adjudication and, 192, 201–11, 213
  ambiguity and. *See* ambiguity
  context and, 73
  declarations and, 192, 212
  deferentialism and. *See* deferentialism
  effectives and, 192
  illocutionary intentions and, 230, 236n1, 250
  legal speech and, 191, 200–201, 212, 219, 242 , 252, 268n13, 277–78
  perlocutionary intentions and, 10, 230
  police interactions and, 70–71
  threats and, 72
  verdictives and, 192
Sperber, Dan, 71, 192, 196, 198, 199, 204
Stanley, Jason, 27
stare decisis, 11, 41n17, 93, 199, 262, 267n6
Steinmetz, Sol, 139–40
stipulated content, 245
substantive canons of construction, 199

techne, 162
textual canons of construction, 199. See also *ejusdem generis*

textualism
  bright line standards and, 47
  deferentialism and. *See* deferentialism
  definition of, 29, 242
  ejusdem generis and, 40
  externalism and, 110–11
  legislative history and. *See* legislative history
  ordinary meaning and, 118
Thomas, Clarence, 113, 126n27
Tiersma, Peter, 5, 16, 34, 37, 72, 73
Traynor, Roger, 108–11, 114, 124–25n14

underdeterminacy, 4, 21, 39–40, 76–77
  US Constitution and, 134–35, 144
United States v. X-Citement Video, Inc. (1994), 17–20
utterance content (utterance interpretation), 193, 196, 209, 212

vague. *See* vagueness
vagueness
  categorization and. *See* categorization
  deferentialism and. *See* deferentialism
  Dworkin, Ronald and, 256
  hermeneutics and, 160
  legal meaning and. *See* legal meaning
  linguistic meaning and, 17, 50, 182n4
  originalism and, 8, 133, 144, 171, 224–25, 229, 237n7, 263
  semantics and, 83
verdictives. *See* speech acts
Vermeule, Adrian, 34

Walton, Kendall, 113, 127n34, 127n35
Wechsler, Stephen, 74, 77
Williamson, Timothy, 33
Wilson, Deirdre, 71, 192, 196, 198, 199
Wittgenstein, Ludwig, 194, 202–3